THE ARCHBISHOP AND
THE LADY

Michael de la Bedoyere

THE ARCHBISHOP
AND
THE LADY

*The story of Fénelon and
Madame Guyon*

PANTHEON

CONTENTS

Part One

THE SCANDAL OF PURE LOVE

Part Two

THE BATTLE OF THE GIANTS

ILLUSTRATIONS

INTRODUCTION

THE STORY that I tell in these pages is unlikely to be familiar to most English-speaking readers, though it is ' required reading ' for any Frenchman with a pretence to knowledge about the cultural and literary history of his own country and of Europe. But in this case culture and history are made easy, and one suspects that the colourful names of Fénelon, Bossuet, Louis XIV, Mme. de Maintenon, as well as that of the enigmatic widow, Mme. Guyon, account for the popularity of the story rather than the important spiritual issues involved in it.

So intensely dramatic a chapter of history, so searching a conflict between fascinating personalities, must have a perennial interest. Nor can anyone tell this story by just repeating it. The people involved, the problems in debate, the revelation of the heights and the depths to which great and good people can rise and then to which they can sink, all of these challenge the story-teller to take sides and to express his own strongly-moved feelings; and they must surely offer a similar challenge to the reader. That is why it is a story that has often been told—and been told in widely differing ways—and that will often be told again. Yet, apart from some excellent chapters in Mgr. Knox's *Enthusiasm*, it is hardly available to the English reader.

The chief actors were people great in their office, intensely human when seen beneath their trappings, and preoccupied here not only with important affairs of Church and State, but with the fate of a strange and puzzling woman. There was the King himself, the " Great Monarch," who supremely embodied the old order of absolute authority and privilege in Europe, when around him in England and Holland, as well as under cover in his own country, new and revolutionary ideas were pointing the way towards a very different world. There was Mme. de Maintenon, the woman who had risen from almost sordid beginnings to become the secret wife of the King himself—a good, clever, powerful woman who was nevertheless much out of her depths in this affair and consequently did nothing but harm. There was Bishop Bossuet, the " Eagle of Meaux," one of the greatest churchmen of all time, whose immense gifts were dedicated to the preservation of the threatened authoritarian State and Church, a cause which, in his view, justified him

7

in outrageous behaviour quite out of keeping with his own goodness and attraction. There was the hero (from my point of view), Archbishop Fénelon, the " Swan of Cambrai," whose much deeper mind and more sensitive awareness seemed to stretch backwards and forwards beyond the passing moment to something more fundamental and timeless in the make-up of man and human society—something which he discerned, strangely enough, in the " Dove," Jeanne Marie Bouvier de la Motte, widow of Monsieur Guyon, the tragic heroine, through whom the whole trouble began.

This is certainly one of those cases when it can be said that a woman made history, a woman, possessing a rare power, yet in herself of little importance as the great world goes. But for this woman, the chief actors would probably have pursued their destinies in mutual harmony and friendship, hardly aware of the spiritual depths which divided them. But Mme. Guyon's influence on Fénelon acted as a catalyst that brought to the surface the subconscious patterns and driving forces, values and ambitions, in both Bossuet and Fénelon, so that they became locked in a furious and classic battle, while the world, awed, mocking, saddened, watched. It was Mme. Guyon, too, who tested the real character of Francoise de Maintenon and found it wanting; who created the scare that a spiritual conspiracy was brewing, endangering Court, Church and country; and who forced to a clear focus very deep religious divisions over the true relationship of man to God and thus over the real meaning of religion itself. Few women have done so much, and without really meaning to do so, to probe the souls of the great.

Posterity may be grateful to her for this, but in her life she derived no reward. On the contrary, both before and after her brief hour of triumph, she was hunted, bullied and persecuted for conscience's sake, spending many of her years in prison, including five in the dreaded Bastille itself. The most moving theme of these pages must undoubtedly be the remarkable loyalty of Fénelon, Archbishop of Cambrai, to the friend whom Church and State deemed a heretic, immoral and half-crazy. This loyalty of a great bishop and noble of the Court, in whose care lay the education of a future king, imperilled the most promising career of the day and caused an oversensitive personality intense suffering. It made him ridiculous in the eyes of the world and it drove the mighty Bossuet into such a frenzy of rage against him that Europe itself was amazed. Yet the " Swan," bruised and shaken, withstood the plunge of the " Eagle," and in the end saved the " Dove."

One of the most attractive aspects of the story is to be found in the fact that the chief characters were neither saints nor villains. Even though the foreshortening of history tends to make posterity see Bossuet as the hero and Fénelon the villain—the older view—or Fénelon as the hero and Bossuet the villain—the more popular view to-day and one which I am unable to reject—there is no getting away from the fact that both men had great virtues and great weaknesses. While drawing firm conclusions, I have tried to bring this out and to be fair to these remarkable people. I feel, too, that there is far more to be said for Mme. Guyon than most of my fellow Catholics, even Mgr. Knox, will easily grant, though perhaps less to be said for her than her highly-placed friends at the time and some of her Protestant admirers afterwards, believed.

But whatever view one takes of Mme. Guyon, the story is, among other things, a story of the defence of the liberty of an individual's conscience in an age when individual consciences counted for little. For this defence, Mme. Guyon should be better known among the roll of women heroes and Fénelon better known as a champion of the long race of the bullied and the browbeaten.

The story, it will be seen, is not wanting in colour and human drama, but I must confess that it is the deep spiritual theme which runs through it that has most fascinated me: the meaning and destiny of human life; the nature of man's access to a truth, a love, a dimension, a reality, on a plane infinitely higher than anything our mere senses and our utilitarian reasoning can reach; the very heart of spiritual endeavour in this mortal life; the relationship of man to God.

But these are profound matters, not easily treated and explained in a book that is meant to be popular rather than learned. Happily, to-day such questions interest many people, for our world, which affords us so many answers to so many problems which have been wrapped in mystery for æons, has certainly made no progress in answering the fundamental ones: "What is man?" and "What is God?" With the power to destroy man himself and the planet on which he lives within human grasp, the answers to these supreme questions become more, not less, important.

I cannot help hoping that while these matters have been treated in this book as shortly and as simply as possible, consistent with the unfolding of the whole story, they will not be felt by the reader to hold up the action, but rather stimulate him to further interest in the problem of human destiny that so fascinated both Fénelon and Mme. Guyon two hundred and fifty years ago.

I have appended references, not to suggest that this is a work of scholarship, which it is very far from being, but to help the interested reader to find out more about it all, if he will, and also to enable him to test the value of my own conclusions.

One last word. Though the scene is set in France and Rome, it so happens that both the Archbishop and the Lady found many adherents to the core of their spiritual views among non-Catholics outside France, not least in Britain. Mme. Guyon, in fact, has been more of a heroine to English and Dutch Protestants than she ever has been to Catholics, though I completely agree with Mgr. Knox that she was herself stubbornly Catholic. Fénelon, one of the half-dozen most creative minds of his day, has been widely viewed as a kind of " spiritual father " of the romantic movement, of the Enlightenment, and thence to Socialism, Marxism and modern democracy. He would have been horrified to know it, but one cannot help feeling that if more attention had been paid to his spiritual teaching, the world would have progressed along happier and more constructive lines.

MICHAEL DE LA BEDOYERE

PROLOGUE

The Swan Meets the Dove

ONE DAY early in October, 1688, the Abbé de Fénelon was introduced to Madame Guyon in the salon of the country house of the
Duchesse de Béthune-Charost, at Beynes, near Versailles.

The scene is easy to imagine, and we may permit ourselves to
set it. The half-light of the autumnal afternoon would be in keeping
with the dark and ample clothes of the ladies, relieved, in the case
of the Duchess, perhaps, by a soft-coloured lace shawl and a muslin
fichu at her neck. She would be good-looking, rather than aristocratic in bearing, for she was born of middle-class stock, albeit
wealthy and powerful, and we can imagine her greying hair rising
high above florid features. She was the daughter of a great man—
of the once all-powerful Fouquet, Louis XIV's Minister of Finance,
that brilliant juggler with the nation's wealth, whose cleverest tricks
had been played in order to line the pockets of his own family.
From power, honours and riches, enjoyed in the magnificent
château of Vaux-le-Vicomte (to this day a mecca of Parisian holiday-
makers), Fouquet had fallen headlong into twenty years of prison
and to death in disgrace. He had been dead eight years before the
scene we are describing took place.

Quietly as his now middle-aged daughter was dressed, for she
belonged to the coterie of the great ladies of the Court who were
setting a tone of grave piety where royal mistresses had once been
in fashion, she would have looked a woman of the world, as compared with the old friend whom she had now invited to meet the
priest. Mme. Guyon, a pious widow, would have looked demure,
though far from forbidding, with her black stiff dress and hood,
fastened together under her dimpled chin, enclosing a once very

11

pretty and now still chubby face in which the eyes had a soupçon
of a twinkle. Near them the ascetic-looking Abbé would be
standing, his black cassock relieved only by the white of his stock
at the neck. Unforgettable, however, must have been the long,
intelligent, angular, handsome pale face, with the fine, delicate nose,
the firm, ascetic lips, the large dark eyes, as he looked with courtesy
and lively interest at the widow, about whom he had heard such
unexpected things.

Fénelon, well under forty, was still young, and with his career
yet to make in the dramatic and gilded world of the Throne and the
Court—if career there was to be. Saint-Simon, that indefatigable
recorder for posterity of all that failed to meet the casual eye in the
privileged circles of royalty and great nobles, tells us that at this
time Fénelon was still little known. He tells us, too, that Fénelon,
despite his virtue, meant to be known. He aspired high, and no
effort of mortification would ever succeed in entirely dominating
his appetite for greatness. Saint-Simon exaggerated, but he was not
entirely wrong.

Mme. Guyon was a little older. Nobly born, like Fénelon, she
had once been a great beauty, but her face was now disfigured by
pock-marks. She was indeed a woman with an astonishing past,
and it was curiosity about her which had brought Fénelon to Beynes
on this day. Better known than the priest, Saint-Simon observes,
she was not yet well known in Paris. If so, the deficiency was all
too soon to be remedied. The Duchesse de Charost at least knew
a great deal about her and had not been slow to tell the Abbé all
she knew.

Yet none of the three, as they talked together that afternoon,
could have dreamt that this meeting, arranged solely because of the
spiritual interests which they shared in common, was to prove the
prelude to a drama that would involve the greatest personages of
the kingdom and scandalise both Church and State. Still less could
they have imagined that it was to be the beginning of a relationship
between one of the greatest churchmen of history and an enigmatic
woman that would throw a long, deep shadow over his uniquely
distinguished career and deliver an innocent person to years of
persecution and prison for conscience's sake. Had these two not
thus met " near the feast of Saint-Francis in October, 1688," as

Mme. Guyon herself recorded in certain key pages of her auto-biography, this tragic story would never have been enacted.

It was one of those cases when the unforeseeable combination of circumstances was needed to compound the particular explosive mixture and to fire it. But for Mme. Guyon, the Abbé de Fénelon's life would have been placid, his fame that of a great writer and guide of chosen souls, of the first prelate in the land, perhaps even of an influential statesman; but his name would have been revered by posterity rather than he himself remembered as one of the most vivid and interesting personalities of ecclesiastical history. As for Mme. Guyon, she, without Fénelon, would have been remembered at best as a curiosity in the roll of minor spiritual writers of strange and doubtful inspiration. Had Mme. Guyon never met Fénelon, Mme. de Maintenon, Louis XIV's improbably pious and secretly-married wife, having peacefully (and relentlessly) swept from the Court all traces of the illicit reigns of La Vallière and Montespan, would easily have got rid of this new and dangerous prophetess and reigned complacently as unchallenged spiritual mother of a reformed Court. Louis XIV, King of Church scarcely less than of State, would not have been called upon to denounce, with tears in his eyes, impieties and heresies reaching to his very household and his grand-children or to pronounce the ruin of the holiest prelate of his not very holy kingdom. The great Bishop Bossuet, Eagle of Meaux in contrast with the Swan of Cambrai, as Fénelon, his friend and disciple came to be called, would never have made of this friend his greatest enemy. An enemy whom he so feared and suspected that he did not hesitate to soil an immense reputation by the methods to which he resorted in order to eradicate an influence that he believed to be destructive of the very being of the Catholic Church and of the order and peace of human society.

Thus were personal destinies of the highest importance and interest to be affected by this meeting. But there was more to it than that. For underneath the open duel between the greatest bishops of their day, the persecution of the innocent, the close involvement of Church and State in France and of the Holy See itself in the affair, there was the unique relationship between the priest and the woman which gave to the issues in dispute their fascination for posterity.

From the moment of the meeting at Beynes until the end of his tragic, yet fruitful and, in its last years, peaceful, life, Fénelon's mind and behaviour were to a great extent inspired and dominated by this woman whom he only saw at infrequent intervals during a period that lasted but a few months. Yet in that time Mme. Guyon's inspiration, doomed in all probability to sterility if left to itself, took root in the rich and mysteriously compounded soil of Fénelon's spirit. The consequence was that his own genius, modified by her daring feminine intuitions, was able to express itself in a life and a literary *œuvre* that raised, in the artificial setting of the *Grand Siècle*, all the relevant questions about the relationship of man to God and, therefore, about the true nature of man and of human society. Theology, political philosophy, and above all, men and women themselves in their deepest selves, seemed to be mysteriously affected by this influence. Great revolutions succeeded this last phase of classic Europe, and one finds to this very day the seeds of so much that mankind has since lived embedded in Fénelon's writings.

2

What did Fénelon and Mme. Guyon know of one another when they met that afternoon at Beynes? Presumably, roughly as much as Mme. de Charost had told each of them, for it was she who had arranged the meeting—and with definite plans in mind, for the pious duchess knew them both separately, and judged how valuable a friendship between them would be.

Though she was the daughter of Fouquet, she was a close friend of three younger duchesses—it is well to remember that this story moves from first to last among the highest in Church and State— daughters of the great Colbert, who had helped to ruin Fouquet and who had replaced him, administering the kingdom's finances less corruptly and with far greater success. They were the Duchesse de Beauvilliers, the Duchesse de Chevreuse and the Duchesse de Mortemart, splendid and attractive heiresses, the first two married to dukes who play a leading role in this story.

Nowhere else and at no other time, surely, would it have been possible for such great ladies of worldly rank and fortune to perfume a quarrel of priests with the odour of sanctity and of the most famous royal court of history. But so it was. For them and their friends, their priest of predilection was this Abbé de Fénelon, one of whose major gifts throughout his life was to command the trust and devotion of women of the highest society. He gave himself wholeheartedly to the spiritual direction of such women, and his greatest and most instructive legacy to the world is probably the mass of letters which he wrote to these fascinating friends and penitents.

The Duchesse de Charost, unlike the other Duchesses, knew Madame Guyon of old. When Fouquet, her father, fell from power, she had found refuge with M. and Mme. Guyon in Montargis, the pleasant country town some sixty miles south of Paris where Mme. Guyon had been born and where she had married in 1664. If, as one must suppose, Mme. Guyon was as torrential a talker as she certainly was a writer, there could have been little of the life of Jeanne Marie Bouvier de La Motte (Mme. Guyon's maiden name) which the Duchess did not know. In the next chapter, we shall try and convey in a few pages the strange life which it took Mme. Guyon herself many hundreds to describe.

But Fénelon, when he met Mme. Guyon at Beynes, would have been less interested in her astonishing spiritual experiences—he was never, in fact, inclined to inquire too closely into them—than in what happened to her shortly after her husband's timely death. For in 1671, this rich widow had answered God's call and had abandoned her family responsibilities in order to go to Calvinist Geneva and there help its bishop by assisting in the foundation and endowment of a community of *Nouvelles Catholiques*.

The object of this confraternity was to confirm the new-found faith—if faith is in many instances the right word—of semi-enforced converts from the Huguenot or French Protestant religion. It was from that time that a series of very odd adventures befell Mme. Guyon, and these, as we shall see, were to have a considerable bearing on the subsequent fate of Fénelon. By an odd coincidence, Fénelon himself also at this time was closely associated with the *Nouvelles Catholiques*. He was something of an expert in the Huguenot question, having been chosen to serve on special apostolic missions to them in parts of the country where their strongholds lay.

Let us not, by the way, make the mistake of supposing that because
Fénelon was the most " modern " of his Catholic contemporaries,
this quality included toleration of heresy. In that sense, no one was
tolerant in the France of his day, not even the free-thinkers.
Protestantism endangered the unity and strength of the greatest
kingdom of Europe, and this fact, quite as much as the question
of spiritual faith made tolerance unthinkable. But we may add that,
to his credit, Fénelon at least realised that no conversion was worth
anything unless it was genuine, and his activities were intelligently
—they were " intelligent " and " gentle "—directed to making real,
not forced, conversions. He was now living in the Paris house of
the *Nouvelles Catholiques*, of which he was the Superior, in the rue
Sainte-Anne. This was not far from Mme. Guyon who was living near Notre Dame.

" Day and night," a priest wrote years later answering calumnies
about Mme. Guyon, " she followed the cathedral services, even in
the depths of winter and to the detriment of her health. Many of
the poor lived on her great generosity." We shall find that this
woman, calumniated by the mob and the great in Church and
State, was always admired by those who had really known her.

Mme. de Charost would have testified similarly to her old
friend, and we may be sure that she would have given Fénelon many
a detail about her friend's recent forced detention for eight months
in a Paris convent from which she had only just been released. It
was an unhappy story of injustice and chicanery on the part of the
ecclesiastical authorities, and only a combination of Mme. Guyon's
indomitable resolution and considerable good luck enabled the
prisoner to be released in good time for that October meeting.

Fénelon would not have been disposed to challenge the view that
Mme. Guyon had been unjustly imprisoned by M. de Harlay, the
Archbishop of Paris. Was he not to describe that wordly prelate
as " corrupt, scandalous, incorrigible, false, sly and double-faced " ?
But he may have needed more persuading about Mme. de Charost's
glowing tributes to her friend. After all, he had been trained at
Saint-Sulpice where orthodoxy, poise, effective zeal, inconspicuous-
ness of the individual were the ideals for the formation of priests
and the steady reform of the Church. Saints like Francis of Sales
and Vincent de Paul were the models put before him. Nobility of

birth and his sense of the high status of a dignified and trained clergy prejudiced him against novelty, against the crank, against the woman out of her due social place. Gossip about this woman, he knew, had little of good to say about her. Had she not intemperately deserted her children? Did not people even whis er that she had run away with a priest? The stories were circumstantial. She had been seen riding behind him on horseback. On another occasion an accident to a carriage had revealed the two of them together on a compromising journey. The mob, they said, called her a witch. The better educated had a graver and far more plausible explanation of the stories. Mme. Guyon, it seemed, was a disciple of the sinister Molinos who had taught dark and horrible doctrines about God's power to elevate chosen souls so much above temporal things that it no longer mattered when they yielded to impure temptations. That priest—was he not called La Combe, strange, mountain-bred Barnabite?—was said to subscribe to their horrible travesty of the spiritual life.

If the fastidious Fénelon had heard these stories, nothing could have been more calculated to repel his severe piety with its attractive overtones of simplicity and romantic melancholy. He had been curious enough some time back to make inquiries at Montargis about the woman, when he was returning from a mission to the Protestants. But all he had heard of her in her native town had been good. She had always been a model of virtue, the people who had lived with her told him, and her charity to the poor had never been forgotten, especially in the hard times that the glorious King's victories were apt to bring to the common man. And now the Duchess was hinting at some remarkable things. Indeed, would Mme. de Charost, would the other Dukes and Duchesses, his close friends, would Mme. de Miramion, that remarkable woman of good work in the Paris slums who had once said: "We shall have all eternity to engage in contemplation; this life is made for work" —would any of these enlightened and devout women have had anything to do with a person such as the scandal-mongers and the riff-raff were describing? Mme. Guyon's story was not the story of a hypocritical fraud or, at best, of a deluded neurotic woman. No, indeed, it was the story, said these friends of his, of a rare saint, a new mystic, in the high tradition of Blessed John of the Cross, of the gentle, kindly Saint Francis of Sales and Madame de Chantal. No sensational ecstasies, no suspect illuminism, no, surely vulgar, external manifestations of extravagant piety and exhibitionist penances; but, instead, a quiet, inner, complete dedication of the self to God in utter self-abandonment so that the too, too human substance of flesh and spirit was changed in the crucible of the divine into oneness with the All-Real whose pursuit haunts, but mostly eludes, ordinary sinful man. Here was someone who knew the true secret of life, the key to an inner peace, to a new awareness far removed from the puzzles and trials of ordinary life.

If there was anything in what his Duchesses had to tell him about this woman, Fénelon knew well enough that rare souls called to such a destiny are commonly misunderstood and hated by the mob, whether lay or clerical, for the mob instinctively mocks and persecutes what to it is the eccentric, the crank, and it will resort to any cruelty to drive such from the flock. Was Mme. Guyon the subnormal eccentric, common enough in ecclesiastical and secular history, or was she the too rare above-normal, God-chosen eccentric, the rare jewel among the common stones? Such questions would at least have keenly aroused his curiosity. For him only the very best was ever good enough, and so, that October afternoon, he keenly watched the lively, mobile face, the large round eyes, that flash of excitement, the burning desire to please, the super-vitality within the chaste and demure frame of an almost nun-like hood and habit.

But what was going on in Mme. Guyon's mind while the priest watched? She would have known much less of Fénelon than he could have known of her. One little point must have made a great impression on her. She always loved symbols, those little coincidences, little oddities, that seem to bear so much significance in a too rational world. Was he not François de Salignac de La Mothe Fénelon? And was she not Jeanne Marie Bouvier de la Motte Guyon? The same name, though sometimes spelt differently. Then, too, his name was François, and she was meeting him " vers la Saint-François."

In her autobiography, she says she first heard of him the day before they met at Beynes. This seems unlikely, and Mme. Guyon's lively imagination was always apt to make her dramatise in retrospect the too insignificant current of life as it is lived. But the point is not of importance in comparison with the certainty that what Mme. de Charost had to tell of Fénelon immediately awakened all her curiosity and interest. Here was a priest sought after by the really great, the friends and advisers of the King himself. His position alone must lead him to success and to immense influence; his intelligence guaranteed the brilliance with which he would fulfil his destiny; but far more important in her eyes were the things she heard about the quality and breadth of his spiritual outlook, based as it was on a natural gift for self-analysis and for the analysis of others, an analysis which revealed the depths of self-deception to which the human character is prone.

Here was a man who was surely ready for the truth which her mystical experiences had revealed to her—a man who, into the bargain, was supremely well fitted to carry it from the little un-influential coteries of the provinces, to which she had preached, into the very heart of the great world itself, into the court of State and Church of the greatest country of Christendom.

Experience had bitterly taught her how limited was the scope of a woman's action, even when that woman possessed an irresistible will to achieve and to preach the truth, as revealed to her. Her poor Barnabite friend, a soul akin to hers, though not without a certain spiritual obtuseness, had already met an even worse fate than hers. She had been liberated from prison, but he still lay there and likely to remain for many a day. With this Abbé de Fénelon, noble, clever, powerful and a saint of the inner life, it would be a very different story. God was about to fulfil the destiny He had entrusted to her. " A few days after my liberation," she wrote, " having heard tell of Monsieur l' Abbé de F., I found myself suddenly thinking of him with great intentness and sweetness. I felt that Our Lord was uniting me with him with great intimacy, and more with him than with anyone else. I was asked to consent. I consented. Then it seemed to me that a spiritual filiation took place from him to me." It was in such spiritual language as this that the workings of her subconscious aspirations and plans always expressed themselves.

What was said at that first meeting we shall never know; but at least we cannot doubt of the powerful stirrings of her will under the conventional manners of a first introduction. Not surprisingly, the Abbé did not seem very impressed. The fastidious in his being must have instinctively recoiled before her exuberance, the single-minded outpouring of her feelings. She realised it. " He did not relish my company." " I could not tune into him "—we would be inclined to-day to read into the French phrase *je ne trouvais pas de correspondance*. But Mme. Guyon's most obvious trait throughout her life was never to take no for an answer, and with her hostess conspiring with her, all was by no means lost. When the moment came to leave, it was suggested, oddly enough, that the priest and Mme. Guyon should drive away together—with a chaperone, of course. They were said to have driven to Paris; but the strange night drive could hardly have been farther than the few miles to Versailles.

In this privacy, she could let herself go—or perhaps she judged that Fénelon needed a more skilled and reserved approach. Anyway, she had the chance of explaining to him the main principles of her spiritual doctrine, and no one, it was admitted, " could talk better of the things of God." Her intense desire to succeed at this critical moment, which could mean all to her, must have inspired her in the darkness of that carriage, as they bumped along, to give of her very best. Fénelon was probably spared, as Mme. Guyon's readers, alas, are not, the torrential flow of imagery, metaphor, reminiscence, self-absorption in intense and rapidly changing feelings, so powerful that they seemed to create a world of their own. Consequently, he could, more easily than we can, distinguish between much soundness of matter, much genuine spiritual perceptiveness, and the very bizarre manner. Nor can we doubt, knowing what was to happen after, that something in him was powerfully attracted by this carriage companion. At this stage, she, doubtless, responded in some way to his longing for spiritual adventure and for the re-assurance of an indisputable spiritual experience, within strictly orthodox bounds. At the end of the drive, we are told, he answered her anxious queries about whether he had followed her meaning by assuring her that it had all gone into his head by the main door. But it was said partly in politeness, for he was as yet far from being won over.

However, they met again next day. With Mme. Guyon no time was ever lost. " We were together for some time without speaking," she wrote, " but the cloud lightened a little." In fact, eight more days—an incredibly short time when it was a case of two such diverse minds and situations—were needed for the cloud to disappear and for the Abbé " to be as I wanted him to be." Her will-power, already well exercised on a great variety of far easier subjects, had achieved in a flash its greatest triumph.

" Since then our union has increased in a pure and ineffable manner. I think my soul is entirely linked with his; and those words of David about Jonathan that ' his soul was knit to David's, seemed appropriate to our union. Our Lord made me understand the great designs he had for this person, and how dear he is to Him." Saint-Simon phrased it more shortly and rather more eloquently: *leur sublime s'amalgama*, which might be translated: they were one together on the heights—or rather in the depths, those inner depths of the soul where physical distance, and even years without direct verbal communication, cannot weaken the bond. For the truth is that from this first meeting until the end of Fénelon's life as Prince and Archbishop of Cambrai, twenty-seven years later, there was never to be any separation, at least in Fénelon's spirit. To her he clung; carefully, and sometimes scarcely honestly, concealing the truth before the world; always true to her in the face of persecution, calumny, disgrace; stubbornly, though not gladly, risking reputation, authority, power for the woman who so deeply intertwined herself into his thoughts, his values, his personality, that to deny her became tantamount to denying himself. The Swan, destined for a life of stately and placid grandeur, had turned aside, lured by the Dove to explore the mysteries of Pure Love; and when she lay, wounded and bleeding, he was to stand by her and defend her secret.

PART ONE

The Scandal of Pure Love

CHAPTER ONE

MADAME GUYON AT HOME

WE SHALL have little difficulty in getting to know everything about this strange woman who had thus crossed the path of the pious, learned and fashionable priest of whom so much was expected by men and women of the highest possible standing in Louis XIV's kingdom. Mme. Guyon herself has done all that is needed to satisfy our curiosity. Despite the supposedly hidden nature of her spiritual life in God, she has left us, in addition to a vast number of spiritual treatises, over 700 pages of autobiography. These were written, she tells us, at the request of her spiritual director. Most of the autobiography was in fact written during those months of convent-prison from which she emerged shortly before meeting Fénelon.

It is one of the most extraordinary documents in spiritual, and indeed psychological, literature. Like stretches of earth and rock in a shallow but raging torrent, objective and unadorned narrative, as well as much religious common sense, shapes its, at times, homely, at times highly dramatic, pattern within a profusion of spiritual emotion and mystical doctrine. And indeed the puzzle of Mme. Guyon will always lie in the juxtaposition in her life of that hard, sane, deeply spiritual sense which was to appeal so strongly to Fénelon, and the extravagant sensibilities which disgusted and scandalised the unromantic Bossuet.

Jeanne Marie Bouvier de La Motte was born in Montargis in 1648. She was the child of an old father, twice married, and the family was of sufficient rank and influence to have the entrée to the best aristocratic society. Both parents were extremely devout, many of their children dedicating themselves to religious vocations. Her mother, indeed, was so pious that her religious exercises prevented her from looking after her daughter, a point which leads Mme. Guyon to make some very sensible observations—entirely in the spirit of Fénelon himself—about the wrongness of parents neglecting their children and, in particular, the wrongness of devout parents imagining that they are pleasing God by praying when they should be serving God by carrying out their motherly and domestic duties.

This excellent advice came much too late for Jeanne herself. An ailing and, clearly, oversensitive child, she lived from the age of two and a half in one convent or another with intervals of being looked after by the servants at home. But she was an intelligent child, pretty and popular. Her old and puzzled father delighted in her company when he was allowed to enjoy it. In fact, he was strong-minded enough to refuse the invitation of the exiled Queen Henrietta-Maria, widow of Charles I, when, on a visit to Montargis, she offered the charming eight-year-old girl a court education. Retrospectively, Mme. Guyon thanked God for her escape from the dangers of a life at court, but it might have been better for her had the grand offer been accepted. Much of the latent purpose and ambition in her nature might have been canalised into more normal channels of feminine life. Instead, she was left to the insecurity and instability of an upbringing which turned her to idle dreams and idle reading, haphazardly absorbed by her quick, but very lonely spirit. As she grew up, her beauty was to attract many suitors, each of whom her doting father rejected. Her own imagination, it seems, was far more impressed by a priest-cousin who visited the family on his way to the Foreign Missions in Indo-China. She was then twelve.

This cousin's dedication to God's work stimulated in her a first immature conversion. "Will it be said of me that I alone of my family will be damned," she said to her confessor. She changed her reading from the distracting stories of romance to the works of Saint Francis of Sales and the life of Madame de Chantal, his friend who founded the Visitation nuns. In these the adolescent girl discovered *l'oraison*—Prayer with a capital P, in other words, the soul's indwelling by its Divine Lover. Naturally, she knew nothing about it, and no one in Montargis was competent to guide her. She had to be content to try to follow in Jeanne de Chantal's footsteps and test her vocation with the Visitation nuns in Montargis. But even in this she was frustrated, for her father could not bear to part with her, while her mother was now thinking of showing off the neglected child, whose beauty was causing general interest. So she passed through another period of worldliness, returning the suit of " an accomplished gentleman," making the social rounds of Paris, devouring more novels, but all the time suffering from bitter scruples about her infidelity to *l'oraison* and the pure love of God.

Reading between the lines of her autobiography, one senses that despite the retrospective spiritual significance, which she attributed to every event and every emotion, her childhood was not so very exceptional for a highly-strung and naturally pious Catholic girl, lacking education, discipline and domestic stability. But her strong *attrait*, when still so young, for the inner personal religion of which she had read and which corresponded to her introspective emotional nature rather than to the visible external pieties of religion marked her out.

Shortly before her sixteenth birthday she was married off to Jacques Guyon du Chesnoy. It was a business match with a rich and noble neighbour nearing forty whom she saw for the first time two days before the wedding.

The marriage brought her face to face with reality, and, naturally enough, she recoiled from it. " The marriage caused universal joy in our town; and in the general rejoicing I alone was sad. I could not laugh like the others, nor eat, I felt so sick at heart." She gives her reasons. One was her natural modesty. Another was the excruciating realisation that she should have become a nun. And the third, more obvious but much harder to overcome, was the *famille Guyon*. She had passed from the free air of her easy-going, if somewhat feckless, parents into the constriction of a home ruled over by a miserly mother-in-law in which her husband, soon to become the victim of gout, had no other merit but that of successfully administering his considerable wealth. Such households in provincial France, then and now, have to be seen to be believed. It needs a Balzac or a Mauriac to evoke the staleness and oppression of the air breathed within them.

Mme. Guyon's torrential chapters possess a vividness, an actuality, a sense of humour which makes it impossible to believe that conscious invention plays any great part in them. Nevertheless, it is always difficult to discern how far what she has to say is plain fact, how far a kind of projection of the subconscious urges in her fanciful and complex personality. During these years of unhappy marriage there is in her story a theme of persecution at the hands of her mother-in-law and even of the servants which cannot but make one suspect a strong element of persecution mania. But the reader will learn in due time that few people can have suffered more in their lives from persecutions whose authenticity is entirely beyond dispute.

In her account she is rarely well. Illnesses are sudden and often felt to be mortal. Recovery would seem to be almost as sudden. Later she was to write : "Doctors are little used to illnesses like mine." It may be that an oversensitive nervous disposition translated into illness, imaginary or real, her excessive reactions to unkind-nesses, scepticism about her claims, even perhaps lack of being sufficiently esteemed. Feminine vanity, which later tended to express itself in strange ways, is discernible in its more natural form at this earlier stage in her accounts of her natural attraction and her charm in the eyes of others both in Montargis and in Paris. But within these different currents, there is always the steady stream of sense, goodness and high mystic aspiration. In marriage she certainly sought to perform her wifely duty and in all sincerity, to love, cherish and, more and more, nurse the husband God gave to her, all of which M. Guyon seems to have desired to return to the best of his limited nature. The modern reader cannot but smile occa-sionally at Jeanne's naïve account, as when she explains the difficulty to her of the marriage relationship, reporting her husband as saying, surely not without a touch of irony: "Anyone can see that *you* never lose the sense of the presence of God." And, in the face of her unhappiness and frustration, it is this last motif which comes more and more to dominate the story: her turning with ever-increased absorption to God within her soul.

External events occasioned a second conversion, this time, with only brief moments of weakness, for good. This took place during the months when the Duchesse de Charost had taken refuge, after her father's fall, in the Guyon home. She understood Jeanne's need for God. Then her cousin, the foreign missionary, came home.

From him she heard of the spiritual reputation of the Benedictine, Mère Granger, who fostered a simple, inner, silent and constant waiting on God with the will, a spiritual technique, called Quietism, then greatly in vogue. Hardly had her cousin gone, when a Franciscan visited her father. The old man thought that this holy person might well help his daughter. Having just completed a five-year retreat from the world, the friar shied violently at the idea of meeting a beautiful young woman, while Mme. Guyon had made the admirable resolution never to meet strange priests alone. When at length both were persuaded to come to the rendezvous, they faced one another in a long silence of intense awkwardness for both. At length the ice thawed sufficiently for Mme. Guyon to tell him of her troubles. "The trouble, Madame," he said to her, " is that you are looking outside for something you can only find within yourself. Get used to seeking God within your heart, and you will find Him." So he spoke, she tells us: "I felt within me a very deep wound, as delicious as it was loving; a wound so sweet that I wanted it never to be cured."

From then onwards nothing was easier for her than prayer. "Hours sped like seconds, and I could not stop. . . . The highest faculty, the Will, swallowed up the other two (Reason and Memory) and took away their distinctive characters the better to unite with them. Not that these did not continue in being, but they did so as unknown and passive; it was the light of Faith which, like the Sun, absorbs lesser lights and makes them dark for us, its own light so far surpassing all others."

Asked why she loved God with such intensity, she replied in all simplicity: " I loved Him without any motive or reason for loving, for no thoughts passed through my head, even in the deepest part of my being." Was it because of His goodness, His mercy? She answered: " I well knew He was good and full of mercy. His perfections were my happiness. But I did not think of myself in loving Him. *I loved Him and I burnt with love, because I loved Him. I loved Him in such a way that I could only love Him; but in loving Him I had no motive but Himself.*"

Later, when Fénelon and Bossuet and the theologians were to battle before the world, on the rights and wrongs of " pure love " and " passive prayer " over the imprisoned body of this woman, they never succeeded in expressing more simply and touchingly the instinctive reaction of a soul in love with God than did the young Mme. Guyon in those few moving and beautiful words. It is because Mme. Guyon, in the midst of verbiage, delusions, strange fancies, apparent will to power, could illuminate again and again in the tradition of the great masters of the spiritual life the soul's relation with God, that her life and character can fascinate us—as they fascinated Fénelon. However odd the setting, the jewels within shone with an authentic radiance.

Her further experiences followed the same classical pattern. If one allows for the immaturity of an ill-educated and highly-emotional girl scarcely out of her teens, the pages of the Auto-biography record her progress through the mortification of her senses and of her reason and will so that God could fill her denuded spirit, and all this according to the pattern that repeats itself again and again in the great mystical writers, Denys the Areopagite, the author of *The Cloud of Unknowing*, Saint Catherine of Genoa and Saint John of the Cross. If, in this young woman's case, it was all delusion, she must have had an uncanny gift of hitting the right mark and even discovering it.

The effect of this kind of blind waiting on God is often to make the normal prayers and exercises of the Christian life difficult or meaningless. Because of this, such " higher " prayer is suspected by the more conventional—and Mme. Guyon was to suffer the consequences. But at this period her record shows her fidelity to the sacraments and devotions of the Church, even to fruitless attempts to go through the religious exercises prescribed for gaining indulgences. Not less worrying to her was the reaction of her bewildered husband. One of her confessors, seeing how things were, sharply reproved her for a way of loving God that hardly seemed to square with her duty to love her husband. Her distress was painful, but happily a Jesuit was found to reassure her.

Among the misfortunes—traditionally the fate of the good—which she recounts, there was one at least which she could not have invented. Smallpox broke out in Montargis. She and her three young children caught the dread disease. Her three-year-old second boy died. " As soon as my eldest son was a little better, he got up and came into my room," she writes. " I was astonished at the extraordinary change in his appearance. His face had been one of extreme delicacy. Now it was like a piece of earth cut with furrows. The sight of it made me eager to look at myself in the mirror. I found myself so changed that the sight terrified me. Then I realised the completeness of the sacrifice which God required of me." Her beauty had gone for ever, and there is much pathos in so feminine an account of what was a disaster on the natural plane, but an ecstasy of self-dedication on the supernatural.

And so, under the jealous eyes of her sour mother-in-law, the years of her youth passed, as she bore what she called the cross of marriage. She had become the object of some scandal in the little world of the gossiping town which had watched the evolution of the gay and lovely girl into the woman, mutilated in body and, as many must have thought, in mind.

When she was twenty-eight, her husband mercifully died. She evaded her mother-in-law to nurse him personally to the end. He gave her as good a testimonial as any of those who during her life were to stand witness to her goodness when, after she had begged his forgiveness for all she had done to displease him, involuntary as it had been, he answered: " It is I who should ask forgiveness. I was not worthy of you." But after his death she very feelingly exclaimed with the Psalmist : " Thou hast broken my bonds, O Lord ; and I will offer thee a sacrifice of praise."

The marriage responsibilities were not, however, entirely broken. She was now a widow with two infant children on her hands. Despite the great wealth which was now hers, together with large sums held in trust for her children, she continued to live for a time with her mother-in-law, suffering not only the crosses inflicted on her by that curmudgeon, but also the far heavier crosses of that sense of utter abandonment by God which precedes the supreme, naked, inner union with God by faith alone, the " cloud of unknowing," the " dazzling darkness," of the English mystics, the " dark night " of the Spanish. " When I had lost all help from creatures and even all Divine assistance, I found myself in the happy necessity of falling into the pure Divine. . . . In losing all that is given, I found the Giver; in losing you, my God in me, I found you in your very Self in the changeless—never to lose you again." Once again, Mme. Guyon was finding the words that classically stamp the authentic adventure of the mystic's experience of the Divine.

2

Among the many priests and spiritual directors whom Mme. Guyon met in these early years, there was one who was destined to play a decisive role in her life, just as she was destined to play a tragic one in his. One of her half-brothers, the Père de La Motte, had joined the Barnabite Order in Paris. When one of his Barnabite colleagues, the Père La Combe, was sent by his superiors from Paris to Rome, there to teach theology, La Motte asked him to stop on his way south at Montargis and there deliver a letter to his sister, Mme. Guyon. La Combe was a tall, bony Savoyard of about thirty, selected for his learning and special promise to hold high positions in his Order.

It is well to remember this, because he seems to have gone down to history as having been always something of a visionary lunatic. When they met, they made a deep impression on one another. La Combe, born in the mountain air, must at that time have been climbing towards the rarified air of higher spirituality. He found in this young woman, as a much greater than he was to find later, someone who already seemed to have discovered what he was still searching for. Mme. Guyon says in her always excited way, " He has confessed to me since that he left me changed into another man." She also says that she never expected to see him again. Indeed, why should their paths have crossed, with him in Rome and she a housewife in a French country town? Why?—unless the subconscious will of this woman drove her to find him again. Was it the haunting memory of La Combe which turned her thoughts after her liberation from marriage to his native country, to Geneva? Geneva was of course the Calvinist Rome and the special object of the apostolic endeavours of the Annecy diocese whence La Combe came. But there is nothing to suggest any specially ardent spirit of proselytism in Mme. Guyon's spirituality —rather the contrary.

Anyway, five years after her husband's death Mme. Guyon made up her mind to the fantastic plan of leaving her younger child, leaving France itself, and journeying with her daughter to the outer Protestant darkness of Geneva. La Combe happened at the time to be the Superior of the Barnabite house at Thonon, twenty miles from Geneva.

Her own account, naturally, allows nothing for such motives as renewing her acquaintance with La Combe. She says it was a priest in confession who warned her that God had a special mission for her and it was she who protested that a widow with children could have no such mission. It was a Dominican who told her that it was God's will that she should do God's work in Geneva, not, however, without consulting its bishop. The bishop himself, M. d'Aranthon, one need hardly add, happened to be in Paris at the moment and ready to be consulted. He was a holy, if not very strong-willed old man, and as he was planning a foundation of *Nouvelles Catholiques* at Gex, near Geneva, he must be forgiven for supposing that Mme. Guyon with her wealth was God's answer to his prayers for money and help. He begged her to come.

Her fateful decision has been universally criticised, and it was one of the things which prejudiced Fénelon against her. In natural terms it was in fact indefensible. But at least she fully realised this, and it was certainly not callousness nor any lack of maternal feeling which accounted for the decision. If her subconscious motive was to see La Combe again—and this, of course, is surmise—she seems consciously to have persuaded herself after a real battle that the will of God was more important than her natural feelings. And she certainly went through the orthodox motions of leaving the final decision to the Bishop. She wrote to her brother that the education she would have given her children was bound to be a narrow and limited one. Now they would be in better hands—God's hands! Nor did she hesitate to sacrifice a great deal of her money, together with herself and her natural duties. She may have been deluded, but she certainly felt herself to be acting from the highest motives she knew. The great adventure of her life was starting.

CHAPTER TWO

MADAME GUYON ABROAD

In THE summer of 1681, Madame Guyon arrived, with her young daughter, at Gex, the little mountain town, some ten miles north of Geneva and some thirty miles around the lake from Thonon, where La Combe was settled. There, four empty walls awaited the little community of *Nouvelles Catholiques*, and the poor mother burst into tears at the thought of what lay in store for her daughter.

For some time she seems to have been torn between her motherly feelings for her child, thus translated from the comforts of a rich home to the austerities of a poor, religious house, and her supernatural maternal feelings for Père La Combe who was sent by the Bishop to console her. Her daughter, however, was taken care of, on La Combe's advice, no doubt, by being sent across the lake to the Ursulines in Thonon for her education. La Combe himself gave her far worse headaches. As she got to know him better, she discovered that he was, to her thinking, altogether on the wrong way of prayer. His was the way of *illuminism*, that is, of clear light, of direct inspiration and certainty, attributed to a special and very exceptional revelation from God. " Since he had been moving up till then by a way which was all light, ardour, knowledge, certainty, assurance, feelings " in contrast with " the little way of faith and denudation, he found it extremely hard to adjust himself." " The little way of faith and denudation " presupposed so complete a surrender to God's will, that the soul was necessarily left in darkness and desolation. In fact, there was a sharp conflict of spiritual wills between them which was probably the cause of a breakdown in her health, though the discomforts and deprivations of her new life must have played their part. For some time, however, she was ready to let La Combe have his way. She, too, it seemed, had her " revelations," among them that she was called upon by God to become, like Peter, the corner-stone of a new work within the Church. In her spirit of obedience to La Combe, she allowed herself to benefit not only from his spiritual direction, but from his powers to cure her afflictions. He would rest his hands on her head with his blessing to make her sufferings pass, and he even rounded off the good work by ordering her cough to cease when she crossed the lake to spend some days with her daughter at Thonon. Many similarly surprising curative effects of the priest's administrations towards his ever-ailing disciple are recounted, during these first two years of exile.

It was a strange interlude that could as easily give rise to the plaudits of the mob acclaiming the spiritual wonder of the two saints as to murmurs about the association between the pretentious widow and the visionary priest. How the choice would go might well depend, as so often in this life, on money. The Bishop could not have been too pleased to learn that his new protégée had signed away much of her estate to her relations, and this without consulting anyone. In his eyes and those of others on the spot a surprising amount of her value had thus disappeared. Then she managed to get on the wrong side of her confessor, a priest who was called the " Little Bishop " because of his diocesan position and the confidence he enjoyed with his superior. He strongly disapproved of the paucity of his penitent's confessional matter, even though she, always ready to make a joke—it was one of her more attractive traits—pointed out there were not many opportunities for sinning within the walls of a convent. Much worse was to come when Mme. Guyon thought it her duty to protect a beautiful young nun from the " Little Bishop's " too marked attentions. The " Little Bishop " took what revenge he could by depriving her of her servant and ordering her to do the chores of the house. She accepted all this willingly, and edified still more the little community by doing so without protest. Her tormentor was now in a dilemma. He would like to have driven her away, but she was a woman of influence and spirit whose talk could do him harm. Yet if she stayed, his own prestige within the convent would be weakened. So he persuaded the Bishop to ask her to become the convent's superior. As superior she would be far from popular, and the money allowed her by her relations was not to be sneezed at. Her connections would help to make the new work more widely known and to attract alms from Paris. But she parried this attack by insisting that her plans were far from settled, and who had ever heard of a convent superior who had not even made her novitiate? La Combe was asked as her spiritual director to order her to obey the Bishop. But he stood firm, even defying a threat of suspension from his priestly ministry rather than give his friend this unjust order.

The fat was now in the fire. Mme. Guyon knew that she would never be forgiven her interference between the "Little Bishop" and his favourite and fair penitent. So she left Gex for the Ursulines of Thonon, and the first of the many slanders which dogged her life began.

Letters about her relations with La Combe were sent to Paris, suggesting a good deal more than they actually said. Puzzled answers from Paris to Thonon were intercepted so that there could be no defence. But in Thonon itself, Mme. Guyon's patent goodness was winning through, as it was to do time and again later. Her charity and good works abounded, and her spiritual views were spreading. By this time, the spiritual clash between La Combe and herself was rapidly moving in her favour, as it had to. Hers was by far the stronger personality and hers, too, was the authentic mystical tradition. Those who have criticised Mme. Guyon on many counts, one of them being the way in which she always succeeded in spiritually directing her own directors, do not allow enough for the plain fact that with all her oddities, exaggerations, self-will and even heterodoxies, she was fundamentally right. Later, Fénelon, whom she also ostensibly directed, understood how to extract from the useless and even dangerous mass the rich vein of spiritual treasure.

Given the slightest chance, Mme. Guyon found ways and means of surrounding herself with disciples and, through them, of introducing her mystical teaching to religious communities and others. The spiritual fascination she could exert on people was always extraordinary. So it was now, and soon the good Bishop grew anxious. In the summer of 1683, two years after she had left Paris, he wrote: " I cannot approve her making her spiritual teaching universal and her introducing it into monasteries, to the prejudice of their rules. That sort of thing divides and upsets even the holiest communities." It was a wise judgment on M. d' Aranthon's part, for we must never look to Mme. Guyon for tact and moderation in her religious zeal. But at the same time the Bishop said: " Apart from that, I esteem and honour her beyond all imagining." This was a reference which proved of the greatest value to Mme. Guyon and to Fénelon much later. But in the circumstances she had no option but to leave the Ursulines at Thonon. Few people could live with her for long, but then few people like to have their ideas disturbed and their habits changed by prophets and prophetesses.

At first she knew not where to turn. She could only find a temporary refuge with her daughter in a primitive cottage where, she tells us, she was never happier. But petty and grosser persecution began again. Stones were thrown at the cottage. People came to destroy the little garden she was cultivating. Her half-brother in Paris, the Barnabite de La Motte, was furious with her, perhaps, as she suggests, because he was annoyed by the way in which she had disposed of the family fortune, perhaps because of his fellow Barnabite La Combe, probably because of the unpleasant rumours affecting his natural and his spiritual kin. Matters grew so bad that the Bishop forbade her to live in his diocese and dismissed La Combe.

A lady of rank and influence in Turin, the Marquise de Pruney, invited her to that city. As La Combe had been asked by the Bishop of Vercelli to help in the administration of his diocese, near Turin, Mme. Guyon, too, thought it would be a good thing to make her way across the mountains. So off they went in a strange cavalcade, La Combe, another priest and a boy on horse-back, Mme. Guyon and her daughter in a litter behind them. The rough journey must have been little short of 200 miles. It was meat for the scandal-mongers. " Our enemies," wrote Mme. Guyon, " first reported to Paris, and a hundred ridiculous stories about the journey were put out. It was a real fairy-tale, with completely invented fables, all as false as possible. Père de la Motte passed them round. Perhaps he really believed them; but if so, charity should have made him keep quiet about them. They said that I was alone with Père La Combe running from province to province and a thousand other stupid stories."

Though the aged Bishop of Aosta made known his approval of Mme. Guyon and of La Combe to the extent of expressing his wish that the latter might succeed him in his See, La Combe planned to see his friend safely established in Turin, while he himself went on to Vercelli. Despite the approbation of Italian bishops, where the Quietist genre of spirituality followed by the widow and the priest was highly popular, matters once more did not work out happily for Mme. Guyon. " The Marquise de Pruney," she confesses, " grew tired of me." This, she tells us, was because of the stories in circulation about her and the accounts of Bishop d'Aranthon's criticism of her mode of apostolate. It seems much more likely that the real problem lay in a conflict of wills between La Combe and herself. The poor Barnabite could not have relished the trouble brought on him by this odd association. What was, in the widow's eyes, a trial sent by God further to denude her self-love looked to the less *exalté* La Combe like pride and jealousy which arose whenever he tried to stand up to her or whenever he shared his spiritual favours with other, and more ordinary, penitents. Mme. Guyon was at this time at her worst, exclaiming in a fit of irritation against her supposed spiritual director: " Don't talk to me any more about humility. The usual rules about virtues no longer apply in my case."

In Turin she had the famous dream which was to cause her so much trouble later. In the dream, she and a friend climbed a high mountain, surrounded by a raging sea. Above this mountain was another encircled by a hedge in which there was a locked gate. They knocked, and the Master opened. Her friend disappeared, but she entered in. The Master, who was the " Spouse," took her by the hand and led her to a room in a wood. In it there were two beds. Who are they for, she asked, and He answered: " One is for my Mother; the other for you, my bride." Wild beasts lived there together in friendship in an atmosphere of candour and innocence. In the room she saw a twelve-year-old boy who was bidden find out if anyone had returned from the wreck. The Spouse told her that He had chosen her, His bride, to gather together all persons with courage enough to pass through the stormy sea and endure shipwreck in it.

We cannot really be surprised that Bossuet when he came to read these sort of confessions by the woman who so deeply influenced his fellow bishop, Fénelon, hardly knew whether he was standing on his head or his heels. But it was Mme. Guyon herself who innocently handed over to the great prelate this strange emotional and mystical jumble, and it was she who later wrote that jealousy in spiritual matters is the worst kind of self-love and that she herself had in the past suffered the most unbelievable tortures through it.

However this be, the Turin adventure was brought to an end, and La Combe received an order from his superiors to take her back to France. Mme. Guyon notes that La Combe obeyed " with some distaste." In fact, he took her across the mountains, and left her in Grenoble.

In these strange wanderings which were to last five years Mme. Guyon's sojourn in Grenoble has a particular importance. The dream related above clearly symbolised her sense of having been given a special apostolic vocation—of the highest order—to spread the mystical doctrine of finding God *within* the soul, through the loss of all self-love, even the loss of the enjoyment of Divine consolations and guidance. The destruction of everything human was the passport to pure love. Grenoble was the centre of rough and irreligious country, which was said to need missionaries more than China. It was spiritually ruled by a prelate of distinction, Bishop (later Cardinal) Le Camus, who had learnt how to deal with sinners through having himself been converted from a wild life at court. True, he used to say that his sins of the past were as much exaggerated as his present reputed virtues. However, here was a place where great things could be looked for through the preaching of Mme. Guyon's simple and God-centred spirituality.

Whatever other doubts there may be about this complex woman, of one thing we can be certain. She possessed a genius in drawing people to her and in entrancing them with the way she spoke of God and of the life of the spirit. " I visited no one," she writes, " but I was most surprised when a few days after my arrival several people who stated that they belonged to God in a special manner came to see me. I at once realised that I had received a special gift from God to read into souls and to give what suited each one. I felt myself suddenly clothed with an apostolic state."

Men, women, religious, priests and even a flock of Capuchin and Carthusian nuns came under her spiritual sway. One day, an influential person who had come to consult her noticed the manuscript of a spiritual book lying on her table. He picked it up and read the title: *Moyen Court et très facile de faire Oraison* (A Short and Easy Way of Prayer). He asked to be allowed to read it, and was so impressed that he had copies made and, in the end, had the little book printed. Mme. Guyon had written it in Thonon. The book was approved by the ecclesiastical censors, and soon it became the rage among the devout.

These successes in Grenoble, based as they were on her conviction that she had been granted a spiritual motherhood of souls which worked in a way analogous to that of the Holy Spirit communicating the Word to men, undoubtedly prepared the way for her later influence, through Fénelon, on the circle of court *dévots* and *dévotes* who were in a position to influence the young duc de Bourgogne, second heir to the throne of France. One day, so it was hoped, that prince would renew the spirit of France, prostituted by the ambitions, greed, sensuality, and pride of the " Grand Monarque," Louis XIV.

However, if many flocked to this spiritual mother, a good many more were once again determined to ruin her work by persecution and calumny. This, she tells us, forced her after some months to take the advice of the Bishop and leave Grenoble. In fact, exactly the same thing happened here as in the Geneva diocese, only on a much larger scale. Le Camus, though wise, tolerant and broadminded, realised that you could not have inspired women taking the place of the clergy and even religious superiors and generally breaking up the pattern of organised spiritual life. Grenoble might be as un-Christian as China, but he at least was not prepared to let feminine mysticism loose in his diocese. In 1685, he wrote to Bishop d'Aranthon that while he admired La Combe, he had had experience of these devout women who so easily attach themselves to their priestly directors, unless they are firmly handled. " She needs to be greatly humiliated and held down. I do not know whether she will stand such treatment, but it would certainly do her much good." But he did not doubt her sincerity and good faith. His testimony was later to prove important in the *cas Guyon*, but it may be that she would have done better to heed his sane advice about the need for humility.

Soon she was being towed, with Le Camus's chaplain and another priest, down the Rhone, encountering, of course, special hazards due to bad navigation and swirling waters. The poor chaplain, she explains, had a terrible fright when the boat struck a rock and was holed; but he, she adds, afterwards said that her abandonment to God's will enabled her to go through the experience without batting an eyelid.

At length, they reached Marseilles where a new, but very important, variation in her experiences took place. The hue and cry against her was this time organised by Jansenists who had got hold of copies of her *Moyen Court*. Jansenists, dedicated to the hardest and most exclusive way of finding salvation, could not stomach this short and easy way for all men to find God. They were always to remain bitter enemies of both Mme. Guyon and Fénelon. However, she was consoled by meeting the blind mystical writer, François Malaval, author of another and highly popular " Easy Way " of higher prayer, whom Bossuet later contemptuously dismissed as " that layman without theology."

From Marseilles to Nice where " I knew not what I would become, on what side to turn, being alone and abandoned by all, without knowing, my God, what You wanted me to do." On and on, Across the sea to Genoa—and the day's sail, it need hardly be added, turned out to be twelve days of dangerous storm. Genoa, recently attacked by the French, was in no mood to welcome a French visitor, and charged her exorbitant prices. A bad litter, a wicked muleteer, robbers, mountains, precipices, a lodging-house full of rough men, another where she was taken for a prostitute, discomfort is heaped on discomfort, horror on horror, in her account of this journey. And it ended with a trial which cost her more than all that went before. She could only make arrangements to go to Vercelli, not to Turin. In Vercelli, La Combe was now established as the Bishop's assistant. It is hard not to suspect that this was the real cause of her finding herself there. But when she reached the town, she found that her priest-friend was far from pleased to see her. The poor man, whose admiration for her and devotion to her were unquestioned, as the sequel shows, was nevertheless terrified at getting into further trouble through a too close association with the widow. Worldly wisdom was never a characteristic of this God-directed prophetess. However, as it turned out, the old Bishop was graciousness itself. He smoothed everything over, and even sent her presents of fruit when she was feeling unwell. He declared that she was an angel and planned to keep her in his diocese.

All this was too good to be true. It could not last. Her half-brother in Paris, the Père de La Motte, had been made Barnabite Provincial Superior. Determined not to stand for any more of this spiritual affection between his sister and his religious subject, he recalled La Combe to Paris on the grounds that a preacher of his quality was urgently needed in the French capital. "Who wouldn't have believed that his words were sincere," Mme. Guyon exclaims. Her health which seemed to register as accurately as a thermometer the degree of spiritual frustration which she experienced broke down completely. So it was arranged that La Combe, in the Barnabite's words, " should accompany his dear sister and help her in her illness and long journey " back to Paris, where, of course, she could more easily be controlled and, maybe, put out of harm's way. At Chambéry the paths of the returning pilgrims of the Infinite and that of Père de La Motte, on his way to Rome to elect a new Barnabite General Superior, crossed. " Though he pretended to be friendly," Mme. Guyon comments, " it was not hard to see that his thoughts were other than his words. He had planned to destroy us."

After this litany of almost incredible misadventures, the return journey after nearly five years of exile from Montargis and Paris was strangely, indeed ominously, peaceable. At Grenoble, the pious widow was once more fêted by her disciples, and Bishop le Camus, soon to be made a Cardinal for his good Christian sense in various issues of the day, not least his criticism of the King's revocation of tolerance towards the Protestants, gave her some excellent fatherly advice. He told her she would do well to give up her striking attachment (*attache éclatante*) for La Combe and to interest herself more in her own family and her personal affairs. He told her to dogmatise less and to be more careful how she explained her spiritual doctrine. Later he was to refer to her " virtue and piety," and it seems clear that this wise prelate was in no way scandalised either by her behaviour or her teaching. He had in fact little difficulty in distinguishing between her real goodness—a not too common quality in his pastoral experience, and the exaggerated way in which she talked and acted. Hard priestly sense is apt to be bored —and suspicious—of the excessive piety of zealous, one-track minded women who want to reform the world.

Thus, the two travellers, surely the oddest couple abroad in Europe at that time, reached Paris in July, 1686, after apostolic wanderings, unique—if we are to believe Mme. Guyon's lengthy and detailed accounts—for the hazards encountered, the hatred and persecution they generated, and the spiritual enlightenment they achieved among those humble and generous enough to appreciate the "easy way" of discovering, attending to, and disinterestedly loving God so that life ever after was, as it were, spiritual plain sailing.

2

Fénelon himself was later to admit that Mme. Guyon was "a person of the mental type given to the exaggeration of her experiences." The reader who works his way through the endless pages of the Autobiography, here summarised into a few paragraphs, will not be inclined to quarrel with that judgment. In fact, he will want to know whether it is a pack of lies. At this stage a quick answer may be given, because the whole story would be robbed of its real interest if, in fact, Mme. Guyon were to be thought of as no more than a mentally-deranged, hysterical visionary. She herself, we have seen, was to hand over the whole account to the formidable Bossuet, and to do this voluntarily. Bossuet, the most powerful churchman of his day, believed her to be a major danger to both Church and State. If the prelate could have proved to the world that she was a liar and if he could have shown that any of the appalling calumnies spread about her by her enemies had any foundation in fact, he would have utterly destroyed her once and for all and with her the powerful personages who came virtually to stand or fall by her reputation. Yet he never succeeded in breaking her story, in demonstrating any of it to be untrue, and least of all was he able to destroy her personal reputation. After years of dramatic and public struggle, with the whole world avidly following the battle, he had in the end to acknowledge that nothing could be proved against her character and her good faith. This is enough to show that even though Mme. Guyon doubtless considerably over-dramatised and romanticised the story she had to tell, her account is substantially true, and not maliciously weighted in her own favour.

But there is another difficulty which requires a preliminary answer. Mme. Guyon is very much her own heroine. If she was as humble and good as we are led to believe, why does she leave us in so little doubt about the fact? The answer to this is not so easy. We certainly have to allow for the fact that she conceived herself to have been ordered by her confessor to write the fullest possible account of her life for his personal enlightenment. For such spiritual autobiographies, there were plenty of precedents. Further-more, as Fénelon pointed out, the saints often do praise themselves, and for this reason. Their detachment from the flattery of human praise and from the false self-regarding humility of lesser mortals, who like to be thought modest fellows, enable them to see them-selves not as *they* made themselves, but as *God* has made them. This would apply to a person like Mme. Guyon (whether genuine or deluded, or a mixture of both) whose spirituality was so essentially based on an utter self-abandonment, come what might, and on her continuously reiterated insistence of the spirit of childlikeness, even infancy, under God's all-powerful and all-embracing power and presence within and about her.

These explanations suffice to suggest that unless she was a com-plete fraud—and we can promise the reader that when he has heard the whole story he will not think that—she was only *conscious* in telling her story in the way she did of obeying her confessor and carrying out God's will. But what was really happening in her *subconscious* may well be a very different story. There is indeed much to suggest that until she met Fénelon, a good deal of her behaviour expressed a subconscious will to dominate others and to make herself into a figure of importance, through the remarkable psychic or spiritual gifts which she must have possessed. The little girl whose first dreams were given shape in the romances which she read with such eagerness was realising underlying ambitions through her spiritual power. If this is part of the explanation, it

derogates neither from the genuineness of her gifts nor from a goodness, even possibly a sanctity, which expressed itself in the admirable
way in which she suffered persecution all her life for justice's sake
and the way in which she learnt from experience.

We need to have these thoughts in mind as we embark on the
next phase of her narrative, for, despite the fact that it took place
in Paris under the public eye, involving personages of rank, power
and importance, it is even less credible than what we have so far
heard. But it, too, let us recall, was to be subject to Bossuet's
eagle eye, scrutinising official files which should have been available
for examination, unless indeed they were destroyed by those whose
interest it was to destroy them.

In Paris, Mme. Guyon settled down for some months to lead a
quiet life in the *cloître de Notre Dame*, where, as we have seen, she
edified people by her piety and her almsgiving.

Her friends were the friends of the Duchesse de Charost, good
women of the best society. They met together in twos or threes,
and certainly attracted no special attention. La Combe, meanwhile,
was earning a reputation as an outstanding preacher at a time when
preaching was a much more important affair than it is to-day. It
was the age of preachers, because preaching was the nearest thing
to free speech and free entertainment in that controlled and rigid
society. Preachers like Fléchier, Boileau, Masillon, La Chaise met
the sort of demand which to-day is satisfied by political speeches,
lecturers, reviews and magazines. A popular preacher was a man
of fame, and he might well be one of power and influence. Jealousy
between preachers was inevitable, and Mme. Guyon's brother, who
had his preaching ambitions, was not pleased to see his fellow
Barnabite's *renommée* in this field mounting. Soon old and new
stories about dark associations between the widow at Notre Dame
and the Barnabite preacher began to spread. A forger and his wife,
it seems, were told to go to confession to Père La Combe. Having
done this, the woman went from confessional to confessional,
pretending to be a *dévote* scandalised by the things she had been
told by La Combe. Forgeries made their appearance—among them
a letter from Marseilles addressed to the Archbishop of Paris in
which it was stated that Mme. Guyon and the priest had slept in the
same room in that city. La Motte showed a copy to his sister. She

only smiled, and told him that the forgers should at least have taken the trouble to get their facts right. The only time she was in Marseilles, the priest was in Vercelli, preaching the Lenten sermons there. These stories were to haunt her life and that of the more unfortunate La Combe.

Mme. Guyon believed that her brother was at the back of this fresh conspiracy, and his behaviour lent countenance to the horrible idea. The widow, however, had more powerful and more anonymous enemies than her strangely-behaving brother. Now for the first time the dread name of Molinos, the Quietist, comes into the story —Molinos who seems to have been regarded as the Rasputin of his day. La Motte warned his sister that papers containing terrible accusations against La Combe had been lodged at the Archbishopric. In them, he was denounced as a heretic and a follower of Molinos. When he spoke to La Combe himself, he said that similar charges were being laid against his sister. At length, he came to the point. Both were accused, and her safety could only lie in immediate flight from Paris.

No one can accuse Mme. Guyon of cowardice. Now, as ever after, she stood her ground. Either the stories were true, in which case she should be punished; or they were lies, and then she had no reason to fly. She had not failed to realise that her flight from Paris would put the final touch to the case against the unfortunate La Combe who was as innocent as the day.

Mme. Guyon now tells us a story with such vivacity that it is impossible to believe that she could have invented it. Her brother planned to enlist the services of the tutor of Mme. Guyon's children in order to help him make representations to the Archbishop personally. The tutor happened to be a Parliamentary Councillor, and as such a person of some weight. We do not know what the nature of those representations were to be. In any case, La Motte failed to find him at his home. Only the tutor's sister was there when he called. Suspecting the worst, she warned her brother. Next morning, both La Motte and the tutor hurried to the waiting-room of Archbishop Harlay so as to be first in the audience queue. The priest won the race; but when he saw the tutor hurrying in before the audiences began, he first turned pale and then scarlet. Then he tried to persuade the tutor not to see the Archbishop, as it was none of his

business. The tutor insisted on going in. Then followed a panto-
mime between them as to which should go in first, settled in the
end by allowing the Archbishop to call the one he first saw. The
tutor turned out to be the lucky one.

Saint-Simon gives posterity an unforgettable picture of the
worldly Archbishop and his times when he tells us how the good-
looking and gallant prelate used to walk about his grounds with a
favourite duchess, while a gardener, walking some distance behind
them, raked the ground for their return along the path. Fénelon's
violent charge against Harlay has already been quoted. But he was
an able man who enjoyed the King's favour and earned the dislike
of the King's wife, Madame de Maintenon. On this occasion, he
listened in some surprise to the tutor's fervent defence of this Mme.
Guyon, and told him that he had never heard of her, though he
had heard of La Combe. He was shocked to hear that he had
advised this woman unknown to him to leave Paris for her own
good. When La Motte entered, the displeased Archbishop asked him
who had been spreading such false information. La Motte left, his
tail between his legs, furiously murmuring that he would get his
revenge.

If the story is true, the revenge was certainly not long delayed.
This time the appeal was direct to the King, who was as jealous as
any archbishop about what he considered to be good behaviour
and right doctrine in the Church of France. Dangeau in his *Journal*
refers in this connection to certain " secret relations with the Court
of Rome," and this may provide a significant clue to what happened
afterwards, for Louis, the Gallican king, was always suspicious of
Rome's interference in French ecclesiastical affairs. " The kings of
France have made themselves Popes, Muftis, Grand Pontiffs and
Princes with absolute authority over sacred matters," wrote a
contemporary.

A report was sent to Louis on La Combe's alleged crimes,
Molinost leanings and, it seems, secret dealings with Rome. The
King, quite properly in the circumstances, as Mme. Guyon herself
insists, ordered the priest to remain in the Barnabite house and to
be questioned by the ecclesiastical chancellor or judge.

But the trap was neatly set. The accused man was not in fact
informed of the royal order, so he naturally went about his external

priestly duties, as usual, thus disobeying the order. The chancellor, who was in the plot, conveniently made his retreat so as to delay the start of the examination. To make sure that La Combe would go out, fake sick calls were arranged. La Combe, informed of the inquiry, was persuaded by La Motte to hand over to him all the papers emanating from the Inquisition, the Sacred Congregation of Rites and various cardinals approving his spiritual views. Such papers would be more than enough to answer any Parisian ecclesiastical inquiry, he was assured. Needless to say, the papers were never seen again.

La Combe was arrested on 3rd October, 1687, and he soon found himself in the dreaded Bastille. He was apparently questioned, and he maintained the orthodoxy of his teaching and the propriety of his conduct. The report of the *Nouvelles Ecclesiastiques* or Church Gazette summed it up: " He was judged without any formalities, convicted of being opiniated, of being too attached to Papal interests, speaking only of Rome and the Roman censorship to which he had submitted his book (*Analysis of Mental Prayer*), and condemned to perpetual imprisonment."

We shall meet La Combe again when, driven half-way to insanity by the years of captivity, he was persuaded to admit grave moral faults with Madame Guyon of which they were both most certainly completely innocent. But as we carry our story along, we must surely shed a tear for this son of the open mountains, sincerely dedicated to the loving service of God, gifted beyond the average, who got himself accidentally involved with great affairs of Church and State, and, without reaping any sympathy or glory from posterity, spent the rest of his many years in prison, more than half of them in madness. For once in her life Mme. Guyon was guilty of an understatement when she commented: " Only in eternity shall we know which are God's friends."

After La Combe's disappearance, there was little chance for Mme. Guyon against whom the *prima facie* case of pursuing the fallen priest and spreading suspect teaching was a good deal stronger. Only favour from the highest quarters or flight could save her from enemies who, in her own words, were determined not to spare her accusations of any " crime of infamy, unorthodoxy, sorcery and sacrilege." The firmest ground was heresy, and so the King was

Jeanne Bouvier de La Motte Guyon known as
'Madame Guyon'

told that she had written a dangerous book. It was, of course, the *Moyen Court*, which continued to be ecclesiastically approved and published, even when she was in prison. She observed, very much to the point, that usually dangerous books were suppressed while their authors remain free; in her case, however, she was to be imprisoned, while her book was freely circulated. Louis was also shown a letter purporting to be in her writing and told that she had had much correspondence with the infamous Molinos, " I, who never even knew that a Molinos existed on earth, until I learnt of the fact in the *Gazette*."

So on 29th January, 1688, nearly four months after her poor friend, director and disciple, had been seized, she was ordered by royal *lettre de cachet* to be confined to the Visitation Convent in the rue Saint-Antoine. She was to be separated from her children, who were in the hands of relatives, and not allowed to see or communicate with them or anyone else. She could have little hope of a better fate than La Combe's.

3

A heretic in a convent! Little imagination is needed to imagine the way in which the good nuns viewed the guest who had been forced on them. The sister deputed to look after her—her gaoler in fact—made no bones about calling her every name under the sun, so long as it was within the wide bounds of Christian charity; and when the prisoner was taken to the chapel, her nun-gaoler knelt behind her sighing heavily. This is another touch which Mme. Guyon was clearly giving from life.

The usual questioning soon began. It was conducted by the Archbishop's chancellor, assisted by M. Pirot who was a kind of theologian-in-ordinary. Pirot does a good deal of questioning in this story, and he was an honest, if weak, man. The prisoner solemnly declared that she had never departed from the teaching of the Church for which she would give her blood. Protestants who later tried to make an Evangelical heroine out of this woman, at whom the Catholic Church looked askance, never realised that her Catholic orthodoxy was as incurable as her mystic call. If she had written anything in her books subject to misunderstandings, she pointed out, the books had been submitted to the Church and to persons of experience and knowledge, and been approved. The examination was an amateur proceeding, and the prisoner easily held her own, answering, for example, the accusation that she had sought to abolish vocal prayer by pointing out that what she meant was that a single " Our Father " properly said was worth more than twenty recited without attention.

She was faced by a much graver matter when she was shown the letter that had been read by the King. This letter involved her in heresy and sedition. " It is not in my handwriting," she protested. She was told that this was only a copy. " The original is certainly in your handwriting; you can see for yourself that with a letter like this, you deserve to be thrown into prison." " Certainly," she answered, " if I had written it."

Mme. Guyon's own account is confirmed at this point by the discovery in the Archives of the Bastille of the letters she wrote in protest to the Archbishop and his Chancellor—letters to which she refers, without quoting them, in her Autobiography. In these letters she complained that if forged letters were to be used in evidence against her, her troubles would never end.

Next, they tried to trap her by asking her for her manuscript writings in which she commented on the Bible—this endless commentary had filled quiet hours during her sojourn abroad, and she promised to do so as soon as she was liberated. Declaring themselves satisfied with this promise, they then drew up an indictment accusing her of rebellion on the grounds of her refusal to give up these papers. When this indictment was read over to her, she protested at the trap, and told her accusers where the papers were to be found.

The first round was won, and by Holy Week, 1688, she was allowed ' freedom of the cloister,' that is, freedom of movement within the convent, but with no alteration of the rules forbidding any contact with her family and the outside world.

The next round sounds unbelievable, but Bossuet who read her account never showed her up as a liar. She was promised complete freedom if she would only give her daughter—an heiress—in marriage to a good-for-nothing, penniless nephew of Archbishop Harlay. The young man had given up the practice of his religion.

Of course, she refused. Her inquisitors, like so many of their kind, then and since, apparently never troubled to study the character of their victim.

The last step was the old, old one of trying to obtain a confession in the shape of a letter of submission to the Archbishop with an expression of sorrow for the mistakes she had made. With such a letter in their hands, her enemies would need nothing more. She could join her friend, La Combe, and posterity would forget her, as it has forgotten him. She was too clear-headed to be deceived, and now, as many times afterwards, she refused to sign letters of submission phrased in a compromising way. However, this refusal did not greatly worry her accusers. They simply had the letter they needed forged. Its contents were spread abroad and communicated to her relations. It could only be a matter of time before she was definitely thrown into prison—and left there.

Only one thing, it seemed, could save her, and that was the lucky chance of influence being brought to bear on the King from the highest quarters. " God who never abandons those who trust in him " told her, she assures us, that all would yet be well.

Certainly help came, and from two quarters.

Mme. Guyon had a brilliant, gay and devout young cousin, Mme. de La Maisonfort. This attractive creature, of whom we shall hear more later, had caught the eye of the all-powerful wife of the King, Mme. de Maintenon, who associated her with the work she had most at heart, the education by new pedagogical methods of the daughters of the war-ruined nobility at the convent of Saint-Cyr. La Maisonfort interested herself in the fate of her persecuted cousin and soon discovered something of the truth. The Archbishop's manœuvres to get his nephew married off to Mme. Guyon's daughter were not calculated to edify the up-and-coming circle of dévots at the Court who, anyway, loathed the worldly Harlay. Mme. de Maintenon spoke to the King. But Louis did not share his wife's dislike of Harlay and professed himself to have a horror of both heresy and mysticism. The two obviously went together. The whole affair smelt, too, of Roman intrigue. So the plea failed.

But one of the regular visitors to the convent was that queen of good works, Mme. de Miramion. She had organised a tremendous work of charity, medical care and education for the destitute in the capital, and she especially interested herself in the orphans. Soon, the great families associated themselves with this work, and Louis himself distributed his alms through her hands. Though Mme. de Miramion was a friend of the duchesses and of Mme. de Maintenon, her active disposition did not prejudice her in favour of the mystical prisoner. But Mme. Guyon, as always with those who really knew her, had won her own gaolers over. The whole convent testified to their prisoner's " piety, sweetness, resignation, conversation and the spiritual inspiration she afforded it." Mme. de Miramion was deeply impressed. She confirmed the reports of Mme. de La Maisonfort, and Mme. de Maintenon once again approached her royal husband. It is most likely that all this pressure from the pious court circle was not so much due to admiration for Mme. Guyon as to their detestation of Archbishop Harlay under whose authority the prisoner was held. The King could no longer resist, and on the eve of the feast of St. Louis (24th August, 1688), he ordered her release. It was not a day too soon, for Mme. Guyon's accusers were daily awaiting the King's signature to the order transferring the prisoner from the convent to a State prison far from the capital, where she would have been forgotten.

Thus, by sheer chance, Mme. Guyon's first period of imprisonment had ended, only a month or so before her meeting with the Abbé de Fénelon at Beynes which was to set the course for storms in Church and State and for human tragedies which went far beyond the range of even Mme. Guyon's soaring imagination.

CHAPTER THREE

FÉNELON ENTRANCED

COMPARED WITH the forty years of adventurous life of Jeanne Marie Bouvier de La Motte, widow of the dull M. Guyon and provincial *mère de famille*, the thirty-seven years of François de Salignac de La Mothe Fénelon's life had been almost banal, despite the romantic aura that attached to his name and birth. In Perigord, there stands the partly medieval château, with its ancient keep, where this latest scion of a family going back to the mists of history came into the world. Yet we can pass over the years of clerical education and early priesthood with their atmosphere of enlightened and dignified piety both in the entourage of his family and of his Jesuit and Sulpician tutors, because it was his birth and his family connections, not his successful studies, which gave him the entrée into the most distinguished society of the capital and court within which alone he was to be truly at home until his last years. Given a certain talent and either ambition or piety, such a man, entering the priestly state, would in those days be born to the episcopal purple. Before Fénelon was raised in his forties to the princely, though provincial, See of Cambrai, and considered the obvious nominee for Paris itself, he had already refused minor episcopal promotion on two occasions.

But Fénelon had much more than talent; he had genius. But with his genius went a complexity, indeed a mystery, of character which makes the complexity of a Mme. Guyon almost simple by comparison. Mme. Guyon was like a volcano throwing out a mass of energy, good, bad and indifferent, an activity which to her credit she learnt to control. Within Fénelon there were mysterious depths about which men will always argue.

His Gascon temperament gave him a dreaming, romantic, idealist side, as well as a sense of the ironic—of the proper lightness with which much of our pretty miserable human life should always be taken. An early letter describes both comically and ironically how he went to take possession of the Priory of Carenac, whose modest revenue was to be his only private income—a matter of great edification in those days. The letter ends, referring to the orator of the occasion: " He compared me to the sun; a moment after I was the moon; all the brightest stars then had the honour of resembling me; thence we passed to the elements and the meteors, and happily finished with the beginning of the world. By that time the sun had set, and therefore to complete the comparison between the sun and me, I retired to my room to do the same." An earlier letter, written at the age of twenty-four, suggests his romanticism, his piety and his dreamy love of the classics. Its style combines a lightness of touch, even a certain shame, which he was never to lose, about too seriously expressing his feelings and ambitions. " A number of accidents have kept on delaying my return to Paris; but at last I go—indeed, I fly. The thought of this journey makes me think of a much greater one. All Greece opens to me; the Sultan falls back in fear; already the Peloponnesus breathes in freedom, and the Church of Corinth flourishes again: the voice of the Apostle will once more be heard. I feel myself carried to those beautiful places and amid these precious ruins. . . . Already, I see the Schism at an end, the Orient and the Occident united . . . the path of the Saviour, watered with His blood, liberated from its profanators and clothed again with new glory. . . ."

But all through his life his inner stability and, perhaps at times, his moral sense, were out of step with his reason or the Catholic imperatives to which he gladly bound himself. Such a complexity was bound to give rise to painful tensions. And in particular juxtaposition of romantic impulse and a certain mental and bodily instability with an acquired rational clerical discipline were to result in what might be called an unconscious but resourceful diplomacy in his reactions to faith, life and people.

Looking back to his own youth, he wrote one day when he was nearing fifty: " My early years have been passed in sweetness, freedom, liberty; they have been filled with pleasant studies and in my relations with charming friends." This idyllic memory which was in reality the memory of the happier and lighter side of his nature led him also to write in subtle fear: " As for me, when I suffer, my sufferings are boundless, so that when happier times return, my nature fears to enjoy the sweetness lest it be a kind of treason that will turn by contrast into a worse suffering when the crosses return." He could write, too: " My life is sad and dried-up like my body. . . . Happy the day when we do not foresee the morrow. . . . There is in me, it seems, a fund of self-interest and lightness which makes me ashamed. . . . God opens to us a strange book indeed for our instruction when He lets us read into our own hearts." Fénelon was indeed a throw-forward in mood and temperament from the classic stability of the seventeenth century to nineteenth and twentieth-century man, increasingly an enigma to himself.

For such an introspective, sensitive, self-sympathetic and spiritually experienced priest there could be no more congenial a life's work than the direction of other people's souls and lives by personal intercourse and endless correspondence. His greatest power undoubtedly lay in his discernment of the only thing that, after all, really counts, the world which is each man's and each woman's consciousness, character, person, just as his deepest natural and spiritual wish was to help enlighten and enrich each such living world and individual human being. There is no reason to suppose that he consciously picked and chose among those he wanted to help, but he was not the man to refuse the opportunity to concentrate on souls, especially feminine ones, of choice distinction in the land. That was his natural millieu, and such souls, with their culture and associations, were naturally infinitely more interesting and agreeable to him than, say, " the last of men," the rough Flemings of the See he was to rule with, however, complete conscientiousness.

Saint-Simon said that Fénelon " wanted to please everyone " and that " he had long been knocking at every door without making them open to him "—this in contrast to his " giant's steps " when the great doors did finally open. This view has been almost universally accepted ever since. But was it really true? Fénelon was, no doubt, ambitious with the ambition of a powerful and wide-ranging mind born and trained in the world where success alone counts and where history is made. But such ambition was only one of the facets of that " self-interest " which haunted his conscience and which, under Mme. Guyon's guidance especially, he sought, never quite successfully, to kill. In his priestly character as a whole it expressed itself in an apostolic zeal on the clerical and social level which was his by birth, by talents and by taste. Such a zeal was to be judged, not by a call to retire from the great world, as would befit a monk, nor by the tally of souls gained, as would befit a Jesuit, but by his spiritual usefulness and his example in the station in which God had placed him, as befitted a unique son of Saint Sulpice.

The many sides of his nature made him essentially an experimentalist, a pilgrim, in life; and because this attitude, more especially in a great churchman, was in the sharpest contrast with the unyielding, brittle strength of the great French clerical monarchy, whatever Fénelon wrote and did became, unconsciously, a challenge and a scandal to his contemporaries. Though he could hardly be said to have written a book in the ordinary sense of the word, he left to posterity thirty and more large volumes of his writings. He always wrote for the occasion, for a practical purpose, to work out an idea; and without his realising it, his writings contained the seed of the yet unborn world of the eighteenth and subsequent centuries. Generations of bored French schoolchildren have had to study *Télémaque*, his best-known work, yet even this was only written to help educate and enlighten the King's grandson whose upbringing was in his charge. The better world, rather too beautifully described in that fable, was a half-practical, half-Utopian vision of a world of nature, brotherhood and peace, born of the classical and the Christian traditions, projected into a self-questioning world. It was in startling contrast with the classic, conventional world of the Grand Monarque, and prophetic of the romanticism of the eighteenth-century hopes. As such, it embodied a severe, though disguised, criticism of the rule of the absolute King and of the France which no one was supposed to criticise.

By the time he met Mme. Guyon he had already written an essay on the Education of Girls, at the request of the Duchess of Beauvilliers to help her in the bringing up of her large family.

Though conservative in tone, it is remarkable for the simplicity, detail and the almost scientific nature of its psychological and practical analysis of the problem, with its emphasis on such subjects as health, hygiene, domestic economy and the rest. Nothing could have been more alien to Fénelon's seventeenth-century mind than modern ideas like the equality or rights of women, or the ways which we call democratic, or still less any questioning of the traditional philosophy of the Church, yet in his determination to analyse the problems presented by human nature and human society, he was preparing the way for values and ideas which were bound to challenge, or at least by-pass, the traditions and conventions of his own time, most of which he himself, in fact, accepted without question. Louis XIV is said to have called Fénelon's writings " the cleverest and most fantastic in his kingdom." If so, that monarch showed considerable perspicacity, but the person most surprised by the royal judgment would have been the author himself. Between the certainties of the reactionaries and of the revolutionaries, Fénelon felt his way forward to the realities of God, and man.

In his spiritual approach and his spiritual writings, no one could have been more orthodox and no one could have accepted with a fuller faith the authority, the doctrine and the values of the Catholic Church, yet within this solid core, his adventurous, experimental and sensitive mind was searching for a living spirit within the magnificent frame—a spirit intimately related to life as we know it, to *our* life, to the life of our neighbours, to human life. Nothing he wrote has worn better than the spiritual letters through which he guided the Christian life of his friends. This appetite for the living spirit, for God, for the All-Real behind the riddle of human life and changing appearances, was so much the essence of his spiritual approach that, unbeknown to his conscious self, it was fundamentally far more important to him than his undoubted loyalty to, and complete faith in, the Catholic system which in his view necessarily went with that personal religion. Hence that stubbornness, that fighting spirit, that unshakeable devotion to ideals and ideal friends, that readiness to face disappointment and disgrace, that carefully analysed submission to authority which make up the central theme of the story we have to tell. Hence, too, the peculiarity of his relation with the mystical adventuress to whom the Duchess of Charost had just introduced him, for it was she who was to provide the key to the puzzle of his own complex aspirations, and character. It was she who gave him the clue to the deepest mystery of human life.

2

Let it be at once made clear that there was nothing in the spiritual friendship between Mme. Guyon and the Abbé (later Archbishop) de Fénelon which has even a remote suggestion of what we call ' sex,' though, as we shall see, circumstances and Fénelon's character lent the relationship something of the furtive and even comic quality of the traditional illicit love-affair. Some early French writers tried to romanticise the whole affair by, making out that the widow was a good deal younger than she was, or by emphasising her reputation as a great beauty. She was described, for example, as " sentimental and romantic and of alluring beauty—the most charming heretic that ever was." Later writers have coldly retorted that a pock-marked widow of forty was unlikely to appeal in that way to the younger and handsome priest, as though a person of Fénelon's type would fall, if he fell at all, through such physical considerations. But the evidence that there was no physical element at all, and hardly any of the normally sentimental and honestly affectionate is far too strong to be doubted. They only met on the rarest occasions, and it is even doubtful whether Fénelon was even attracted by her—whether, for example, he was half as attracted by her as by the King's wife, Mme. de Maintenon, who in the end turned so viciously against him. Yet, throughout his life and in the face of the hostile, mocking social and clerical world, in the face of the great who could fulfil his highest ambitions or destroy him, the relationship persisted. It was unique in itself and it joined together two unique personalities.

As for Mme. Guyon, she was a natural mother, not a natural lover. Her affection for her children, despite the flight to Geneva, was extremely strong, while her whole taste, piety and self-dedication to God precluded any spontaneous tenderness or physically-based friendship or love between herself and others. Suspicions of sexuality repressed or expressed, in her life or in her spiritual doctrine could hardly have been farther from the mark. Spiritually, she was the mother of a new people of God, a creator of new life, not a sharer of life with anyone less than the Divine. " I confess," she wrote to Fénelon, " that my heart has a kind of maternal feeling for you—a feeling that you would find it hard to understand without further experience. But it is so real that I am sometimes forced to say to Our Lord on your behalf and those of your friends [' your,' not ' our ']: have I not carried this people in my womb ? Yes, I have carried you there, and in a way which He who made it understands. One day, you too will understand." Fénelon, in his turn, was expected to be " the father of a great people." Her expressions of intimacy were always purely spiritual. " I am one with you in Him who is all." " There are times when your soul is seen to be so near mine, that I find nothing between them, I say nothing."

Perhaps Fénelon expressed their union best when he wrote: " I feel nothing for you, and I am closer to no one than to you."

What was the secret of this unfelt intimacy which sprang up so suddenly after that first meeting and expressed itself for some months in an extraordinary correspondence unknown to Fénelon's early and official biographers ? The answer is to be found in one word. Mme. Guyon was one thing only to him, but that one thing was supremely important. She was his " saint." She somehow polarised for him that unanalysed sea of spiritual yearning in which he wanted to find the answer to the heaped-up and insoluble perplexities of life.

Fénelon, we have seen, was avid of experience, eager to bypass the dead bones of theologisings and philosophisings about Him whose very essence it was to exist, to be actual, to be reality itself, to be as truly in the heart of man as to be in the farthest heavens, to be here-and-now as much as to be in eternities. But with this will and feeling for the living God went the long, logical, conformist priestly training in which in fact he was himself a brilliant theorist. Had he not denounced the Oratorian, Malebranche, for selling the pass to the Socinians and Deists ? Worse still, his natural temperament was unstable, nervous. His lightness, his laugh, his very deep human feelings for his family and his friends, his delicacy and sensitiveness, his social grace were gay and charming flowers grown in a dark and dry soil. He was essentially a cerebrotonic, nervy, restless, self-doubting, melancholic. " Dryness," " coldness," " reserve," " repugnance," " lassitude "—such are the words which qualify his disposition in his more intimate letters, and not least those to his friend. In other words, he was by temperament anything but sanguine, comfortable, optimistic in himself, however much he might dream romantic dreams. However desperately such a man may seek the Divine, his disposition will cut him off from what might be called the primrose path to sanctity, the path which such a self-confident and sanguine personality as Bossuet could so easily follow. He was neither expansive nor credulous. He had little self-assurance. Too capable, almost, of distinguishing the counterfeit from the genuine article, at any rate in himself if not in others, he had no easy vision of God, no taste for the spiritual consolations and joys which carry along the jolly, as well as the fierce, saints. He had indeed hoped once to experience the " sweetness " of the Divine touch, and he had recommended others to seek it, but he had despairingly failed to find it, and he came to warn others against it.

And now he suddenly found himself face to face with someone who, he believed, had manifestly experienced the authentic Divine, someone who had trodden the true road along which the great mystics of the Church had climbed through clouds into Reality, someone, above all, who could explain his spiritual restlessness. " I am convinced," he wrote to her, " that you possess an eminent power, in the light of experience, for the inner ways, which is extraordinary, and I am very certain of the way of pure faith and abandonment, along which you walk and enable others to walk." His famous remark is always quoted: "We should believe Mme. Guyon about this [the ways of the inner life]. She has experienced them. True, she is but a woman, but God reveals His secrets to whom He will. If I wanted to travel from Paris to Dammartin, and a local peasant were there to guide me, I should follow and trust him, even though only a peasant."

The reader should remember that he already knows a good deal more about Mme. Guyon's past than Fénelon ever cared to know. He persistently refused to do more than dip into the writings which were to scandalise Bossuet so deeply. Maybe he feared to do so, but writings, his own as well as those of others, were secondary compared to the living person which fascinated him.

Mme. Guyon for her part very quickly sensed Fénelon's mind and qualities. Here was a priest from a world utterly different from poor La Combe's. He was a priest with a splendid future, sent to her by God as the agent of the great spiritual work she was called upon to do; but he was also a well-trained, learned priest with whom one would have carefully to choose one's words. On the other hand, now that the great doors were about to open to him, Fénelon was just ready for her little way of darkness and self-abnegation which would counterbalance and almost justify the opportunities and dangers of life at Court. Unlike La Combe with his natural love of air and light, Fénelon needed an inner refuge when horizons were broadening. The whole point of the " little way " was that it would sidetrack the complexity of his nature, his appetites, his learning—traits and gifts which overcame him with a spiritual depression about himself, because he felt them to be barriers between his inner self and God, and yet he felt that he could not but choose the way of so congenial a greatness. So she taught him the way to become a little child again in the spiritual life. He must be " led in faith and darkness, and the motive force of all that moves you is in the will; walking must be in blindness of spirit by the very pure and certain light of faith." What a liberation for a spirit like his whose essential defect lay in straining and constricting itself by trying too hard and in the wrong way, by concentrating so much on the self in the search for God that God's guiding hand could not break through, by confusing self-love with love of God. " Each person has his own divine *attrait*," she assured him with a new flexibility that allowed for all his secret wishes. " Yours is and will always be docility and littleness, not only in general, which will be easy for you, disposed to it as you are, but for the detail, exacting of you a thousand things and then not exacting them, so that you may be made more supple and that your reason may not affect the conduct God wants of you." " God wishes to exercise your pliability in your quest for the Infinite."

It was masterly in its subtle application to Fénelon's psychology, but it was also honest for it sprang directly from the teaching of

the *Moyen Court*. In that book she had explained that the pheno-
menon of "conversion" or "second birth" which in one form or
other affects the lives of serious Christians, was anything but a
matter of feeling or illumination. It was far from the Evangelical
idea of a sudden, spiritually buoyant new life with God, with the
sense of inner spiritual certainty never afterwards to leave one. On
the contrary, it came from the realisation that man's true relation
with God is neither a matter of *feeling* good nor of saying prayers
nor of trying to effect a junction between ourselves here and God
acting out there. Still less is prayer a mere matter of thinking about
God or talking to Him or feeling about Him. There is need for
these things, especially where beginners are concerned and in a
secondary way. But the secret lies in inverting, as it were, the
normal process. You must first detach or disinterest yourself from
yourself and from all creatures—even from the consolations of God
and religion as ordinarily understood, so that the hidden God, ever
present in the depths of your being, now purified from self-love
and distraction, can attract you " as the sun attracts the heavy mist
and refines and purifies it." This acquired habit of letting *God* act
within you, which is in fact the essence of true prayer and spiritual
progress, will come to change all your values. God, not the im-
potent, enigmatic, confused, ever-changing " you," will effect the
spiritual progress you seek. The God of sweetness you previously
sought was only an idol, another projection of self. Externally,
visually, nothing seems changed. Life continues as usual—no visions,
no transformations, no exceptional asceticisms, no haloes, no flight
from daily life; but the meaning and relevance of it all will be
transmuted from within—from *God* within. Life is seen at last from
in-outwards, from God-outwards. The principle, as she says, is dead
easy, as all really great and deep truths are in themselves easy. It
is we, with our pervasive self-love, not God, who make the
difficulties.

To many, as we shall see, it all sounded much too easy—a sort
of quiet sleep in God, while normal life is enjoyed as usual. Worse
still, it could be interpreted as affording a spiritual passport to
fatalism, agnosticism, moral laxity, as though nothing mattered any
more except to fix the deepest will and attention on an inner
divine X. But Mme. Guyon at her best—and she was always at her

best when aware that Fénelon's trained, rational mind was her audience—never meant to convey any such caricature. " There is such a thing," she warns Fénelon, " as an *all-devouring* fidelity in order to overcome the repugnance of our natures; we need an infinite faithfulness and suppleness in order to follow the touch of grace. Without this extreme pliability, you will always remain under the empire of your human will, however much you may believe that you have killed it; you will be following the way of reasonable man, not the way of God alone." The difference between the real thing—death to self and all for God—and the fake— substituting self-indulgence for a will to God—was enormous, yet psychologically so subtle that the way seemed as difficult to walk as a tight-rope.

Fénelon understood this only too well. In a sense this distinguished priest, now beginning to climb the ladder of greatness, was practising the " little way " by submitting himself to the spiritual direction of an untrained and ill-educated woman who, he believed, had found the road to God. But all the time in these first months of correspondence and occasional furtive contacts within a confessional a double process was taking place. While the woman was teaching the priest, the priest was all the time rationalising and purifying the woman's inspiration. He shows, for example, how the denuded soul is filled with an inner, direct, yet naked, certitude or light which is not subject to judgment or reason, so that one can never say of it: " I have or enjoy this certitude or faith." He relates it to Saint Paul's faith which " gives substance to our hopes, which convinces us of things we cannot see." He shows how it all works in with the teaching of the Church and submission to that teaching: " souls deepest and most tried in the night of the faith never cease to have a complete certainty about the way they are going, which comes to the same thing as the rule of faith decided by the Church and as the simplicity of children filled with submission." " We see and yet do not see "; " we have courage and yet it is not courage "; " we are afraid and yet are not afraid "; " we move and do not move "; " we lose and yet we do not lose "—such expressions, recurring again and again in these letters, are the only way of expressing in human, conceptual language the realisation, within a new divine dimension, of what has been sacrificed (and yet not

lost) in the ordinary human dimension of normal thought and
behaviour. It evidently has an analogy with the Hindu *Advaita* or
Non-Duality, which sees human relationship with the Divine as
being neither the relation of identity, nor that of difference, but
something beyond our rational way of thinking—a kind of " Yes,
and yet No," more creatively fruitful in grasping this unique
relationship than mere affirmation or negation. And it is, after all,
but an attempt to realise the Scriptural warning, " Unless the seed
die . . ." Life with God is the fruit of a death which yet is not a
death, but a resurrection to a new order of being. Human life
cannot be satisfactorily enclosed within the ordinary categories of
thought—how much less the human relationship with the Divine!

Endless pages of Mme. Guyon's Autobiography and letters
develop the theme of this teaching; the degrees of progress attainable through it right up to the " passive" and " unitive" way
which is only just short of the vision of God, just short only because
it is impossible to have the actual vision while we are imprisoned
in the order of time, space and sense-perception; the subtleties and
varieties of its application; and its adaptation to varying people
and to different needs. Most triumphantly and most sanely was it
now applied to Fénelon under Fénelon's own covert distillation of
her outpourings. " I am quite sure," he wrote, " that I am very far
indeed from understanding properly certain very delicate and deep
matters which can only be made clear by *experience* itself. But for
the principal stages of your [spiritual] way, I feel I understand them
thoroughly from start to finish, at least in the main and in general,
so that I can easily reduce them to the true principles of the holiest
orthodoxy. Nothing therefore scandalises me there. My inclination
to see scandal would be about your general state. You follow
spontaneously your inner taste with such vivacity or—better—with
a force that carries you along so swiftly. I fear this movement
which is, in any case, so contrary to my own state of deliberation
and caution. In fact, I should horribly fear to be driven along like
you on a course that would destroy my wisdom in the eyes of the
world and risk my whole reputation." How well he knew himself!
And again: " I have never doubted for a moment of the purity
and absolute honesty of your intentions. . . . But for the special
movements or views which God may reveal to you about people

François de Salignac de La Motte Fénelon,
Archbishop of Cambrai

and happenings, I am really in no worse position than you. You have assured me that you side-tracked these things without judging them, passing them over to me simply as you received them without making any decision. I do the same. I do not believe them to be true—or false. It is not because of these things—even when your views have been shown to be right—that I hold by you. I hold by you in the way of inner faith, which is entirely in conformity with the most precise teaching of the Gospel, by the simplicity that I can discern in you, and by the adaptability to God's will which is the fruit of this way. The rest is well above me and concerns spiritual states that are far removed from mine."

Again and again, he puts his difficulties, not least those of knowing *when* God truly speaks within one and when we only imagine this to be so. Mme. Guyon always seemed to know! She knew, too, how to adapt her inspiration to his far more rational mind. But her need to accommodate herself to his trained mind indirectly resulted in the priest influencing her views so that while it looked as though she were directing him he was actually directing her. Thus it came about that the Mme. Guyon whom Fénelon knew was a different person from the Mme. Guyon about whom Bossuet was to read in her own early, unsophisticated manuscript writings. And Fénelon's disinterest in any part of her mind which did not help him added to the misunderstandings which were to blaze out later.

Why then, it may be asked, all the secrecy and conspiratorial tone about the friendship? Why the precautions about the transmission of letters and the careful hiding of them? Why the use of codes and ciphers for the names of people referred to, including Fénelon himself who is often referred to in the third rather than the second person? Why the secret assignments in the shadows of a church?

There were two obvious reasons. We know the fate of La Combe. We know that Mme. Guyon would probably have shared his fate had not Mme. de Maintenon rescued her mainly to annoy the Archbishop of Paris. The State was totalitarian; spies abounded; theology was very much part of politics; politics depended on a *simpliste* theology which kept man in his proper place. Mme. Guyon's whole way of thinking had, as we shall see, become suspect, and it was particularly disliked both by Gallicans and the powerful Jansenists who liked tidy, neat and hard ways of religion suited to political and social ambitions. Fénelon, on the other hand, was very much of a coming man, and no one realised it better than Mme. Guyon who was pinning her spiritual hopes on his career. Already he was the friend of the great in State and Church, and during the course of this correspondence which lasted from 1688 to the end of 1689 he was to be given the appointment which opened to him the great doors and led to the " giant steps " of which Saint-Simon spoke. Above all, his future must not be compromised by his ostensibly sitting at the feet of a suspect woman with a doubtful past. Nor must he be thought of as the kind of priest who puts dangerous and fancy ideas into people's heads.

But there was another reason. Fénelon, the man of the world, the aristocrat, the deeply sensitive person, would have been intolerably hurt had the great world laughed at this odd spiritual intimacy. The fact makes the liaison and his public defence of it later all the more courageous; it underlines, too, the deep seriousness with which he viewed Mme. Guyon's teaching and spiritual experience. The fear was all the greater in that there was a secret part of his nature which welcomed the simplicity, the relaxation, the childlikeness involved in Mme. Guyon's teaching. But what would have been his pain if the court and the gossips got to hear that " when alone, I sometimes play like a little child, even when praying. Sometimes I jump and laugh alone, like a madman in my room," as he wrote to his friend. There are reticences about one's inner self which may be shared with one person who will understand, but which one would blush to tell the world. " Pure love," as Bremond has said, " has its suitable privacies as much as earthly love " and never more so than when the intimacies of one's personal religion are concerned.

There is no doubt that this secret correspondence, consisting of 38 letters from Fénelon and 101 from Mme. Guyon, and revealed to the world so long after Fénelon's death, explains much of Fénelon's subsequent conduct. Mme. Guyon, pruned, without her fully realising it, of the excesses of her earlier excitement and exaggerations, was a revelation to the gifted priest, endowed with an imagination and sensitivity not easily fitted into the normal ecclesiastical life in the great world of those days. The doctrine of the *Moyen Court*, with its wonderful spiritual promise, its privacy, and its almost infinite subtlety in adapting itself to the most complex needs and natures, gave him the strength to face life boldly and yet suffer all its disappointments, not least those of his ailing, introspective make-up.

It had the answer to everything. The fulfilment of secret ambitions was but the will of God, and Mme. Guyon was tireless in enticing him with the promise of greatness in God's work. " I promise you that everything will be given to you as you need it. You must exercise your faith in this, for it would be wrong to imagine that naked faith only works in denuding yourself of everything; it is also exercised in believing nearly unbelievable things. . . . How great God is and how we can glorify Him in different ways." On the other hand, failure, and especially the sense of spiritual failure, is equally well accounted for. The ultimate goal, which is union with God, necessarily seems to recede as progress is made, since the more one progresses, the more clearly one realises how far short one is from the better understood ideal. Besides, the more naked and dry the faith, the higher its quality, so that depressions, morbidities, aridity, inability to pray can be the direct result of progress, as, of course, they can also be signs of failure. " Do not be astonished at the lack of death in your mind in prayer," Mme. Guyon could assure him. " Our imagination is always darting about—and this, in fact, is necessary: first in order to detach the soul from everything that would hinder it, if perceived; second, in order to hide from it God's work and keep it out of its knowledge; third, to bury the soul more and more into the centre. The more you progress, the more will your mind escape you, and the less will you be its master."

It proved an astonishing specific. Though Fénelon's letters are filled with complaints about his own shortcomings both in spiritual progress and in that buoyancy of soul and body, so characteristic of his opponent, Bossuet, he held on like a tiger, persistent in the way of detachment from self-love, yet ever pursuing his hidden urges to do great things. It taught him the spiritual value of never looking back, never turning in on oneself, yet to be ever anxious about his own state of mind. It allowed him to fight fiercely for his rights and for his friends, yet to be almost excessive in protestations of submissiveness and docility to others. Yet, somehow, it is impossible to accuse him of the slightest hypocrisy or duplicity. It all hung together splendidly and it moulded him in the end into a most attractive holiness. And if perhaps he never succeeded in really understanding himself, he was little short of a psychological genius for his times in understanding others and particularly those for whom he wrote the immortal letters of spiritual analysis and direction, making of most them intimate friends, but of one a powerful enemy who sought to destroy him.

CHAPTER FOUR

PIETY AT COURT

THIS INTIMATE correspondence between Fénelon and Mme. Guyon preludes the few months of glory and hope in which these spiritual adventurers must for a moment have seemed to themselves destined to effect a spiritual and moral revolution in France which would have been unique in itself and which might have altered the course of Christendom's history.

Let us picture the scene. When Mme. Guyon was released from her convent-prison, King Louis XIV was just fifty. Few monarchs are better known to posterity. But one day—presumably after the Great Famine of 1694—Fénelon for some reason doubtless connected with the prospect of reform at court, put his thoughts about the King's true character on paper in an anonymous letter to him. Naturally he did not send it to the King, but he apparently sent a copy to the King's wife, as she described it in a letter as " well-written, but such truths are not calculated to bring him back." The portrait Fénelon drew was far indeed from flattering the monarch who lived on flattery. Telling the King that the writer's only interest was " the truth, free and strong," he goes on: " You are scarcely accustomed to hear it. People inured to flattery easily mistake for complaint, harshness and exaggeration what is in fact no more than the plainest truth. . . . You were born, Sire, with an honest and just heart; but those who educated you taught you the art of ruling only in terms of suspicion, jealousy, setting virtue aside, fearing oustanding merit, looking only to ambitions and sinuous men, interesting yourself and taking pride only in your own interests. For about twenty years . . . men have no longer been talking of the State and its laws; they have only talked of the

King and his good pleasure. . . . You have been exalted to the skies, and this, so they say, because you have blotted out the greatness of all your predecessors together—in other words, because you have impoverished all France for the sake of introducing to the court a monstrous and incurable luxuriousness. Enough, Sire, to show that you have passed your whole life away from the road of truth and justice, and therefore of the Gospel. . . .

"Meanwhile your people whom you should love as your children and who until now have loved you passionately, are dying of hunger. . . . It is you yourself, Sire, who have brought these troubles on to yourself; for now that the whole kingdom is ruined, you have everything in your hands, and not a soul lives but through your gifts. Such is the great kingdom, flourishing under its king who is daily pictured to us as the delight of his people—this, indeed, would be so, if flattering counsellors had not poisoned him. . . . God will know how to raise the veil from your eyes and show you what you would wish to avoid seeing. For long He has held His hand raised above you; but He is slow to strike because He has pity on a prince who all his life has been obsessed by flattery, and whose enemies, besides, are His own. But He will well know how to divide His just cause from yours, an unjust one, and how to humble you in order to convert you; for you will never be a Christian save in your humiliation. You do not love God; in fact you only fear Him with a slave's fear. You fear hell, not God. Your religion is but a matter of superstitions and trifling pious practices. You are scrupulous about little things and hardened to terrible evils. You only love your glory and your comfort. You refer everything to yourself, as though you were the God of the earth and as though everything had only been made so that it may be sacrificed to you. But God, on the contrary, put you into the world for your people. Alas, you cannot understand these truths; how then could you relish them? You do not know God; you do not love Him; you do not pray to Him from your heart; and you do nothing to get to know Him. . . ."

This was the reading of the *Grand Monarque's* character from which the spiritual reformers proceeded in their vision of a new spiritual age. This was the man whom Mme. de Maintenon had secretly married in 1684, a year after the death of Queen Maria

Theresa to whom the "Very Christian King," as his official title stated, had been so ostentatiously unfaithful. And Mme. de Maintenon was now the obvious pivot for the work of reform.

Few women in history can have played their cards as well as Francoise d'Aubigny, later Marquise de Maintenon. She was born in a prison. Her father was an ardent Protestant. She was brought up in poverty as a Catholic, taken to the West Indies, returned penniless to France as "the beautiful Creole," and married at sixteen and a half to the forty-two-year-old poet and wit, François Scarron, rather—so it is said—than go into a convent. It was in one respect a lucky marriage for this girl of no natural expectation but for her beauty, because the Scarron house in Paris, modest as it was, became "the *rendez-vous* of all that was elegant at the court and among the cleverest people in Paris." In such company, the attraction and charm of the young wife were effectively displayed; nor were they forgotten when Scarron died when she was but twenty-five. Her grief was not excessive. Given this start, she was well able to cultivate the fashionable society whose apex was the court. Honour and position she avidly sought rather than wealth and power, and there is something *snobbiste* in the way this parvenue sought to establish the nobility of her birth. Through the company she kept, she was introduced to the Queen Mother. Through another connection she was brought to the attention to the King's Mistress, Mme. de Montespan, who gave into her charge the children she had borne to the King. Legitimised in 1673, these children were the means of bringing their governess to the entourage of the King himself who at first took a dislike to her. But her whole experience had taught her the value of patience when one knows that one possesses the goods. Meanwhile, she strengthened her standing as a lady of position by buying the property of Maintenon, near Paris.

Gradually, Montespan fell from royal favour, and Louis discovered not only this fine figure of a woman, but a new sort of relationship, a relationship of friendship and affection in place of the passion which had hitherto governed him. He was about forty at the time and she three years older.

It is a mistake to suppose that Mme. de Maintenon was brought up to piety or even that she rapidly became a *dévote* after establishing herself with the King. She was, indeed, conventionally good and shrewd enough to appreciate the wearing qualities of respectability with the maturer Monarch. She judged—and there is nothing derogatory in the fact—that her hold on Louis, with all that it meant to one who had climbed so very high from such depths, would be most securely established through the influence of religion. It was not in the nature of that strong, handsome face to do anything by halves or without fully meaning it. Thus, she gradually became religious, with perhaps very little to contribute from herself, just as she had become noble and then the King's good wife with only a little of nobility in her and nothing of the tradition and sureness of status which distinguishes blood royal from the paler variety.

However, there was at that time a rather different type of piety in Paris and at court. The spiritual school in which Fénelon had been trained under M. Tronson, as Tronson had been trained under M. Olier, grew from the broad main stream of the Counter-Reformation, and was only one of the many examples of the re-ordering and deepening of the life of the Church which had been proceeding steadily, not least in Paris where the labours of St. Vincent de Paul had been so fruitful. To one side of this stem was the straight, hard, dark and spiky branch of Port Royal and the Jansenists with its stern and pessimistic insistence on the difficulty of salvation and the consequent need for the elect to live apart from the ordinary, and probably damned, run of mankind. To the other side was the long and flexible branch of the Jesuits, so easily breaking out into green life, with its so much gentler and more human spirit, even though its enemies saw evil in the fact that the Company of Jesus reserved for itself the hard and selfless dedication to the end which, so they alleged, justified many doubtful means. And, above them all, floated the subtle, shimmering foliage of the mystical outburst of the seventeenth century with so many individualistic, saintly souls eagerly seeking—and some finding—in a direct experienced union with God the only answer to the troubles and riddles of the times.

With such spiritual strictness, hope and fervour in an air, already threatened by corruption, free-thought, and the dangerous political and religious views of England and Holland, even though only a small minority in the country were affected, it was not surprising if men and women of rank should have found the opportunity of self-dedication even in the highest positions and thus insensibly created what less pious observers dubbed the "Convent of the Court" or the "Cenacle".

We have already been introduced to the four duchesses around whom many other titled women flocked, but more surprising were the characters of two of their husbands, the Duc de Chevreuse and the Duc de Beauvilliers. As a younger son, Beauvilliers had hoped to become a priest, but the death of his brothers made it necessary for him to take up the social position of his family. The spiritual training he had received from M. Tronson, his lifelong friend, bound him closely to Fénelon and always left in him something of the clerical though when young he enjoyed good living. A good deal may be learnt about a man even by the slightest of anecdotes. It was thought rather amusing in those times that Beauvilliers was wont to apologise to his coachman when he had kept him waiting. Saint-Simon spoke of his virtue, his sweetness and his courtesy, and did so without mocking. He had integrity rather than intelligence and the fact that in spite of his meticulous, practical, and conservative disposition he should have stuck to Fénelon in the battle to come is a fine testimonial to both friends. Chevreuse, his brother-in-law, had been educated with the Jansenists. He was far more intelligent than Beauvilliers and was reputed to possess the kind of mind which could argue itself into anything. But Saint-Simon who tells us that also says: "No man possessed his soul in peace as he did." Again, it was surprising that despite the Jansenist influence he should have fallen far more heavily than Beauvilliers to the optimistic spiritual views of Mme. Guyon as well as to Fénelon. These two grandees had impressed the court by their polite, but firm, detachment from the then all-powerful entourage of Mme. de Montespan [the King's mistress], and Louis is said to have conceived his special affection for Beauvilliers because he came to symbolise the new ways which began with the rise of Mme. de Maintenon.

These Dukes, with their Duchesses; Bossuet, the greatest churchman of the kingdom and of Europe; Mme. de Maintenon and her highly-placed spiritual directors; and Fénelon, the enigmatic, were the heart of the reform which came to possess, especially under Mme. Guyon's influence, an unusual character.

Mme. Guyon herself wrote that she was not called to work for the external propagation of the Church and the conversion of heretics, nor even for the sinners' change of heart, " but rather to stimulate those already desirous of conversion to that perfect conversion which is the inner Spirit." Thus the court cenacle was essentially a movement of the *élite*, an island of perfection whose example and influence, coming from the very apex of the absolute régime, could gently spread the spirit of spiritual reform and purification not only in space but in time, for the eyes of all were on the future when Louis would have gone to his reward.

Mme. Guyon in her letters to Fénelon had prophesied the great opportunity that was so soon to be his and had conceived of the spiritual future in terms of a fanciful spiritual conspiracy. Her friends would be enrolled in the service of the " Little Master " (Our Lord), and under the protection of Saint Michael—she called them " Michelins "—they would work for a world renovated through her teaching with Fénelon at their head. " The Michelins will be under the hand of my Little Master like a weathercock moved by the wind or a rag in the mouth of a dog," she wrote. These Michelins would, as children of " pure love " be distinguishable by their littleness, their joyfulness, their gaiety, their weakness, their childlikeness, in contrast with the, oh, so grand, grave, self-esteeming, serious types whom she called " Christophets."

In August, 1689, the King chose the honest and dependable Beauvilliers to be the Governor of the household of his seven-year-old grandson, the duc de Bourgogne, eldest son of the Dauphin and second heir to the throne and his brother-princes. Beauvilliers, in his turn, had proposed Fénelon as Preceptor or tutor—though the word tutor is far from conveying the dignity and importance of the charge to which the King thus appointed Fénelon. He was to be responsible for the whole education of a future heir, and his position was more like that of the headmaster of the most important and select school of the kingdom whose star pupils were the sons of the Dauphin. It was said of the Dauphin, father of the young princes, that " it is hardly possible that in the whole course of history a prince has been born to equal eminence." Bossuet himself had fulfilled for him the role that now fell to Fénelon where the second generation was concerned, and Fénelon, as a noble, enjoyed a status far beyond that of the plebeian Bossuet—a cause, it is said, of the latter's latent jealousy.

When the news was announced, Bossuet was first to congratulate him on the promotion of a " virtue which had been hidden with sure care." M. Tronson, who well knew the weaknesses of his old pupil wrote warningly, "We cannot deny that in the ordinary course of events our elevation makes our salvation difficult. It will open to you the doors of earthly dignities, but you must beware lest it close to you the doors of the substantial greatnesses of heaven." As for Mme. Guyon, for her it was all spiritual sunshine, and her destiny fulfilled. " Your natural talents," she insisted, " will only serve you in this task in so far as you make your soul docile to the movements of grace. Believe me, the education of a prince whom God wishes to sanctify—and I am certain that He will make a saint of him—must be done in complete dependence on the movements of the sanctifying spirit. That is why God makes use of people capable of discerning these movements. You will do better in this by dying to yourself than in any other way. And though in view of his extreme youth you will not yet see all the fruits which you can expect, be sure that it will prove an exquisite fruit in due season. Of this I have no doubt: he will rebuild by the true spirit of faith what is now nearly destroyed and moving towards total ruin. This is certain: God has on this prince designs of singular mercy." Fénelon's reply betrays his excitement: " I can scarcely breathe, so pressed and busy am I . . . I have hardly time or sufficient calmness to pray, though I feel I am often praying without knowing it. . . . Your letter has given me much pleasure. It has made me recollected again. . . . As to all the things you say to me, my fixed answer, from the bottom of my heart, is *Fiat mihi secundum verbum tuum.* I feel that God wishes to carry me as a little child, not knowing how I can take a step of my own without falling. . . . I am dying to see you—I ought to speak more politely; but I cannot with you."

By this date the spell which Mme. Guyon had worked in obscure Grenoble and Vercelli was now working in the entourage of the King himself. Mme. de Maintenon herself had met Fénelon at the Beauvilliers', and through him had come to know and appreciate the woman whom she had been instrumental in liberating. Saint-

Simon gives us the pictures of the evenings at the Beauvilliers or the Chevreuses when the group supped together, the bell on the table instead of the servants waiting as usual through the meal, and the conversation about God and the spiritual life continuing until a late hour. On Sunday afternoons after lunch, it was Fénelon who gave a conference to a fuller gathering of ardent souls, carrying their copies of the *Moyen Court* in their pockets.

One must pause once again to take note of the astonishing power of this spiritual prophet who could thus decisively impress and carry with her men and women whose every natural instinct must have suggested to them the utmost caution in the face of the woman who had only lately been liberated from what might have been perpetual imprisonment for the heresies suspected in the very teaching she was spreading among them. Not only that, but her behaviour in the past had given rise to so many sinister rumours that any person of the world might have been forgiven for taking the view that there must have been some fire to cause all that smoke. Yet in the face of her charm, her will and, surely, the goodness which was manifestly in her, all that seemed forgotten. It must, however, be noted that Mme. Guyon, like Fénelon, though in a lesser degree, carefully adapted her teaching to the needs of different people. In instructing her own daughter, for example, she used conventional methods.

Now that Fénelon's first " giant step " had been taken and Beauvilliers controlled the destiny of a future king of France, it must have seemed as though anything would ultimately be possible to them. The petit Prince [P.P. of the letters] would be the head of a new empire of Christian love and " my saint [Saint Michael] will be his protector," as Mme. Guyon wrote. Sometime in the future France would be given a Louis XVI (both the Dauphin and the little Prince were called Louis) formed and trained to spiritual as well as earthly glory in the broad school of the excellent and many-sided Fénelon, spiritually vivified by the Holy Spirit according to Mme. Guyon's gospel. This immense hope and prayer, doomed to destruction in earthly terms by the early death of Louis XIV's son and grandson which led to the succession of the " after me the deluge " Louis XV and to the guillotine on which the head of the real Louis XVI fell, was like a vision of the new Jerusalem, not only to Mme. Guyon, but to many of the pious circle. These people, we must remember, saw the *Grand Siècle* with very different eyes from those of French history.

Fénelon's real feelings are very hard to assess. For him the rosier the dream, the greater his natural caution. The fact that right to the end of his life he remained indirectly at least in touch with Mme. Guyon and still seemed to hope that his ill luck in fulfilling his destiny would change makes it hard not to believe that somewhere in his heart he shared his friend's divine optimism. On the other hand, he never lost his sense of proportion. His work with the princes was not only a full-time occupation in itself, but it imposed upon him the need for the greatest caution in not publicly mixing himself up with anything strange or suspect.

But two further reasons forced on him an outward conduct in considerable contrast with his inner feelings. As a priest and spiritual director, his head was never turned. From the beginning he took the view that Mme. Guyon's spirituality was only suited to a small and exclusive number of people. It was dangerous stuff that could be immensely helpful to himself and some others, but deadly dangerous if broadcast to all and sundry. Furthermore, the nature of her teaching made it something deeply personal and logically quite distinct from the romantic dreams of spectacular success which Mme. Guyon could not help nursing.

It was of the essence of this doctrine of abandonment, naked faith and pure love that *visible* results were of no importance. Its goal was union with the hidden God, a union as fully realised in disappointment and loss as in success. It was the hardest way, not the easiest, as too many superficial disciples were apt to think.

All these motives, in fact, led to such caution on Fénelon's part that but for the evidence of his later-discovered correspondence with Mme. Guyon no one could have suspected the degree of intimacy between them. Yet without them his early biographers had no explanation of the stubborn way he allowed himself to be ruined and his strongest ambitions disappointed simply because he would not renounce his loyalty to a persecuted, and apparently heretical and not quite sane woman of no serious consequence. Driven into fury and into the adoption of unpardonable tactics, as Bossuet was to be, by such stubbornness, one trembles to think of what the great

man would have done had he ever put his fingers on that correspondence!

Meanwhile, Fénelon had his hands full in wisely directing, on
the Guyon recipe, the souls of those who had entrusted themselves
to him, as well as in settling down to the tough job of bringing up
a horrid little prince—bad-tempered, cruel, mulish—the words, and
many others, are Saint-Simon's who added: " he looked upon other
people from the heights of heaven as atoms with whom he himself
had no resemblance." Luckily, with his spoilt character there went
plenty of intelligence and docility, so that Fénelon was to achieve
a pedagogical triumph in turning the boy into an heir to the throne,
better prepared in mind and soul to govern France than any the
Houses of Valois and Bourbon had ever produced. Compare Saint-
Simon's words with Mme. de Maintenon's report: " Since the
First Communion of the Duc de Bourgogne [at the age of twelve
in 1694], we have seen little by little disappearing those faults of
his which in his infancy gave cause for so much anxiety about the
future. His progress in virtue was marked from year to year. The
laughing-stock of the whole court at first, he came to be admired
even by the libertines. He continues to take severe steps to get
entirely rid of his defects. His piety has so changed him that his lack
of self-control has been changed into moderation, sweetness and
affability. It seems as if these are part of his character—virtues
natural to him."

Fénelon adopted methods of teaching religion, by demonstrating
its effects and its beauty in both history and the individual character,
rather than through dry doctrine and cautionary morality, and his
horizon as a priest-teacher was very broad. Here he was doubtless
helped by a Guyonist inspiration which, of course, he was most
careful to keep from his young and inexperienced pupil. The Prince
in fact learnt that God's will was not something sectarian and
clerical, but that it included the immense variety and richness of
God's creative power in history, in the great civilisations, in literature, in the art of just government, in the hopes of a fairer and
kindlier world where love, rather than force, could rule. And Fénelm
insisted that it is the world itself which is the first to grow sick
of those who fail God and His creative breadth. " If this Prince
were allowed to follow his own heart, far from God and the graces

he has received, everything in him would dry up; and the world, which was his excuse for forgetting God, would prove to be God's instrument in avenging such ingratitude." If Fénelon was the spiritual father of the Enlightenment and the romantic movement, the spirituality of his inspiration was very much overlooked by his actual progeny.

2

But the plot of the tragedy that was so soon to break out was really hatched, not in Paris or Versailles, but in Saint-Cyr. After herself and the King, Saint-Cyr was the greatest interest in Mme. de Maintenon's life. The woman who had done so much to educate herself by her wits, her tenacity and her *savoir-faire* in grasping and holding an influence greater than a queen's—did they not call her Mme. de Maintenant, to symbolise her tenure of power, and the Pantocrat, to symbolise its range?—had founded a great school for girls at Saint-Cyr, near Versailles. This establishment for the education of the impoverished daughters of the fighting and nobility ruined in the King's wars was to be in the sharpest contrast with the traditional convent schools about which Fénelon himself had written that the girls in them had suddenly to emerge from the depths of cavern-like darkness into the blinding light of the world as it really was. At Saint-Cyr they were to be trained for that world, trained to be mothers, and there would be no more nonsense about the convent prudery that caused girls to giggle whenever even the word marriage was mentioned. School-work throughout the year would be tempered by breaks arranged according to religious and secular feasts, each with its special ritual of enjoyment. "I would like to see comedies acted and *mascarades* during the four days before Lent, the Saturday to prepare everything and the other three days for the fun," Mme. de Maintenon wrote in pages of direction and advice almost as torrential as Mme. Guyon's spiritual gospels. In fact, she derived enormous enjoyment from running every detail of Saint-Cyr with its religious community of Dames de Saint Louis who as nuns wore a secularised teaching habit which must have been even more of a " new look " for that generation than similar experiments in ours. Only one feature was consistent, and that was the fierce discipline which the Foundress imposed on the daughters of soldiers who had to take their pleasures as well as their pains at her nod. They were even expected to marry according to her plans. The emancipator of feminine education who could furiously denounce the stupidity of the kind of education which made girls snigger at the word trousers could threaten to use the whip even to drawing blood: " I would tie them to a post in the dormitory the better to whip them, and leave them there a long time; it is annoying to have to be cruel, but the punishment must be such as to terrify them."

When Mme. de Maintenon fell under the spiritual spell of Fénelon and Mme. Guyon, it was inevitable that she should wish to introduce something of the new spirituality into her beloved Saint-Cyr whose effective spiritual director she had made herself. This was all the more natural in that her special favourite in Saint-Cyr was the brilliant young mistress, Mme. de La Maisonfort, the cousin of Mme. Guyon who had striven to rescue her from the convent-prison. By all accounts there must have been something very remarkable about this young teacher who was usually called the Canoness because her small income was derived from a canon's benefice in Lorraine which her father had bought for her. . . . " I am sure that it pleases you to see how all the precious pearls which you have spread here are gathered together and how you deem it a special grace of God that a Canoness has taught to young ladies destined for marriage the principles of honour, virtue, modesty and good conduct," the Superior wrote to the foundress; and Mme. de Maintenon described her as " the most charming saint of the world." The great visitors to the school, French royalty, the exiled English royalty, nobles, dramatists like Racine who wrote the plays the demoiselles of Saint-Cyr acted were all captivated by this young woman. We can imagine her, tall and gracious, romantic and sweet, the embodiment of the teaching seductress who, through the ages, has captivated the hearts of young girls and created bitter jealousies all around her.

With such a cousin in the school what more natural than that Mme. Guyon should call more and more frequently at Saint-Cyr. Mme. Guyon was in fact quite certain that her cousin had been placed by God at Saint-Cyr as a sign of His special love for His prophetess. Saint-Cyr, Beynes, Versailles, all within a few miles of one another, even the geography of this story seems to have been providentially charted. Best of all, here was a community of girls and young women, two hundred strong, reaching for the stars, whether in the piety of married life or within a religious vocation. Only one thing had been missing, a spiritual teaching geared to the other-worldly worldliness so well suited to the transition of ideas from the Counter-Reformation to the Romantic movement. Mme. Guyon was all too ready to supply the need with the " religion without tears " of the *Moyen Court*. Or rather she was ready to supply the real thing that could so very easily be interpreted as a " religion without tears " by young ladies avid of fresh experiences and spiritual thrills within the long walls that enclosed their overstimulated expectations from life.

However, it is only fair to insist that Fénelon above all, but also Mme. Guyon herself, envisaged an indoctrination that was to be confined to a few chosen and more spiritually advanced mistresses. At the start it was a secret confined to five or six of the *Dames*, since, as Mme. Guyon herself insisted, only chosen souls could truly understand the way of union which she taught. But who, with any experience of an enclosed convent atmosphere, could have imagined that the secret would long be kept? If anyone at this stage was rash, it seems to have been Mme. de Maintenon herself who habitually carried the *Moyen Court* in her pocket, lent it and praised it. She hoped to learn it by heart and recommend it for women destined to live in the world. Copies, of course, were furtively passed, with a delicious sense of spiritual abandon, from person to person, for who could bear to deprive her best friend of the latest spiritual thrill? Let us read Mme. Guyon's own brief account: " Since I left St. Mary's [her convent-prison] I had constantly visited Saint-Cyr. Some of the young ladies of the house, having told Mme. de Maintenon that they found in the conversations I had with them something which drew them nearer to God, she allowed them to confide in me, and many times she said that she had no reason to be sorry that she had done this in view of the change in some of them with whom up till then she had not been too pleased. During this time she was very good and kind to me. This lasted for three or four years during which I received all kinds of proofs of her esteem and confidence in my regard."

In Saint-Cyr, Mme. Guyon had no more fervent disciple than her own cousin, the Canoness, and she in turn sat rapt at the feet of Fénelon, the spiritual charmer. Mme. de Maintenon was delighted to add to the originality of the educational establishment the originality of a spiritual teaching which would add mystical perfection to the manifold fruits of her foundation. It seemed like an idyll. Alas, with Fénelon's favours being fought for by three women, it could hardly last. But in the battle to come far more was at stake than the jealousies and ambitions of women, even women as remarkable as these, and to understand this it is necessary to leave Saint-Cyr for a time and to turn to the wider considerations which must be understood if the rest of the story is to be followed.

CHAPTER FIVE

TROUBLE BREWING

THE MODERN reader may well be forgiven if he wonders why Père La Combe and Mme. Guyon were pursued with such bitter hatred and finally imprisoned, the one for life, the other only escaping a similar fate by the accident of having powerful friends. Odd they may both have been, but their worst oddities hardly constituted a breach of the peace. Both had enjoyed the favour of high dignitaries of the Church, and their published books were formally approved of by both Church and State.

Part of the answer to this problem and to the problems we shall shortly be in a position to study lies in the word ' Quietism,' the name given to the school of spirituality to which they belonged because of the spiritual climate of the times, rather than through formal discipleship.

The name ' Quietism ' was apparently chosen by a group of Italian disciples of the great sixteenth to seventeenth-century mystics, Saint Catherine of Genoa, Saint Teresa, Saint Francis of Sales, Saint Jeanne de Chantal, Saint John of the Cross and many others, honoured among Catholics and others as saints or near saints.

It was a most unfortunate choice, and one that greatly helped to ruin the reputation of this loosely-linked revivalist movement in Italy, Spain and France. For the word suggests repose, sleeping, letting oneself be acted upon, giving way, not making any active efforts, above all, *not* praying and *not* resisting temptations to sin. Associated vaguely with an expression like " pure love " or with the favourite symbolism of mystical writers, ever since the Canticle of Canticles, in which the intimate union of man with God is described in language derived from marriage and carnal love, it was very easy to associate Quietism with a hypocritical non-resistance on the part of self-constituted pious peoples to sins of the flesh. Once this idea started, not a few churchmen, vowed by their vocation to complete renunciation of the even legitimate use of this instinct in marriage, seemed to find an escape from their constraint in the righteous denunciation of the kind of horrors that must, they felt, be lurking under the cloak of such false pietism. Whilst for the mob generally there is always a particular satisfaction in dwelling on the picture of would-be saints indulging, not merely in the ordinary weaknesses of sinful men, but in the kind of debauchery that would surely result from this apparent permission to sin whilst in the highest flights of prayer and devotion. In the case of a priestly spiritual director of women penitents, the imaginative possibilities were endless. The moral satisfaction of the mob, would be completed only by the denunciation and pursuit of such hypocrites until they were cruelly punished.

Unfortunately, the scent which the mob-hunt picked up was not always false. The whole relation between religious exaltation and some form of sexual feeling is a complex one; nor can we be altogether surprised if the restraints which religion imposes should sometimes lead to excessive preoccupation with the instincts that have been more than normally repressed or if the intense feelings of liberation, dedication, love and ecstasy which the more emotional and illuminist type of religion can give should in some cases spill over into this powerful and, in its own order, also uniquely expressive instinct.

A number of so-called Quietists undoubtedly sinned in this way, and in those days there were no psychologically experienced confessors to help them sin no more. On the contrary, there was only prison or the fire. But, as it happened, the real Quietist outlook was, of its nature, particularly unsuited to this sort of excess.

The whole point of Quietism was a turning away from the self and the self-indulgence of any spiritual or physical emotionalism and consolation; still more distasteful to it were visions and ecstasies. In its more elementary stages, it was hardly more than an attempt to exercise the continuous practice of attending with the will to God. Instead of making God, however subtly, serve the will, needs and desires of the self by petitionary prayers, by " feeling good " or even the subtle *volupté* of " feeling bad " when you were not bad, the Quietist tried to want nothing for the self but all for God. It was like seeking a new meaning, a new dimension, in life without changing the outward appearances of ordinary life. The Quietist sought to live with his mind on God, the Eternal Reality, present within him as well as around him and, as it were, lovingly regard Him. The view was that a good Christian life was more easily attainable by this short and simple method of trying to let God act within the real self than by that preoccupation with self which endless efforts to try to rise on one's own shoestrings so readily cause. Modern psychologists would agree. Moreover, this spiritual technique seemed to be admirably adapted for countless good people with no pretensions to special gifts or special sanctity, and the idea of preaching it to all and sundry was one of the notable characteristics of the whole of this mystical revivalist movement. For exceptional people there were the higher " passive " stages by which those specially chosen by God were more easily enabled to reach a degree of union with the divine in which repeated voluntary acts of the will towards God by prayer, especially vocal prayer, became unnecessary and often impossible, since the soul was in fact living in the " one act " of " purely loving " God with God's own " pure love." " I loved Him," as Mme. Guyon said, " in such a way that I could only love Him ; but in loving Him I had no motive but Himself." But for the greater number of ordinary people to whom God had not given such exceptional graces, it was considered possible to weaken their pervasive self-love by thinking a good deal less of themselves, even in their religious devotions, and being content to think lovingly of God and thus allowing Him to work in their souls instead, so to speak, of their always getting in His way with the picture of their so spiritually devout or morally righteous selves.

In all this there was nothing really new. It was in the classic tradition of the saints. But, as is so often the case, the old, presented in a fresh and alluring dress and offered to men and women looking for something spiritually better than much of the normal religious practice (or non-practice) of the times, proved immensely attractive. The movement aroused great enthusiasm and the highest favour within the Eternal City itself. If it meant anything, it meant that many ordinary folk of real spiritual goodwill would henceforth be able to dwell on the lower slopes at least of Mount Carmel, the symbolic mystic mountain whose heights privileged souls and great saints alone could scale. The need for this inner more personal religion was also, no doubt, stimulated through a reaction against both Jansenist and some Jesuit spirituality, as well, of course, as against low clerical standards. It was opening the doors of heaven which the Jansenists were determined to close for all except the elect and it was an answer to the spiritually utilitarian methods of Jesuits who sought too crudely to lure back into the fold the impious and the heretics.

Thus the early history of Quietism was a remarkable success story. Fr. John Falconi, who died in Madrid thirty years before Mme. Guyon's liberation and was the first widely celebrated Quietist writer, achieved such a reputation for sanctity that Rome accorded him the title of " Venerable," which is the first step along the road to canonisation. Later the title was quietly dropped! The writings of Antonio de Rolas, a Quietist secular priest, were approved by no less than nine bishops. Most striking of all perhaps was the case of the Oratorian priest, Peter Petrucci. Though a most prominent apologist for the Quietist teaching in Rome, he was a personal friend of the Pope's and so highly in favour that he was first made a Bishop and then a Cardinal even after the Quietist storm had broken out. Malaval, whom Mme. Guyon met in Marseilles, enjoyed a personal reputation for sanctity which no insults from Bossuet and no condemnation of his famous book could touch. It is fair to say that if Mme. Guyon and La Combe had been born thirty years earlier, they, too would probably have lived quietly and successfully as approved spiritual leaders.

But the most famous and notorious of all the Quietists was the Spanish priest, Michael Molinos, whose arrest, at the time when Mme. Guyon was preparing to return home via Grenoble, suddenly changed the whole picture.

Molinos, best known to Englishmen through Shorthouse's novel, *John Inglesant*, was born in Aragon in 1628 and ordained priest in 1652. His early ecclesiastical career was not distinguished, but his work took him to Rome in 1663. There he achieved a tremendous reputation as a spiritual director. In 1675 his *Spiritual Guide* was published, and in six years its popularity was such that it ran through twenty editions. This book was in the main an elementary treatise on the Quietist doctrine. It was addressed, not to aspirants of the higher spiritual life, but to pious people desirous of a simpler and more fruitful method of prayer. Four Inquisitors and seven Cardinals approved of the *Spiritual Guide*, all of them in fulsome terms, and the Pope, Innocent XI, gave Molinos rooms at the Vatican itself.

Such success made the Jesuits uneasy, and the saintly ascetic, Fr. Paul Segneri, whom Mgr. Knox describes as " the John Wesley of seventeenth-century Italy " wrote a book to put people on their guard. But it was poor Segneri who promptly found himself on the Index and, according to Poulain, " narrowly escaped being put to death." In those days theological controversy was far from being the quiet and relatively safe occupation it has since become.

Then, suddenly, in the middle of a Roman summer's day, Molinos was arrested at the orders of the Holy Office. It was 18th July, 1685. At the time Mme. Guyon, who had never heard of Molinos, was being told by the Bishop of Vercelli that his happiest moments were " when he could spend half an hour chatting with her about God." News travelled more slowly then.

What had happened? There is evidence, not easily dismissed, that it was the work of Cardinal D'Estrées, France's Envoy, undertaken at the bidding of the King, acting on the advice of Père La Chaise, his Jesuit confessor. But it seems strange that Louis should have interfered in this Roman business—D'Estrées had been a friend of Molinos—and strange, too, that the Pope should have allowed himself to be dictated to in this way by that Gallican monarch with whom relations had long been severely strained. The teaching of Molinos was not in question at the time, for though he had his enemies, they had so far proved powerless, and Quietism was still in favour at the highest levels. Though they were probably contributory causes, it seems likely that Mgr. Knox, who has no particular love for the Quietists, is right when he says: ". . . the conclusion is irresistible that those stories had begun to leak out which were to convince the Roman world, from the Pope downwards, that Molinos was leading a double life."

Whether the stories were true or false—the world will never know for certain since the Holy Office is reticent with evidence—Molinos's crime in the eyes of his enemies was that of sexual misbehaviour perpetuated under the cloak of a specially edifying and pretentious spiritual direction. Seventy witnesses, we are told, testified against him and many thousands of his letters were examined. After months of examination, Molinos confessed to the charges brought against his teaching and his morals. One may leave it at that, and perhaps one should—but it ought at least to be said that Molinos's own Quietist teaching could have inspired him to the willing acceptance of the final degradation and humiliation as the supreme test of his own doctrine of utter self-abnegation and conformity to God's will.

Because of this confession, the wretched man was condemned to the relatively light sentence of perpetual imprisonment. But the last lurid scene of his public abjuration, standing on a scaffold, torch in hand, in the presence of the cardinals, officials and an immense crowd shrieking constantly " To the fire with him! To the fire with him! " leaves us in no doubt about the effect on public opinion of this dramatic transformation from public saint to public sinner.

The condemnation of Molinos instantly altered the whole picture of Quietism, and the purge of Quietists and Quietism in Italy proceeded apace. What had been read in one way because it was believed that most Quietists were holy and earnest people, was now read the other way because it was suspected that all were associated with Molinos or were like him. Quietism no longer meant the peace and tranquillity within which God could work on the soul so that God filled it, instead of the self; it meant a state of irresponsibility, of " couldn't care less," of fatalism which blasphemously seemed to make God Himself responsible for the sins, called by the Quietist " trials," which the Quietist happily committed along the way to perfection. It implied making pretentious claims, beyond the reach of sinful man, to a sinless state that would only be realised in heaven when the arduous moral battle of life had been won. Once again it had been shown that the corruption of the best leads to the worst.

Such was the atmosphere which, moving across Europe, had already blotted out La Combe, touched Mme. Guyon and was so soon to darken the days of Fénelon.

2

It is difficult to exaggerate the importance that must be attached in this whole tragedy to the element for which Molinos mainly stands: the sexual immorality of would-be spiritual leaders and guides whom the clericals suspected and over whom the mob righteously gloated.

But who were the real agents ready to set the simple machinery in motion or to make use of it as it constantly ticked over?

Mme. Guyon, we have seen, charged her brother-in-law, the Barnabite priest. But if only part of the persecution she tells of and deems to be the natural and supernatural lot of those who move close to God in utter abnegation of self-love is true, it is inconceivable that this priest could have been more than an agent of whom she happened to know because of the accident of kinship. She herself tells us that she had never heard of Molinos, and we can believe her. But Molinism was in the air, and indirectly she must have been much influenced, as was La Combe, by the Quietist teaching both in Montargis and in the places where she travelled. Dangeau, reporting in his *Journal* the case of La Combe, wrote: " They have arrested a Barnabite accused of being rather Molinist; certain theologians have taken to flight because they are suspected of errors very like those of Molinos." Yet months and even years after, Mme. Guyon was still regarded as orthodox at the Court and in Saint-Cyr!

In the Autobiography there are a few clues which seem to suggest the first set of people who were determined to down Mme. Guyon and her circle and to use any means at hand for doing so. She tells us, for example, how during the years between her husband's death and the beginning of her foreign adventures, she was long importuned by a " person whose doctrine was suspected of Jansenism [the word is left out in her text and added by her editors in a footnote] and whose position in the Church forced me to show deference to him." When Mme. Guyon, seeing that this person was so opposed to the way of inner religion, finally broke with him, " he organised strange persecutions and roused people of his party against me. These gentlemen had a way of finding out very quickly who their friends were and who their enemies. They held together by passing messages to one another. In this way they managed to discredit me in the strangest way." We remember, too, how at Marseilles " the disciples of M. de Saint-Cyran " were all openly mobilised against her and her *Moyen Court*. Saint-Cyran was the father of Jansenism in France. The author of the preface to the book hints at the fact that the Jansenists expected to find in her an ally, no doubt because they saw that her views involved a strong criticism of Ultramontane clericalism and could thus further the cause of the independent Gallican outlook they preferred.

Mme. Guyon was only saved from the hostility of disappointed Jansenists and the bad reputation of Quietism after the fall of Molinos through the influence of the Convent of the Court which hated the worldly ways of the Archbishop of Paris who had had her confined and examined. But her new association with these powerful friends inevitably meant that a fresh set of enemies began to work against her—all those, in fact, who were interested in preventing the dukes and duchesses, together with the King's secret wife, from dominating the King himself. The Cenacle had so far been too highly placed, powerful and irreproachable to be attacked for unorthodoxy or hypocrisy, whether openly by ridicule or covertly by intrigue. But as soon as Mme. Guyon was taken into their circle a weak spot appeared in their otherwise invulnerable position.

Though Mme. de Maintenon never seems to have been wholly happy about Fénelon's mystical woman friend, she certainly worked up at first a considerable enthusiasm for much of her teaching. Of the *Moyen Court*, she wrote to the Superior of Saint-Cyr: " I have read the little book which you sent me; I hope to learn it off by heart. Much of it seems to me suitable for those who are not called upon to live in the enclosure." In another letter she wrote: " The Abbé de Fénelon has told me that the *Moyen Court* contains the mysteries of the most sublime devotion that, apart from a few expressions, are to be found in the mystics," but she added that there were expressions in the book " of which I cannot approve in any way." She apparently also disapproved of the fact that Mme. Guyon when at Saint-Cyr in spiritually unostentatious Quietiest fashion " had arms and neck more uncovered than was suitable for a person who made so great a profession of piety," but the Dames of Saint-Cyr agreed that "she did not understand very much of it [the *Moyen Court*] except that the book greatly moved one to prayer and union with God."

The Court Cenacle was, of course, supported by the zealous in touch with Mme. de Maintenon, especially the somewhat Jansenist-minded Noailles, then Bishop of Châlons and later to be Archbishop of Paris, and Godet-Desmarais, Bishop of Chartres (the diocese wherein Saint-Cyr lay). But these churchmen were far from sharing Mme. de Maintenon's enthusiasm for the suspect Quietist teaching of Mme. Guyon. Naturally, they would have had little difficulty in weaning the King's wife alone from this dangerous attachment and gobbling up an unsupported lone woman. Unfortunately for them, however, another weak spot of very serious proportions had developed. It was the close friendship for this woman of their fellow-priest at court, and one on the threshold of high episcopal office—the Abbé de Fénelon. Moreover, Fénelon himself had come to have great influence over Mme. de Maintenon, over the dukes and duchesses and over the nuns and teachers at Saint Cyr. In the hands of Fénelon, of Beauvilliers and of their friends lay the immense power which the bringing up of the young prince who one day would be absolute king of France gave them. It was an awkward situation, but none of these good bishops could have dreamt how awkward it was in fact to prove. One detail they could never have foreseen: the fact that Fénelon was to prove to be so attached to Mme. Guyon that the whole world leagued against him could not break down that strange friendship.

Around this closely-knit circle, to all appearances so invulnerable but with its grave weak spots, the anonymous enemies watched and waited.

There were the Jansenists, jealous of any power but their own. There were the numberless people who knew that Godliness at court boded no good for them; if Louis fell completely under the influence of his wife and the Court Convent, the future would be closed to all who had flourished under the former corrupt way of life and manners. There were the anti-Quietist clerics whose fears were expressed by the case of conscience put up for discussion by the powerful Sorbonne, centre of theological orthodoxy in France: "Would it be right for a prince to allow a teacher suspect of

Quietism to be in charge of his children?" The question obviously suggested another: "Would it be right for such a prince to keep a wife suspected of the same views?" And behind them all was the mob so easily incited to clamour against anything new, to scent the moral scandal which could so readily be whispered into the ear.

The situation was full of dangers which only tact and discretion could avert. This at least Fénelon fully realised, and, under his influence, so did Mme. Guyon. Fénelon was the very soul of caution. He never deviated from the view that the Guyon-Fénelon teaching was only for a small minority of people, that it should be transmitted individually by experienced hands and that it would do untold harm if broadcast. If everyone had acted with a similar discretion, the coming tragedy could have been averted. Unfortunately, a new factor was to enter into the picture and precipitate the trouble. It was the jealousy and resentment of a woman who from the start had been hopelessly out of her depths in the whole delicate affair—Mme. de Maintenon.

The Abbé Bremond in the most intelligent modern work on Fénelon, *Apologie pour Fénelon*, maintains that the fatal mistake of the pious cenacle was to have included Mme. de Maintenon among its members. Yet it was largely due to her that they owed their high influence and their great spiritual opportunity of forming a devout court and ultimately a devout country. It was through her that Fénelon was constantly seeking to move the King himself to a more serious spiritual perception, and it was partly through her that he and Beauvilliers owed their chance of forming a future king according to the rosy promise of the prophetess. But it is certainly true that the uncrowned queen was not up to the spiritual levels which were taught by Fénelon. She had always possessed the gift of easily assuming the positions and responsibilities which accrued to her with each step of her long upward climb from almost sordid beginnings to that of the first lady of the land—not that real royalty and the great families ever acknowledged any such status. Unguardedly, she accepted with a like ease and self-confidence the climb from being an ordinary Catholic to becoming an extraordinary one. She did this with all the more assurance in that her spiritual guides, Fénelon always excepted, flattered her outrageously.

A spiritual perfection only a little inferior to that of the Apostles was promised to her.

Fénelon, whom for many months she enormously admired, made no such mistake; but he was fatally to make the opposite one of telling her the truth as he, with his exceptional psychological insight, alone could. Early on in their relations he wrote her one of his famous letters which could hardly be described as flattering.

" I shall tell you what I think," he wrote, " and God will make use of my words as He pleases. You are simple and natural. Therefore, you get on very well, without having to think twice when it is a case of people you like and esteem; but you freeze up when it is a question of others. You were born with much pride—the pride that we think virtuous and well-thought-of. But this pride is evil in so far as thinking it good does not make us feel ashamed; a silly vanity is more easily corrected. You still have much of this pride in you, though you fail to notice it. The fact that you are so sensitive about matters that prick you to the quick is enough to show how far from being dead is this pride of yours. You still want the esteem of honest men and the approval of people of good repute; you like to feel that you carry your success with moderation. In a word you like people to think that your heart is even better than your rank.

" Your ego, about which I have so often spoken to you, is still your unbroken idol. You want to go to God with all your heart —but not through losing yourself. On the contrary, you seek yourself in God. . . . Believe me, in your case the slightest attachment even to the best things for you will hold you back even more than all the imperfections you may fear. . . . You are naturally good, and you want to believe (even perhaps too much) in good people whose prudence you are fully assured of [Mme. Guyon]. But the moment you are on your guard, your heart, I think, is too much narrowed. . . . Remember that even the most spontaneous virtue has its little turnings-back on itself, little lookings to its own interests, which it fails to detect. . . . We must never forget that the truest goodness of heart consists only in fidelity to God and in pure love. All merely natural generosity and feelings are no more than a kind of self-love, more refined, more seductive, more flattering, more charming, and consequently more devilish. . . . Madame, be persuaded that when it is a question of correcting one's faults and carrying out one's duties, the point is to labour at the task from within, not from outside. This outside work, even were you to give yourself up to it entirely, would always be too much for you. But let yourself yield to the spirit of God and cut away even to the roots all your egoism, and your faults will little by little disappear."

It was a cold douche, even though his extreme interest in her doubtless flattered her. It is to her credit that she so long remained faithful to him, copying out his teaching in her little red books and constantly quoting him in her own endless letters of spiritual direction to the Dames of Saint-Cyr.

But it could not last for ever, and Saint-Cyr, or rather Mme. Guyon's influence in Saint-Cyr, brought the underlying trouble to a head.

Mme. Guyon, we remember, had the entrée to Saint-Cyr where, under Fénelon's influence, she discreetly propagated her views to a small number of disciples, who did not keep the good news to themselves. Chief among them was her cousin, the delightful de La Maisonfort, the Canoness. To ensure that she should become " the keystone of Saint-Cyr " and, no doubt, to control her immoderate enthusiasm for the *Moyen Court*, Mme. de Maintenon was determined to persuade Mme. de la Maisonfort to join the community of nuns. At this distance of time it is impossible to doubt that the Canoness, despite the name, had no sort of religious vocation, and, had it not been so tragic for her, there is almost a scene of comedy in the way a host of eminent churchmen, themselves swept along by the imperious Pantocrat drove the wretched woman into the vowed dedication of her life to God. Fénelon, alas, was chiefly to blame since him she trusted above all. When she turned to him, he could only write: " All I have to say to you can be reduced to one point: it is to remain in peace and with a full confidence, since you have sacrificed your will to God's and your fate has been decided for you. Vocations reveal themselves as much by the decisions of others, as by our own *attrait*. When God gives us no feeling within to draw us, He gives us an external authority to decide us. . . . You have brought together a sufficient number of experienced people, full of good intentions and without any suspicion of worldliness in the advice they have given you, men

who understand the rules of their profession and who have taken
the trouble to know you. After such an examination, your responsibility is fully discharged before God." Fénelon's teaching
about naked faith and the destruction of self was being applied in
terms of Mme. de Maintenon's will and without reference to Mme.
de La Maisonfort's God-given freedom and responsibility. Nothing
could be more unlike the real Fénelon. In tears, the young woman
met her fate, whilst everyone conspired to persuade her to be
resigned to God's will. Her noviceship was reduced to one year,
and soon after, at the beginning of 1692, she took her vows. Fénelon
grimly recalled the scene in the opening sentence of a letter to her:
" I am delighted that you are in peace, and that you have more
courage than you showed in the parlour when it was a question of
deciding to take vows."

Binding the Canoness to Saint-Cyr by vows had the worst
possible results. If she threatened to be a danger to the institution
through her Guyonist views when she was free, she became a far
greater danger when numbered among those who were dedicated
to its work and service. To make matters worse a Lazarist priest
called Jassault was one of the confessors of the house and as such
possessed considerable influence. He was an admirer of Mme.
Guyon from whom he had learnt the practice of the inner, wordless
prayer she taught. As an excellent and able priest, he became popular
both inside the confessional and in giving spiritual direction outside
to many members of the house. " Practically the whole house
became Quietist. The talk was only of pure love, *abandon*, and
holy indifference. Even among the lay sisters and servants, it was
always a question of pure love. And some, instead of doing their
work, spent their time reading Mme. Guyon's books." So state
the Memoirs of the Order.

The astonishing thing about this rapid spread of exaggerated
views and consequent loss of normal discipline is that no one seems
to have stopped it. Fénelon later said that if he had been given the
authority, he could have put an end to it all in three days. Mme.
Guyon herself had been converted by Fénelon to a discretion of
behaviour that was in startling contrast with her past. Both of
them realised the importance of not giving hostages to fortune.
Had she not very nearly been imprisoned for life? Had he not

been entrusted with one of the most responsible tasks in the kingdom? Why did Mme. de Maintenon fail to exert her absolute authority? Her letters show that she kept on recommending Fénelon's teaching to the community, while rapidly cooling off in her own enthusiasm for Mme. Guyon. "We must keep her for ourselves. She was suspected; and that is enough for people never to leave her in peace," Mme. de Maintenon was writing in 1692, already a considerable change from the days when she carried the *Moyen Court* in her pocket. In the next year Fénelon was warning the Canoness of "the state of mind of those who hope with reason that she (Mme. Guyon) should never appear to have any relations with Saint-Cyr" and discreetly hinting, when asked by her to forward a letter to Mme. de Maintenon, that the great lady's early enthusiasm for Mme. Guyon was not as strong as it had been, even though it was he who had constantly warned her against spreading Guyonist views. His own writings, he insisted, had "a deep truth that was most useful for a small number of people, but they were very dangerous for others who were not up to them." It would be better for him not to forward the letter, and he allowed himself a touch of humour when recommending her to read the New Testament, the Psalms, Saint Francis of Sales and "that other venerable writer," meaning himself.

It is hard to avoid the conclusion that Mme. de Maintenon had been trying to maintain Guyonism in Saint-Cyr for the sake of her Fénelon, while quietly getting rid of Mme. Guyon herself. It was a natural enough reaction when the Fénelon whom she so much admired could write to her stinging letters of spiritual direction under the influence, apparently, of the rival with whom he had remained spiritually infatuated. She was not accustomed to accept second place when a rival woman was in question, and the doctrine of pure love and self-killing was certainly not going to make her change her habits now.

With Mme. de Maintenon, torn between her affection for Fénelon and her jealousy of Mme. Guyon, the troubles steadily grew, and the Canoness was the storm-centre.

Godet, Bishop of Chartres and of Saint-Cyr, became increasingly worried. Saint-Simon describes him as a "lackey in purple," meaning that his piety and talents, though outstanding, were negative and submissive to stronger influences. He was an ascetic, who received the news of his elevation to the episcopate on his knees before the Crucifix in his bare room. "The enemy of all novelties," writes Cardinal de Bausset, Fénelon's official biographer, "and invariably attached to sane doctrine, he fought, one after the other, the two colleagues dearest to his heart, Fénelon and Cardinal de Noailles, without ever ceasing to insist on their virtues." Not surprisingly, the sight of Mme. Guyon (whether willingly or not) inspiring the spirituality of Saint-Cyr scandalised him. If he was troubled by the reflection that Mme. de Maintenon also thought it her duty to be a kind of spiritual mother to the community and school, he was far too tactful to say so. Guyonism in his opinion, was "not bothering about anything, forgetting oneself entirely, never reflecting on oneself, and depending on that liberty of the sons of God which meant making oneself subject to nothing." It was not a very good description of Mme. Guyon's doctrine, but it hit off the Saint-Cyr interpretation and the increasingly reckless attitude of Mme. de La Maisonfort.

In the summer of 1693, Mme. de Maintenon wrote to both Fénelon and Godet: "Since there seems to be a determination to form a singular kind of order at Saint-Cyr, I should like you to put together a little book which would be called *The Spirit of the Institute of the Filles of Saint Louis*." It appears that the first draft of this little work which was to save the institution from the consequences of her own mistakes was her own. Godet who had put out his spies in the convent to report what was really happening made his additions, and the final draft was Fénelon's. When it reached Saint-Cyr, the irrepressible Canoness laughed at it and openly quarrelled with Mme. de Maintenon herself. It looked like mutiny, and on the part of the woman who, above all, had won the great woman's heart. The fat was now in the fire.

Poor Fénelon, so careful and so discreet, did his best to retrieve the situation, but Godet, not he, was the ecclesiastical authority in the convent. He could only write to Mme. de Maintenon, defending La Maisonfort's essential goodness, while making no bones about her stupidities and frivolousness. He neatly pointed out that "it was a strange thing that those who wanted to follow a way which meant being attached to nothing should be so attached to the way itself and those who counselled it." " Mme. de La Maisonfort knows very well that I look upon any prayer and any spirituality as a pure illusion if it does not bring sweetness, patience, obedience and the renunciation of one's own feelings. . . . Prayer and virtue are only solid in so far as they are tested by the Cross and humiliation. We cannot really profit from the best prayer except in so far as we are ready to give it up under obedience. Mme. de La Maisonfort knew it was scandalous to despise spiritual ways so salutary for people in general. . . . At bottom she is, you know, in good faith. Her prayer is innocent, but she had not made a humble and submissive use of it. She is sweet, but God has allowed her to be strangely carried away in your eyes."

In a further letter the degree of his worry is shown by his use of a favourite expression when under stress: " This is what I think before God; I say it as though I was going to appear before Him at this moment." The essence of his teaching was expressed in this correspondence in words similar to those of the later de Caussade: " The freedom which is founded on a true renunciation of the self is a perpetual subjection to the signs of the will of God which is declared at every moment; it is an appalling death in every detail of life and an utter extinction of all self-will in order to act and to will against nature." He declared: " Perhaps I who speak am more prejudiced than others and I favour too much an extraordinary spirituality. But I do not wish to push this spirituality farther than Saint Francis of Sales, the Blessed John of the Cross, and others like them whom the Church has canonised in their teaching and their way of life. . . . Great as is my respect and admiration for Saint Teresa, I should never have wanted to give the public all she has written."

Fénelon, a priest by taste and temperament reserved for the *élite*, spiritual and social, was always consistent in this exclusivity, and considerably more cautious than is customary to-day when books on mysticism are widely diffused. Mme. Guyon's liking for addressing anyone who would listen is nearer to us for whom modern publicity has rendered almost anything accessible.

During all this excitement, Mme. Guyon herself appears to have behaved with the greatest tact and common sense. Whatever her mistakes in the past, she bore no primary responsibility for the present troubles. It was Mme. de Maintenon who had encouraged her relations with Saint-Cyr and she who had insisted on confining her teaching to the few ready for it. It was Mme. de Maintenon, playing for Fénelon's spiritual favours, who failed to prevent her gospel from spreading in the convent. And it was Mme. de Maintenon who grew jealous of her rivalry and her relationship with Fénelon so that all the King's wife's efforts were bent on getting rid of Mme. Guyon and keeping Fénelon, pruned of his affection and dependence on the prophetess.

Mme. Guyon's own account is as follows: " On the excuse of my past troubles and of the Quietism which, they said, was making great strides, they asked the Bishop of Chartres, Superior of Saint Cyr, to tell Mme. de Maintenon that I was disturbing the rule of the house by my peculiar conduct and that the nuns whom I saw were so attached to what I told them that they no longer listened to their superiors. Mme. de Maintenon told me all this with kindness. So I gave up going to Saint Cyr; and I only answered letters which the nuns sent me by open letters which went through Mme. de Maintenon's hands." In this generous version of the affair, there is no suspicion of any persecution complex.

But Mme. Guyon was, naturally enough, not content to remain under vague suspicion of heterodoxy. She consulted theologians on her own account—theologians reputed to be hostile to her views, such as Jansenist Nicole and Boileau. With them, she went through the *Moyen Court* sentence by sentence, and she was advised that the only thing wrong with the book was the lack of sufficient explanation of the terms and the teaching. Never loathe to put pen to paper, this indefatigable woman promptly wrote *A Short Defence of the Moyen Court*, in which she pressed the very important distinction between beginners and those more advanced in prayer—the very point that the Quietists were, as a rule, too apt to overlook. Criticisms, she pointed out, of the view that one must not worry about faults, scruples, repeated vocal prayers might well be justified when it was a case of beginners; but these criticisms were out of place when it was a question of the people for whom this part of her teaching was meant—people already fully determined to serve God with all their hearts and practised in so doing. She insisted that she had never meant the " single act " of always being in a position of waiting on God to be a permanent state that would guarantee anyone from falling into sin. She had learnt well from Fénelon, while ostensibly teaching him. She concluded: " I have always written under obedience, and I have submitted everything, as I submit it still, protesting that I would rather die than separate myself in the slightest from the spirit of the Church."

Alas, rumours of Quietism at Saint-Cyr and the presence there of the suspect Mme. Guyon were not calculated to appease the various kinds of anonymous enemies whose interest it was to undermine the new spiritual developments at court and in the country.

It may be, too, that a general sense in France that the King's victories were piling up troubles for the future, a sense stimulated by the social disaster of a bad harvest and consequent famine, added to the general feeling of grievance and to the need for distraction. Anyway, there were now ominous signs that the net was once more being quietly spread to catch the woman who so lately had enjoyed the confidence of the King's wife and the *dévots* and grandees of the Court. The old calumnies were resurrected and fresh ones added. It was the first step in an all-out attack against the reformist movement.

Mme. Guyon's letters to the Dukes of Chevreuse and Beauvilliers from now on are full of pathos, sadness, resignation and readiness to admit that she might have been deceived, but if so involuntarily. " I cannot pretend to reassure you, if God causes you to have doubts," she wrote to the upright and rather wooden Beauvilliers. " I have always told you that I could not guarantee not to have been deceived; but that my purpose was never to deceive. . . . It is for you to judge whether I have deceived you, and where." To the warmer and more naturally appreciative Chevreuse she could open her heart more fully. To him she spoke of the spate of new and sinister persecutions at a moment " when the angel of darkness was turning himself into an angel of light in order to confuse true piety with crime "; of the fraudulent Sœur Rose who had gained the ear of some of the clergy and turned them against her [later this woman had to be driven out of Paris owing to the scandals attached to her]; of the " Daughters of Père Vautier " who used to confess gross sins they had committed, so they said, because of following Mme. Guyon's teaching; and of other enemies who were certainly agents of the hostile forces sensing that their opportunity was near.

She realised, she told him, that she must leave Paris. "Had Providence left me in peace in my little house, I would have willingly stayed there. But since God does not want this, I must once more become a wanderer, without hearth and home, ill and abandoned by all the world. I consent to it with all my heart. . . . A thousand times I am all to you all."

"I must beg you, in God's name, to let me perish. . . . I am decried everywhere. . . . My Master is strong enough to save me. But if He does not will it, I should be content. . . . A village and a peasant's dress will hide me for ever from man." This depression when the persecutions were renewed contrasts with her wonderful courage best expressed in an amusing and evidently rather later letter which perhaps is not her least effective defence for posterity.

"I must cheer you up," she wrote to the Duke, "by telling you of the news of your great world—I who do not even belong to the world. They are saying that my trial is being rapidly prepared, that Desgrès (Lieutenant of Police) has been commanded to fetch me. Some say that I am to be condemned to bread and water and perpetual imprisonment; others that I shall have my head chopped off. But the most popular rumour is that I shall have to make an abjuration in front of Notre Dame, after which my wrist will be cut off, and then my head. My body will be burnt and the ashes scattered in the wind. All this just suits me and I was delighted for a whole day. . . . If my readiness to accept all this counts for the fact itself, then my ashes are already flying about. Yes, it would be pleasant, but I fear I do not deserve such a favour and dare not hope for it."[1]

The situation being what it was, the Court cenacle worried and perhaps involved; the bishops anxious; Saint-Cyr compromised; Mme. de Maintenon determined to have her way (even if she did not know what it was) and nervous about the King's reactions; the enemies of reform rearing their heads, there seemed to be only one thing to do to save the day. Fénelon, Chevreuse, Godet, Maintenon and Mme. Guyon herself turned in the direction of the ecclesiastical light of France—to the great Bossuet himself whose word was almost an oracle. They could not have made a worse mistake.

---

[1] This letter is dated January, 1694; but the context suggests that it was written in 1695 when Mme. Guyon was arrested and imprisoned in Vincennes.

CHAPTER SIX

THE EAGLE AND THE SWAN

JACQUES BÉNIGNE BOSSUET, Bishop of Meaux, is one of the great figures of ecclesiastical history. As a writer, he is an immortal— and that despite the fact the religious subject of his writings, together with the dogmatism of his treatment, weighs increasingly heavily against posterity's taste for reading him. As a preacher and orator, he was the greatest of an age of great preachers. As a controversialist, in the strictest sense of arguing within limits agreed upon by both sides, he has hardly been surpassed for his rapid mastering of the relevant facts, the clarity of his reasoning and his power of transcending the argument itself so that what he wrote possessed a value wider and deeper than its immediate purposes. He has been called " the last of the Fathers of the Church," and perhaps until we meet the very different Newman there is no Catholic ecclesiastical figure comparable to him, save only Fénelon himself.

But what about Bossuet the man—indeed Bossuet the old man; for it is with him that we have to deal in these pages. He was already in his late sixties when he found himself involved in the affairs of Mme. Guyon and the Quietist movement. In some respects he was a disappointed old man. From the worldly point of view, he had been robbed of his natural crown, the Cardinal's Hat and the See of Paris. The Hat was withheld by the combative Innocent XI because of Bossuet's unsuccessful attempt to resolve the long-standing quarrel between the French Church and the Holy See. He would have gladly been spared the honour of trying to settle this quarrel. But it was forced on him by Harlay, Archbishop of Paris, who foresaw that the thankless task could not but diminish Bossuet's stature, both in Rome and Versailles. Bossuet's devotion to the

absolute monarchy, so brilliantly illustrated in the *Grand Monarque*
went hand in hand with his absolute faith in the Catholic Church
as the sole revelation of Divine Providence for the ordering of
mankind. As such, the best he could do was to produce a compromise which displeased Louis and Innocent. Beneath the surface,
too, he was tired—tired of endless fighting against Protestants,
Freethinkers, and, not least, those within the Church who dared to
question his monumental certainties.

From the personal point of view, Bossuet's life had been something of a spiritual tragedy. Brought up as a young priest under
St. Vincent de Paul, his spirit yearned to dedicate itself utterly to
God's service and to a life of piety and penance. By nature, too, he
was gentle, kind and tolerant. This priestly ideal never ceased to
haunt him, and it always left one side of him humble, attractive and
sweet. But his remarkable talents carried him, despite his humble
birth, to early dazzling success and to the life of the Court where
flattery and compromise were the order of the day. He was too good
at heart to sacrifice and forget his deep principles, but he could not
help play the magnificent role for all it was worth, the role of the
court preacher and oracle whose magnificent and well-relished
sermons were not for a moment expected to have the slightest
effect on the hypocrisies and superstitions of Versailles, Paris,
Fontainebleau and Marly. As the accepted representative of the
Church in its public relations with the State, he had to play another
role, that of the authoritative, forceful, self-confident writer who
could crush the heretic and cause the libertine to blush—at any rate,
on the right occasion. This was the Bossuet of the great Rigaud
portrait in which the pose, the draped robes, the panoply were
merely an ecclesiastical transposition for the trappings of a monarch
or a marshal. Only in personal contacts, as at the death-bed of
" Madame," Charles II's well-loved sister, Minette, or face to face
with the individual living Huguenot, or as bishop in his humble, but
convenient, diocese, or with his old friends, could he be the self-
forgetting, sympathetic priest, rightly named " Benign," bringing
the love and understanding of God to the human soul. This was
the Bossuet of the smaller portrait that still hangs in the episcopal
palace of Meaux and suggests a man of feeling and sympathy, albeit
a successful one who knew comfortable living. Pride of life was

the temptation that oppressed him, he knew it as a temptation and it caused both his enjoyment of his great priestly success and the bitterness he felt in this enjoyment. This conflict within him, as well as the hard crust which the sentimental person is so apt to grow in self-defence are, one feels, the explanation of the lamentable part he played in the story we have to tell.

History thinks of Bossuet and Fénelon as men born to differ and to clash: Bossuet, the " Eagle," dominant, aggressive, sure of himself and of a world eternally ordered and shaped by Christian revelation and ideally set in the frame of the apogee of Christian monarchy; Fénelon, the " Swan," gently and dreamily floating along the tide, conscious of the strangeness and never-ending novelty of man and his world, contemplative, feeling his way, unsure of his goal, yet instinctively pursuing it in graceful circles. But such analogies, while they express part of the truth, are bad guides to living men.

In reality, there was much that drew the older and the younger man together. As a young priest, Fénelon's admiration for Bossuet was unbounded. How could it be otherwise? Bossuet's position and learning suited Fénelon's interests and hopes. His goodness, piety and humanity in personal relations enchanted and perhaps flattered the younger careerist. Fénelon's greatest pleasure was to visit Bossuet in the rural shades of his country home at Germigny where both could talk at ease, rest and enjoy the poetic peace not to be found in Paris. From his exile working for the conversion of the Huguenots in Poitou, Fénelon wrote to Bossuet to plead with those who could recall him to the centre of affairs—and to Bossuet. " If we are held too long separated from you," he wrote in the vein he so enjoyed, " we shall have to suppress the *Ave Maria*, and, maybe, we shall go so far as to become grossly heretical so that the happy consequent disgrace would bring us back to Germigny; that would cause a little storm fit to make a pleasant shipwreck! " In Versailles, Bossuet had gathered together a group of learned priests for the discussion of Scripture and other matters which became known as the Little Council. Among them were friendship, ease and common purpose. Fénelon was of the number, and the youngest. The avenue where the company would walk and talk together became known as the Alley of the Philosophers.

Fénelon's Bossuetist opponents later accused him of currying favour with Bossuet by indulging in fulsome praise of the greater man. The story is false to both their characters, except perhaps in so far as the disciple might, as we should now put it, have pulled the older one's leg for his little vanities by putting on an act of flattering him. To Fénelon, Bossuet was already the "Eagle": "I could see you in your skull-cap, gripping M. Du Pin [a critical clerical writer disliked by Bossuet] like an eagle which holds a feeble hawk in its talons." To Bossuet, Fénelon was the promise of the future. The links between them were very close, a fact that makes the subsequent classical quarrel all the sadder. Both were sincere and devout priests; both were ambitious in their very different ways; both were capable of great personal feeling and affection. And if Fénelon's horizon was different, we must always remember that he possessed something of the chameleon's gift of changing appearances according to his environment. The real differences between the two men were in some ways the contrary of the differences between eagle and swan.

It was Fénelon who was tough beneath the surface; it was Fénelon who sought order and reason and God as the goal to be reached through toil and the struggle against human and worldly distraction; it was he who was to be the Ultramontane, intent on the order and universality of the Church of which the Pope was Head. It was Bossuet who, with all his genius, was carried on the tide of feeling and instinct so that his greatness was dated by the already archaic and doomed Gallican glamour of the *Roi Soleil*. It was he who saw in the artificial stiffness of the trappings of the *Grand Siècle* the marks of the universality and eternity of the Church. It was he who trusted specious appearances rather than unchanging reality. As so often, the true and lasting orthodoxy is not the orthodoxy of the past seen through eyes of the present, but the deeper orthodoxy, below appearances and change, that may seem suspect to narrow minds, yet is destined to endure into the age to come. Consider Newman in his quarrel with Manning, two ecclesiastics who at times recall Fénelon and Bossuet.

The complete trust which Fénelon had for the great bishop who was practically his patron proved to be a dangerous trap causing both Fénelon and Mme. Guyon to rue the day when they looked to him for help. But in the summer of 1693 they both felt completely confident about the submission of the Guyonist teaching to Bossuet's judgment, even though it was known that he had very little knowledge or experience of mysticism and had certainly not read the great Catholic masters of the subject. Mme. Guyon wrote: " Several of my friends thought it a good thing for me to see the Bishop of Meaux, who was said not to be ill-disposed to the inner spiritual life. I knew that he had read the *Moyen Court* and the *Cantique* eight or ten years earlier and had found them excellent." This was possible as the books had circulated freely.

Bossuet's story was that he was reluctant to interfere in a matter which was, after all, not in any way his business. It was for the Archbishop of Paris to pronounce on Mme. Guyon, but this, of course, Mme. de Maintenon wished to avoid. Harlay belonged to the hostile camp. In the end, Chevreuse brought Bossuet to Mme. Guyon's house. He was all smiles, all affability (according to Mme. Guyon). "We talked of the *Moyen Court*. The prelate spoke so deeply on the interior life and God's authority over souls that I was surprised." Chevreuse gave him a history of Mme. Guyon's life which, she says, greatly edified him, and he even took the trouble to write to Chevreuse to tell him that he had just had another proof in the death of a certain nun that " God wished to be served with a total self-abnegation and the loss of all self-love."

In this cordial atmosphere—and there is no reason to suppose that anyone was acting a part, for it was all *en famille*, and it was always Bossuet's nature to be kind and tolerant so long as he could—Mme. Guyon most unwisely offered Bossuet copies of everything she had written, whether printed or in manuscript, including her Autobiography to date. Let him read and study everything for himself. She only made the condition that he should keep everything an inviolable confessional secret between them.

During the following six months (summer, 1693, to January, 1694) Bossuet set himself the onerous task of reading every word of her interminable outpourings and even painfully copying out long passages for collating purposes. The " Eagle " was in fact submitting to the most searching theological examination writings which the " Swan " could never be bothered to read at all. Fénelon

was only interested in the person—the person whom he himself
was all the time influencing through occasional contact and much
correspondence. The rest was a bore and of only secondary importance. Bossuet had hardly any personal knowledge of Mme.
Guyon nor much interest in, or knowledge of, the Catholic mystical
tradition. He liked solidity, definition, and comfortable, well-worn,
human emotions. But she had delivered over to him in her en-
thusiastic way the uneducated, uninhibited, personal expression of
everything she had thought and done, or thought she had thought
and done, since she could remember. Her youth, her strange
adventures, her relations with La Combe, her episcopal critics and
her episcopal friends, and, above all, her romantic hopes about the
future when Fénelon would be the corner-stone of a new Church
and the *Michelins* would crush the *Christophets*. True, she repented
of letting Bossuet see her aspirations about Fénelon and charged
Chevreuse to get them back lest Fénelon be compromised by her.
But it was too late, Bossuet had already read and copied them. It
was all a pell-mell of dream, phantasy, intuition, subconscious
yearnings, with, as we have seen, a golden thread of good sense
and high spirituality.

We can well imagine the literal-minded Bossuet's reactions.
What hair he had left must have stood on his head as he heavily
underlined apparent heresies, even apparent blasphemies and, it
seemed, lunatic dreams about a new world and a new Church.
The Mme. Guyon he got to know through those autumn and winter
months, when the episcopal lamp shone late into the night over
the sleeping citizens of Meaux was, in fact, a very different person
from the Mme. Guyon whom Fénelon had esteemed as a person
advanced in the higher ways of prayer, for the simple reason that
Fénelon's personality, sympathy and learning were all the time
modifying and rationalising her views. Hence the profound misunderstanding between them.

Fénelon's " saint " only caused Bossuet to shudder and write:
" And Thou, O Lord, if I dared, I would beseech that Thou
should'st send forth one of Thy Seraphims with the hottest of his
coals to purify my lips soiled by this recital, necessary as it is. . . . My
stomach was turned again and again as I read the teaching in her
book." To him the analogy, the parable, the dream, the exaggerated

and often silly imagery was sober narrative. To him it was " the pride of the devil " and a " frightful presumption."

Such reactions of Bossuet—and he did not err by cutting short his oratorical flow—were in fact expressed some years later and in the heat of the public battle with Fénelon. But when at the end of January, 1694, he felt he could learn no more from her writings, it was arranged that he and she should meet in a Paris convent. She had not recovered from the heavy depression which overcame her during these months, and she must have been aware that she had made a mistake in handing over to Bossuet the papers which even Fénelon had not read. She arrived in the early morning heavily veiled and arousing the eager curiosity of those present. But Bossuet said Mass and gave her Communion—a rather strange thing to do if his feelings then had corresponded with his later indignation. One must suppose that Bossuet, too, had discerned Mme. Guyon's fundamental goodness and that he was in two minds how to take her: a pious woman, yet given to incredible delusions, or a hypocrite with the gift of writing spiritual jargon. His uncertainty about how to take her was to continue for some time, and it is permissible to think that the second interpretation grew stronger because it was the one that suited the powerful Mme. de Maintenon, ever at his elbow.

However this be, the two of them, on this day, lunched together in friendly fashion, and the serious talk was postponed until the evening. Then, Mme. Guyon tells us, he was quite a different man. She complained that he talked so rapidly and continuously that she could not get a word in. However, " God helped me so that I could satisfy him about everything to do with dogma and purity of doctrine. . . . We left very late, and I came away from the meeting, my head so worn out and so overcome that I was ill for several days." This nervous illness was evidence enough that Bossuet had badly shaken her.

Letters and meetings continued. Bossuet was endlessly patient, while Mme. Guyon tried in increasing bewilderment to explain to a clerical logician that she hardly even knew what she had written in the past. It was not a theological text-book; it was the palpitating story of her inner life, her relationship with God, written under obedience not to omit anything she had felt. If Bossuet said so, then she was wrong, but her mind had not been thinking in terms of right and wrong, but of experiences that had been lived. Part of the trouble was that Bossuet himself was so unfamiliar with the language and experience of the mystics. It all shocked him and, in fact, it would continue to do so. He could easily catch her out when, for example, she maintained that she could not pray for Divine favours or recite vocal prayers. All he had to do was to remind her of the Lord's prayer and order her under obedience to say it. " I can repeat the words," she answered, " but I cannot feel the sentiment in my heart." It seemed like more blasphemy, more stubborn rebellion, to Bossuet, and Mme. Guyon may indeed have been deluded. But her state would have at least meant something to the student of St. John of the Cross who reproved spiritual directors " who have no knowledge save of hammering and pounding with the faculties like a blacksmith " trying to force souls back into normal prayer.

Bossuet was particularly puzzled by her insistence that God had no " graces," i.e. no special illuminations, for her and for some others like her. He could understand the " extraordinary behaviour he had seen in certain persons or about which he had read . . . but this way of simple, little, dark faith . . . was a jargon which he thought came from an empty spirit; such terms were unknown to him and unbelievable," Mme. Guyon wrote. She even had to explain to him that when she used the word " graces " she was not talking of " sanctifying grace," the state of every Christian not in grievous sin, but of the ecstasies, visions, revelations which she mistrusted. That passage rings true, and Mme. Guyon was right; Bossuet wrong. Then again Bossuet was utterly unable to believe that man could love God without any element of self-interest entering into his love. Here again Bossuet's view was to be proved wrong. Then he was convinced that mystical prayer was, anyway, confined to four or five exceptional people at most in the world at any given time. " There are more than a hundred thousand," Mme. Guyon insisted, " and it is for them that I write." Numbers hardly enter into the problem, but to-day theologians would prefer Mme. Guyon's view, at any rate, in the sense that many indeed are called to such prayer, even though we cannot say how many achieve it.

No wonder these interviews left them both dead weary. "I think his head is split, not only by his mitre, but by the trouble he has taken over me," Mme. Guyon wrote to Chevreuse with her usual spirit. "As for mine, it is split into four pieces."

On the whole, it had gone a good deal better than she could have expected. Her charm did its work, and Bossuet, left to himself, never wanted to bully. He certainly insisted that he found it quite impossible to reconcile some of her views with the teaching and traditions of the Church; but he did not doubt her own genuine Catholicity and good faith. He was therefore ready to give her a certificate to that effect and to administer the sacraments to her. The best in him was expressed in a letter in which he assures her of his sympathy with her, notwithstanding their differences: "You have got hold of certain views on prayer and you believe that when you make certain acts of prayer commanded by God your prayer becomes self-regarding and self-interested. However, I remain one with you and I trust that God will make known to you what you lack, all the more so in that you want to be corrected about your mistakes. This is all I have been trying to do out of sincere friendship."

"M. de Meaux," Mme. Guyon wrote more succinctly to Chevreuse, "had the goodness not to believe me a witch or a villain." Indeed though she still remained depressed, and retired completely from the world so that no one knew her whereabouts, there were signs of her spirits reviving. This was due, not only to Bossuet's personal kindness but to the evidence that her friends, and Fénelon especially, were ready to stand by her.

It must not be imagined that the great Bishop would have found the time to make so thorough an examination of the prophetess, had there not been a very important motive. He was already under Mme. de Maintenon's orders to disabuse her Fénelon of his mysterious and increasingly intolerable predilection for the woman. But when he hurried to Versailles to pour out to his disciple and friend, Fénelon, the astonishing fancies, delusions and worse that he had read in Mme. Guyon's papers, "the only answer I got was that since she was submissive about her doctrine, there was no need to condemn the person." He left, as he said, "astonished to find so fine a mind lost in admiration of a woman whose inspirations were so shallow, whose merits so frivolous, whose illusions so obvious, and who pretended to be a prophetess." But once again this was Bossuet writing later in the full flood of polemic, and we may resonably suppose that his real reaction was one of bewilderment at her split-personality. In fact, he accepted Fénelon's view and did not " condemn the person."

2

Once again it seemed as though the troubles, which were still of a private rather than public nature, could have been left to simmer down. True, highly injurious stories about Mme. Guyon were being put about by her hidden enemies. There was the case, for example, of a document supposed to have been written by a priest of high repute who had once been Mme. Guyon's confessor. In the midst of complaints about her teaching and her lack of submissiveness, the following story was insinuated: " I remember only that our interview lasted a long time. Towards the end, whether it was at this meeting or at Mme. de Charost's, she told me confidentially that there were people who did these things [practising Quietism] in an astonishing state, for example, naked to the waist— a detail not to be mentioned to people of quality who could not bring themselves to do it." The document, which was handed about, was so cleverly composed and with so much knowledge of the priest and of Mme. Guyon's relations with him that she herself did not reject it as a forgery. She could only say that he must have been thoroughly confused and suffering from some loss of memory. Yet when Chevreuse investigated this particular calumny, he discovered that it was a forgery, and on one of Mme. Guyon's own letters he wrote: " About a letter of Père Paulin, which he has since disavowed, assuring M. le Duc de Chevreuse that he never wrote it or did anything else on the subject."

But even calumnies like these could not really touch the devout Court circle. It was impossible, especially with Mme. Guyon herself excluded, to accuse people of such high rank and influence of the crime of Quietism. Those who had personally known Mme. Guyon still appreciated her worth, and we find the worthy and strict Abbé Tronson, of Saint-Sulpice, Beauvilliers's spiritual

director and Fénelon's old superior, writing that her retirement
should cause " the rumours to cease and the storms to quieten down.
. . . It is true that she is extremely highly esteemed by those who are
most devout at the Court." In a further letter he wrote: " It is true
that her conversation has caused extraordinary effects of grace among
many highly qualified people at Court, so that it would be difficult
—to judge only by this—not to believe her to be filled with the
spirit of God." Referring then to her critics, he went on bewildered:
" I have not been able to say anything except that her conduct is a
mystery about which I understand nothing! "

Fénelon himself, of course, remained utterly untouched in public
and private esteem. No one, except his closest friends like Chevreuse,
had any real inkling how very close his relations with her had been,
and his spiritual views, most discreetly communicated only to those
who could understand and profit from them, were given as his own,
however much, in fact, they may have been influenced by Mme.
Guyon. With him—it seemed—there could be no question of
open Quietist accusations. On the contrary, there he was, enjoying
the fullest confidence of the Court, of the King's wife and presumably the King, and continuing his fruitful labours, under
Beauvilliers, to educate, with the help of his friends, Langeron and
Fleury, the Prince who would be ' France ' to-morrow. In fact,
the King himself was totally uninterested in such spiritual and
theological niceties and, confident in his wife and in Beauvilliers,
he remained undisturbed, it seems, and anxious, to allow the spiritual
standards at Court to be raised, even if it meant having to put up
with the strange quirks of the fanciful and mysterious Fénelon.
Like all dictators, he only believed what he wanted at the time to
believe. Much water had still to flow under the bridges of the Seine
before his suspicions were aroused.

It was a different matter with his wife. She was determined to
keep the waters stirring, even if for the time being she did not know
exactly what she wanted. For Mme. de Maintenon, the main
thing was that all her efforts with Bossuet had not succeeded in
weaning Fénelon from that rival spiritual intimate, even after the
latter's physical retirement. Not only that, but Fénelon himself was
coming to realise the mischief she could do with her immature
spiritual pretensions, her inability or unwillingness to control in

Jacobus Benignus *Bossuet Episcopus*
Meldensis Comes Consistorianus *antea serenissimi Delphini Præce-*
ptor et primus serenissimæ Ducis *Burgundiæ Eleemosynarius* Ætatis anno 74.
Peint par H. Rigault. Gravé par le Chevalier Edelinck.

Benigne Bossuet, Bishop of Meaux

Saint-Cyr the divisions which had been created, and her growing desire to ruin Mme. Guyon and perhaps Fénelon himself. The difficulties became so acute that in May, 1694, he wrote to her the second of his famous letters in the hope of making her realise the extent of her self-esteem.

"We must see our imperfections," he wrote to the woman who had climbed all the long way to the highest pinnacle of feminine power behind the Throne, "and be ready to see them exposed to the censure of the public. You, and all those who come near you are condemned as incapable of great affairs by every sort of reasoning. You must let yourself be condemned in peace; you must even wish to be blamed wherever you really are at fault. . . . How good it is, Madame, to be deprived of our own self-esteem and of that of honest men. . . . You do not hold by common goods and common honours, but perhaps you do, without realising it, hold by your good standing, the reputation you have among good men, by friendship, and above all, by a certain perfection of virtue that one would wish to find in oneself and which would take the place of everything else. This is the last refinement of self-love which consoles us for all loss. . . . The more perfect we appear to people without true experience who only judge by outer behaviour, the more imperfect we are—for we are full of ourselves, like Lucifer. His sin only consisted in the pleasure of seeing himself as perfect; I mean perfect in the mirror of self-love. . . . If it please God, you will always be very virtuous; but God demands of those to whom He gives much a disappropriation of His gifts, a littleness and an absolute death which millions of perfectly good and humble people know nothing about."

Whether she realised the hideous irony of the fact that Fénelon was piercing her with a weapon forged in Mme. Guyon's arsenal, though sharpened to a fine point by his own ruthless insight, we cannot tell. But it was more than she could bear. She sent the letter to Godet for the necessary antidote in the form of soft spiritual words for herself and a censure of Fénelon's views. Godet did his best, but with some misgiving as he had once assured her that he could answer as much for his friend Fénelon as for himself.

Still aiming to live by the highest spiritual standards, Mme. de Maintenon accepted with sorrow and self-pity, rather than anger, her duty to disentangle herself from the friendship she had so long felt for the cleverest and holiest of the churchmen around her, a friendship which Fénelon undoubtedly reciprocated. She could hope that the time might come when Fénelon would be disillusioned of his painful submission to the fascination of the pretentious little widow Guyon; so for the time being no effort must be spared, no means recoiled from, which could hasten that happy day.

Among the means she used was the questionable one of handing over to Bossuet, without a word to the writer, the letters of spiritual direction she had received from Fénelon, as well as the little red books in which she had copied out that part of his teaching which had most appealed to her. Armed with these private documents Bossuet would be better equipped for the great work of persuading Fénelon that he, too, must condemn Mme. Guyon if he was to pursue successfully the great career that had opened out in front of him.

As for Mme. Guyon, almost any of the celebrated priests within Mme. de Maintenon's call and powerful influence could be used for further examinations of these Quietist writings, together with the appropriate condemnations.

But Mme. Guyon herself, now well recovered from the depressions of the previous autumn and winter, was ready to fight as hard as ever for her cause. In particular she was ready to fight for her reputation as a woman, for she well knew that here was a question of fact and evidence where she was absolutely impregnable. " I take the liberty," she wrote to Beauvilliers, " of begging you to tell Mme. de Maintenon that I demand lay judges, because ecclesiastical ones are not competent to judge of criminal matters and cannot go deeply into them. There is no question of my spiritual teaching since I have submitted my writings in all good faith possible and handed them over to be burnt [if only some of them had been burnt!] if this is judged proper, and, if I have been deceived or fallen into error, I disavow it all and submit myself. . . . I demand men of probity and uprightness, incapable of being swayed by cabal."

Mme. de Maintenon absolutely refused to see her rival's character cleared through such an inquiry, and she did not trouble to hide her reasons. In fact, she wrote to Beauvilliers to explain them. Mme.

Guyon herself tells us the lines along which Mme. de Maintenon was thinking: " She [Mme. de Maintenon] had never believed the rumours current about my morals; she thought them good, but my teaching bad. If my morals were justified, there would be a risk of my views spreading. In this way they would gain some authority. It would therefore be wisest [Mme. Guyon concluded] to have my *teaching* thoroughly examined once and for all, and afterwards the rest would be automatically forgotten."

Mme. Guyon was not for a moment deceived: " I was thunderstruck by Mme. de Maintenon's refusal to allow me judges. I very well understood that they wanted to deprive me of the only resource I had in order to make my innocence known. The only reason they did not want to make this fresh examination was to deceive the public and make my condemnation the more authentic. . . . I knew who my enemies were. It was feared lest my innocence be made public and the methods used to tarnish it exposed. Some even feared to be accused themselves."

Luckily, the King's wife could not get her own way entirely. There were churchmen about who realised that the question at issue was far more serious and far-reaching than Mme. de Maintenon could imagine. Right or wrong in her detailed views, Mme. Guyon was in the great tradition of contemplative, mystical, personal prayer. After all, Saint Francis of Sales had only been dead seventy years and Saints Theresa and John of the Cross about a hundred. Mystical Theology, as the subject was called, had an impressive and also scientific record within the fullest Catholic orthodoxy for centuries, and never had it flowered more profusely than in the sixteenth and seventeenth centuries in France. Of late, it had deviated into paths that had been condemned, but the distinction between true mysticism and false could not be drawn by a straight line from Bossuet's blunt pencil, still less in terms of the prejudices and careers of far less eminent and worthy ecclesiastics. Fénelon himself, above all, realised this, and it was because of this realisation that he refused to separate himself in mind and soul from Mme. Guyon. The aged and scrupulous Tronson, detached from all worldly or fashionable interests, had sufficient courage to point out that a careful reading of Mme. Guyon often showed that a dangerous view, if it was read by itself, was later balanced by a qualification that made it safe and understandable. For example, when she maintained that the soul could reach a spiritual state even in this world in which it could no longer sin—which was heretical in itself —she later qualified the statement by adding "except for the blackest infidelity that ever was"—in other words, the impossibility of sinning was a moral one, not a physical one, and this was sound doctrine. Tronson was impressed, too, by the argument of "by their fruits shall ye know them." She did good to all who knew her and brought them nearer to God.

In the end there was general agreement for a very sensible plan. Let the whole subject be thoroughly, though unofficially, examined by three eminent ecclesiastics about whose nomination all concerned could agree. A court of inquiry of this kind could reach positive conclusions about what *was* true Catholic mysticism and what went beyond the bounds of tradition and orthodoxy. Such findings would provide a yardstick by which Mme. Guyon's teaching could be judged and any suspicions about Fénelon cleared. They would also furnish a charter of orthodox teaching to which suspected people could subscribe, thereby clearing their reputations.

The only difficulty was that any inquiry of the kind should be held under the authority of the Archbishop of Paris, the unpopular Harlay. The King's wife would have no truck with him, and his whole spirit was thoroughly alien to the churchmen of her entourage. So it would have to be something of an undercover family affair in which Mme. de Maintenon would have to trust Bossuet to see to it that the final results would not disappoint her. Bossuet, as one of the examiners, was acceptable to Mme. Guyon herself. He had already approved her good intentions and her virtue. He was still a close friend of Fénelon's, and indeed it was on his advice, as well as that of Chevreuse, that she accepted him. Unfortunately, as she was well aware, his knowledge of mystical theology was very slight and his mind on the subject prejudiced. So it was agreed to bring in Mme. de Maintenon's closest ecclesiastical friend, de Noailles, the Bishop of Châlons.

De Noailles, a member of one of the greatest French families, was an uncle of the Comtesse de Guiche, a prominent member of the Court cenacle and a friend and disciple of Mme. Guyon. But he was not a strong-minded man and was unlikely to stand up to pressure from Bossuet and Mme. de Maintenon who was later to nominate him as Archbishop of Paris in succession to Harlay. Only the third examiner, Tronson himself, could be regarded as fully impartial and fully up to the subject-matter under examination. In view of his age and his retirement from the great matters of the world, he could only be persuaded with the greatest difficulty to accept the invitation. His health did not allow him to leave the country-house of Saint-Sulpice at Issy to the south of Paris. The meetings had therefore to take place in that pleasant retreat, and they came to be called the Issy Conferences. They lasted nine months from July, 1694, to March, 1695.

In Mme. Guyon's strange life nothing perhaps indicates more strongly the influence this lone woman could wield over great people than the Issy Conferences. Off and on, for nine months, Bossuet, the greatest churchman of his day, busied with a thousand cares, made his way to Issy, there to meet another highly-placed bishop and to disturb the painful hours of the venerable superior of Saint-Sulpice, and all for the purpose of concentrating on the spiritual teaching of this little widow dedicated to the spiritual way of self-abnegation and utter dedication to God's will. And into the bargain these great people were all conspiring like children to avoid the attention of the Archbishop of Paris, who was the only competent person to hold any inquiry of the kind, within the Paris diocese.

Mme. Guyon, only saved from life-imprisonment by the accident of the unpopularity of Harlay with the Court convent, could never have commanded such attention if far greater causes than her own had not been at stake. It was only because her influence had so deeply affected Saint Cyr, the reformist movement, Mme. de Maintenon herself, and, above all, Fénelon and the upbringing of the young princes that she was now so fully in the centre of the picture.

Mme. de Maintenon had certainly made up her mind that once and for all Mme. Guyon must be shown up in the eyes of all who had been deceived by her for what she really was, a dangerous heretic.

One vitally important reason for this was her husband, the King himself. Bossuet later wrote that if " a prince so religious, so delicate in matters of faith, so circumspect in filling the great positions in the Church " had for a moment suspected what had been going on, there would have been ruin all round. We can translate Bossuet's eulogies into the simpler fact that Louis detested all novelties, whether in Church or State. In his secret wife he admired most of all what he called her " solidity "—the very last quality one could apply either to Mme. Guyon or to Fénelon, a woman and a man whose minds were at times almost vapourised into strange and enigmatical fancies. Deceived in the past by his mistresses, especially the notorious Montespan, the King was unlikely to stand a fresh deception, however spiritual, from his solid wife.

But of more immediate concern was Mme. de Maintenon's relationship with Fénelon himself. He, above all, must be exorcised of this fatal attachment which had utterly spoilt the charm, brilliance and piety which had captivated her. This private inquiry, conducted by his own close friends must surely finally dispose of Mme. Guyon and face Fénelon with the fatal dilemma: condemn her or be condemned and ruined yourself. One can see why the widow's moral reputation was of secondary concern to her. If that reputation were publicly destroyed Mme. Guyon as a person would be destroyed; but the matter would be irrelevant to the case of the morally above suspicion Abbé Fénelon. Only an utter condemnation of her *teaching*—and that by his own friends—could finally shake him, and restore him to her.

Bossuet himself, who had read all Mme. Guyon's papers and who now had access to Fénelon's private letters to Mme. de Maintenon, had no less forceful motives for ending the whole business with a spectacular condemnation. It was completely in his interests to carry out Mme. de Maintenon's instructions—the Archbishopric of Paris might soon be vacant and it was in her nomination. But even if this latter motive played no great part in dictating his actions, he was certainly completely bewildered by the Fénelon he had so much loved. How could this brilliant and delightful priest, natural successor to his own ecclesiastical authority, tutor to the princes and due for the highest promotions, fall for a deluded woman who dreamt of founding a new Church in France under the inspiration of the Holy Spirit and the mediation of Fénelon, whom she actually compared to a new Christ? Had he not read her words with his own eyes: " Sometimes in order to melt the tension within me I had to cry: " O my son, you are my well-beloved son in whom I am well-pleased . . . I am that stone set by the Cross and thrown aside by all the architects, the strong and the wise who will never acknowledge it, but which will become the corner-stone of the inner building which the Lord has chosen for the construction of that Jerusalem come down from heaven, grand and triumphant, like a bride arising from the nuptial bed." Had Fénelon ever read the words? It seems that he had not. Had Mme. Guyon even remembered the curious excesses of her excited, ardent mind which produced, among other things, such odd images and such odd prose? But there they were in black and white in Bossuet's own hand, faithfully copied from her manuscripts. Any means, surely, would be justified in rescuing Fénelon—and the Church, for he maintained that the whole Church was at stake—from this delusion.

What of Fénelon himself who—let us recall it again—virtually knew a different Mme. Guyon from the one whom Bossuet had studied? Throughout, Fénelon adopted an attitude of submissiveness to Bossuet's judgments and findings which strikes us as almost abject in its expression. He offered to make a general confession to Bossuet of his whole life—an offer Bossuet was to accept, and wrote: " I do not stand by my position [as preceptor to the princes], and I am ready to give it up, if my errors have made me unworthy of it." He would write: " I summon you in God's name, and by the love you have for the truth in its fullest rigour. I shall hide myself and do penance for the rest of my days, after having abjured and publicly retracted the false doctrine that led me astray."

Such was the kind of language he used again and again in his letters, and it filled Bossuet and Mme. de Maintenon with delight. The erring son would be rescued at the eleventh hour, and the whole tragic affair would remain in the family. But Fénelon very well knew what he was about. His rhetorical self-abasement, though doubtless sincere, was hypothetical. The words quoted above were immediately followed by the sentence: " But if my teaching is *innocent*, do not hold me in suspense for reasons of human respect." Far better equipped than any of the others to judge of orthodoxy and unorthodoxy in mystical theology, he was morally certain that his own teaching was not heretical Quietism, but fully within the long tradition of the most fully approved mystical saints and writers of the Church. He could afford to let Bossuet's tempestuous breath strike him with its full force, for he knew that however far he might find it convenient to bend, he could not in the long run be broken. And so letters and explanations and quotations from the great mystics poured from Mme. Guyon and Fénelon like an avalanche on to the examiners, surely perspiring under their perplexing labours even in the winter coolness of rural Issy.

Nothing pleased them less than the belated intrusion of Harlay, the Archbishop of Paris, now justifiably irritated by this episcopal conference held without his authority in his own diocese. He summoned Mme. Guyon to his presence. But she was persuaded not to go. Bossuet surprisingly maintained that Harlay was only acting from jealousy and that all this examination was a private matter conducted within a virtual confessional secrecy. Mme. Guyon later commented that on the contrary Bossuet's loquacity and her silence during these months were the real cause of all her future troubles. However, her agreement not to answer Harlay's summons inevitably led to the censure of her books in the Archdiocese. Though wags said that the terms of Harlay's censure involved his condemning the love of God without ever having heard of it, Mme. Guyon sadly observed that " after the censure there was no limit to the calumnies spread about me."

In the end, Mme. de Maintenon and Bossuet were caught in their own trap. Mme. Guyon submitted to Harlay's official censure, thereby rendering academic and meaningless any private *en famille* charge that she was a contumacious heretic. Nor could they expose her in Fénelon's eyes as they would have wished. They had to confine themselves to showing that she had innocently made mistakes requiring correction, a matter which neither she nor Fénelon had ever denied. Moreover, the tiresomely fair M. Tronson pinned them down to an objective examination purely on the merits of the case. After examining her one day from one o'clock until seven, with Chevreuse acting as secretary, he came to the conclusion that " though it was agreed that her books should be condemned, she has since explained her teaching in such a way that I do not know how one can find much in it to criticise." That from the learned and impartial Tronson!

Nothing seemed to be left, after all, but to find means of proving that her personal conduct had been evil. But Tronson, who from the first realised that her moral behaviour was an important factor in judging of her good faith and soundness of teaching, had made it his business to get in touch with bishops and other people of authority who, according to her own account had approved of her and encouraged her in the past. Why this obvious step had not been taken long ago was best known to Bossuet. He had read all her records and stories. Were they lies? In most cases, witnesses could have been found to substantiate her accounts or to deny them. If she was a liar, this would hardly be compatible with her spiritual pretensions and it would throw doubt on her own moral defence. Did he simply fear that what she wrote was after all true? But Tronson did not hesitate to pursue old M. d'Aranthon, the Bishop of Geneva. D'Aranthon avoided answering for the simple reason that by now no prelate cared to confess that he had given any protection or praise to a person suspected of Quietism and still more of Quietist morals. Relentlessly the old priest pressed the old bishop, a year his senior. Was it true, as Mme. Guyon had written, that he had never accused her of any crime? Was it or was it not true that he had appointed Père La Combe as her spiritual director, saying that in doing so he was giving her another himself? At last, the Bishop's answer came. He avoided the direct questions, but wrote: " I have never heard speak of her but with great esteem and respect, and neither my memory nor my conscience reproach me with having spoken of her in other terms." Then he repeated rumours he had heard about La Combe and about her *outré* Quietist views, and went on: " Though I have always expressed my dislike for that doctrine and Père La Combe's books, I have always spoken of the piety and morals of that lady with praise. Those, in a few words, are the true sentiments I have always had in her regard."

From the Marquise de Pruney, whom we recall as Mme. Guyon's friend and host in Turin, he obtained an eloquent testimonial: " Though Mme. Guyon was frequently tried by great ills, she always showed herself a person of unconquerable patience and of great resignation to God's will." Chevreuse himself in the end forced Cardinal Le Camus, the Bishop of Grenoble, to explain a contradiction between letters of his about the widow. It seemed that the Cardinal himself had been deceived by the stories which the woman Cateau Barbe, Mme Guyon's servant, whose love for her turned through jealousy to bitter hatred, had spread about her immoral behaviour. He said, too, that he had heard from a Carthusian prior that she had taught the condemned proposition attributed to Molinos that the devil could sin in the body of a person rapt in prayer. Chevreuse and Mme. Guyon traced the story like detectives to the prior in question, who confessed: " I have never heard you say anything of the kind, nor anything in the least like it; and, for my part, I have never said anything which could make anyone believe I heard it from you." As for Cateau Barbe, she herself, he understood, had retracted and explained that she had spread such stories out of spite. Though not all her enemies retracted like Cateau Barbe and many continued to do her harm, if there is one thing certain about Mme. Guyon it is that her moral behaviour was always above reproach.

The Issy examiners were making none of the progress which their mistress looked for and which Bossuet had thought certain. Neither in faith nor morals could Mme. Guyon be exposed as evil and contumacious. She had wanted to teach the truth, was by nature stubbornly orthodox, but she had in her ignorance and her excitable nervous constitution said and written many false and foolish things. They might have also noted that since she had know Fénelon and been influenced by him she had ceased to make such mistakes.

Their work was therefore brought back to the very delicate academic study of the technically narrow but vitally important path which separated condemned Quietism from the approved teaching and tradition of Catholic mysticism and personal prayer and intercourse with God. To speed the good work and educate the examiners in the subject-matter about which they were supposed to be pronouncing judgment, Fénelon, who had been assiduously reading the writings of mystical saints and doctors, early and late in the Church's history, inundated them with more texts that came as a most unwelcome revelation to the ecclesiastical-minded Bossuet about the lengths to which the great authorities could go in expressing the directness and intimacy of the relations between the soul and God that were possible in this life. Bossuet, not a little of a Jansenist in his outlook, was scandalised and distressed by this saintly failure to realise the intrinsic corruption of man and man's spiritual impotence unless the whole visible articulation of the Church stepped in to enable man, through the normal channels of grace, to rise above his corruption. But the extracts, the " maxims," of the saints were accompanied by Fénelon's further protests of utter readiness to abide by Bossuet's least word. " My conscience is knit within yours. If I fail, it will only be because you will fail me through failure to warn me. . . . I am ready to be silent, to retract, to accuse myself, even to retire, if I have failed in what I have owed to the Church. . . . Treat me like a little boy; do not think of my position, nor of the kindnesses you have shown me. . . ."

In another man it might have seemed like hypocrisy. But it was not. Though it owed something to rhetoric, to the gentlemanly gesture, it was truly meant, just as his certainty of being right was sincerely believed. One effect it had which, one feels certain, he did not directly intend. It helped to ensure his nomination to the vacant princely See of Cambrai.

CHAPTER SEVEN

THE WAY OF AN EAGLE

ONE MAY well ask why the suspected Fénelon, still at the age of forty-two an ordinary priest, was at this awkward juncture nominated to the important See of Cambrai. This See was in the King's gift for the first time, since Cambrai had been ceded from Spain to France at the Treaty of Nijmwegen in 1678—the Treaty that in fact marked the farthest extension of French aggression under its aggressive monarch. Since the Treaty, Louis had been painfully negotiating with the Pope for the right to choose his own bishop, and the concession had only been granted a few months before the death of the Spanish bishop. These unusual circumstances made the appointment a delicate matter, for Louis would certainly wish to be sure that the first French archbishop of Cambrai would in every way prove worthy of his selection, both in Rome and in France.

The choice of Fénelon was therefore a personal one made by the King himself. Fénelon's reputation as priest, scholar, a man of affairs and yet of holiness made him a well-fitting candidate. Naturally the King consulted his wife who knew much more about Church affairs than he did himself. We have seen that her feelings about Fénelon had become very mixed, but there is every reason to suppose that if he would but separate himself finally from Mme. Guyon and condemn her, Mme. de Maintenon would have been happy to resume the previous spiritual intimacy, despite the harsh things he had written to her for her soul's good. The woman who had done so much to convert the King from his former way of life and had stood out for marriage or nothing was not a religious hypocrite. Her troubles belonged to her feminine make-up and her struggle to reach and hold the incredible position to which she

had climbed almost from the gutter. Now she consulted Bossuet
and Godet, and these prelates had been sufficiently impressed by
Fénelon's submissive letters to feel sure that he was sound at heart
despite his spiritual peculiarities. Both were still very much his
friends. One may also surmise that they thought such a promotion
to be a guarantee of steady behaviour.

But another consideration may have entered into the picture.
Fénelon's closest friends in the Court cenacle, especially his women
admirers, were most anxious to see him obtain the greatest See of
France, the See of Paris, which must soon fall vacant. Apart from
Bossuet, he was the obvious choice, and Mme. de Maintenon could
ensure his getting the plum which would keep him at the beck and
call of his noble disciples at Court. It seems possible that if Mme.
de Maintenon was in two minds about Cambrai, the thought that
this would prevent his nomination to Paris, if there were an early
vacancy there, may have decided her to support the King's choice.
We are told that Fénelon's friends were in despair when the news of
Cambrai was heard, and Mme. de Guiche burst into floods of tears.
Fénelon himself was thought not to have expected this promotion
because it would interfere with his work for the princes. But Louis
arranged that the new prelate would keep the preceptorship and
remain at Court for part of the year, devoting the rest to his pastoral
duties on the North-East frontier.

After the nomination, Fénelon at once resigned the one small
benefice he possessed, an act of detachment so unusual in those days
that the Archbishop of Reims dryly commented: " M. de Fénelon,
thinking as he does, has acted well; I, thinking as I do, have also
acted well in keeping my benefices."

Fénelon's appointment in the midst of the Issy Conferences in
February, 1895, had consequences which no one seems to have
foreseen. In immediately altering his ecclesiastical status, he ceased
to be a simple priest, however outstanding and influential through
his work and his friends; he had become a nominated Archbishop
awaiting his consecration. He was now the peer of Bossuet himself,
of Noailles and of Godet. As Archbishop-Designate he could no
longer be regarded as unofficially on trial in the person of his friend
and protégé. And there was only one way of associating him with
the conclusions of the examiners. That was by adding him to the

self-constituted board. As such, he would not be a sleeping partner, nor would he retain his former submissiveness to Bossuet. In fact, just as Fénelon had decisively influenced Mme. Guyon, while apparently submitting to her spiritual direction, and changed her into a different person from the one Bossuet met in her writings, so he had been steadily educating Bossuet in the elements of mystical theology while expressing his readiness to accept Bossuet's conclusions. The result was that Bossuet had drawn up a list of thirty articles which read very differently from what he had in mind before studying the results of Fénelon's researches into the writings of the mystical saints. Even so, the new member of the board was not satisfied with Bossuet's draft. Some of the articles betrayed the hand of the amateur where the most delicate distinctions were concerned.

In Article 29, for example, Bossuet had referred to the case of " the very few special souls " whom God inspires in such a way that it is unnecessary in their case to insist on normal acts of prayer needed to keep alive their faith and love. He could not deny that such special souls could exist, so he airily dismissed them by saying that " we must leave them to God," adding that the best spiritual writers do not mention them and that the perfection of Christian behaviour is not to be found in this kind of exception. Writing to him, Fénelon now said: " I beg you to consider that I cannot, in my present situation [a nominated archbishop] subscribe to this point through my own agreement with it. I remember too well that when Mme. de Chantal took the advice of Saint Francis of Sales on the acts that are most essential to the Christian religion and to salvation—acts which she could not make as they are ordinarily made with the ordinary help of God—his answers were decisive: she must only make them " in so far as God should move her to do so, and she must remain active or passive in her prayer, according to the way in which God moved her." In a letter to Mme. de La Maisonfort, Fénelon said that he hesitated about the Ninth Article which asserted that a Christian could not be indifferent to his salvation. But since the Thirty-Third added the necessary qualification he would accept the Ninth. The Thirty-Third was one of four new Articles added as a result of Fénelon's promotion, and it stated: " Tried and truly humble souls can be inspired to a submission and consent to the will of God even when—the possibility is, of course, out of the question—God, instead of rewarding them with the eternal blessings promised to the just, were to hold them for His good pleasure in eternal torments without depriving them of His grace and love." This article, in fact, was simply a complex way of saying what Mme. Guyon had long ago instinctively said: " I loved Him in such a way that I could only love Him; but in loving Him I had no motive but Himself."

After such vital changes insisted on by Fénelon in his new status, it was not surprising that Fénelon was able to declare that he would sign " with his blood." This was more than Bossuet was ready to do, since he could never bring himself really to believe that human nature, however spiritual, however much aided by God, was capable of a completely altruistic and completely pure love. In view of the fact that sacrifices of an utterly disinterested nature, of mothers, for example, in regard to their children or soldiers for their duty to their country, are common enough on the natural plane, it is a curious reflection on Bossuet's religious and psychological make-up that he could not envisage a love of God of equal disinterest.[1] However, he grudgingly accepted the amended Articles, and they were in fact signed by all four examiners on 10th March, 1695.

Bossuet and Noailles published the Articles, together with a condemnation of Quietist books, Mme. Guyon's name not being mentioned, in their dioceses. Noailles, hearing that Bossuet had sent a copy of his ordinance to the Papal Nuncio, hesitated to do the same because he had described himself as " Bishop of Châlons by divine permission." So he had a few extra copies printed in which he added to his title " and by the grace of the Holy See," and forwarded one of these to the Holy See's ambassador. It is a delightful reflection on the times.

The long and painful episode had ended in a complete failure to achieve the purpose originally envisaged by the King's wife and the Eagle of Meaux. Mme. Guyon had not been picked out for condemnation, and Fénelon had not been forced to disown her.

The ill-fated woman, however, had no luck. Some weeks before the Issy Articles were signed, she found herself in danger of arrest

[1] C. S. Lewis in his autobiography *Surprised by Joy* notes that his conversion to Theism and Christianity was entirely divorced from any belief in a future life, and he counted this as one of his greatest mercies.

because of Harlay's censures in the Paris diocese. Still trusting Bossuet, she asked him to give her a refuge in his diocese of Meaux. This was to deliver herself into his hands, and he readily arranged for her to live in the Visitation convent in his episcopal city. The extraordinary thing is that anyone could have supposed that a woman with such an infallible gift for doing the wrong thing and creating traps for herself was a dark and dangerous criminal and heretic.

Though, of course, she most willingly subscribed to the Issy Articles in a beautiful profession of faith which ended with her declaration of her resolve " to live the rest of her days hidden with Jesus Christ in any place that Providence might destine for her," she had been deeply hurt by the whole affair. " I protest before God and the whole heavenly court," she wrote to Chevreuse, " that I have never doubted these truths for a minute, and that nothing could be more odious than to turn them into articles in order to persuade people that those given to prayer do not believe in God the Father, Son and Holy Ghost, or in Jesus Christ. It is an invention of Barabbas. As for me, I know how to die as one should die; but I know not how to sign falsehoods and things which could leave the slightest suspicion that I ever doubted these truths about which I have never been tempted. . . . The desertion of all my friends hurts me not a little; what hurts me as it hurts the heart of God is to write articles of faith in God and Jesus Christ as though souls devoted to prayer believed neither in God nor in Jesus Christ."

This passing indignation was really based on a misunderstanding. The Issy Articles in seeking to distinguish truth from error were expressed in the form of a kind of catechism of the Christian faith, and because they stated that every Christian was obliged to have an explicit faith in Almighty God, in the Trinity, in Jesus Christ, and to make acts of faith, hope and charity, it was not really implied that even Quietists denied these elementary truths, but rather that they refined or transcended them in a dangerous way.

But at least she was consoled by a voice from the distant past, for Père La Combe from his prison in Lourdes managed to get some letters through to her. Though his tired head was only fit for gardening, he reassured her, saying that the Articles contained " orthodox truths that must be absolutely safeguarded and in no

Madame de Maintenon

way tampered with under pretext of mystical theology—not that
it is impossible to produce these acts in another way which, if
simpler, more lasting and more united to God's loving look,
remains still very real and satisfies, though more perfectly, the
obligations common to all the faithful." And he added, in reference
to his old friend's submission: "All that a woman can do is to
submit to the shepherds of the Church without being obliged to
resolve scholastic difficulties." For a man going mad, it was a neat
summing up of his old friend's problems.

Though Bossuet was later to tell the world that he was already
at this time deeply suspicious of Fénelon's conduct and views, he was
certainly most anxious to consecrate him personally, even though
this meant some unpleasantness with Godet who as Bishop of
Chartres had the right to do so in Saint-Cyr where both he and
Mme. de Maintenon wished the ceremony to be held. On 10th
July, 1695, Fénelon was in fact consecrated there by Bossuet, with
Noailles and the Bishop of Amiens as co-consecrators, in the presence
of his royal pupils.

2

The immediate reason why well was not left alone is certainly
to be found in the fact that neither Mme. de Maintenon nor Bossuet
could stomach the idea that Mme. Guyon had escaped the condemnation of her teaching at the hands of their ecclesiastical friends
which, so they believed, would have forced Fénelon to break with
her and with the dangerous Quietist associations. Fénelon as an
archbishop now carried great ecclesiastical weight. His influence
over Saint-Cyr, over the pious circle of the Court nobility and over
the household and education of the Princes was bound to increase.
He remained in touch with Mme. Guyon at Meaux through the
intermediary of the faithful Chevreuse, and it was his inspiration
that dictated the tactics of her new struggle with Bossuet. Meanwhile, the outside world, the enemies of the Court cenacle, all those
who dreaded or wished to down Quietist and mystical influences
in the Church, and those whose own future careers in State and
Church depended on weaning the King from his present intimate
friends and advisers were waiting and ready to take advantage of

the signs of disaster within the inner spiritual family circle whose troubles we have been recounting.

It would have been infinitely wiser to hush up the affair and close the ranks, but Mme. de Maintenon seemed determined to save or break Fénelon, while Bossuet could not bear to let Mme. Guyon and Fénelon get away with a spiritual teaching that he believed at heart to be disastrous for the Church and ultimately for the world.

Forthe story of what was to happen while Bossuet held Mme. Guyon at Meaux, we have once again her own account, and it is supported, where Bossuet was to dispute it, by the testimony of the Mother Superior of the Visitation convent where Mme. Guyon lived, Mère Picard. She and her community testified to their guest's "simplicity, humility, mortification, sweetness and Christian patience, as well as a true devotion and esteem for all that is of the Faith, especially as regards the mystery of the Incarnation and of the Sacred Infancy of Our Lord Jesus Christ." Are we to believe that such a testimonial from the nuns of Bossuet's own cathedral town, nuns under his own episcopal rule, is compatible with her telling a pack of lies about what happened under their own roof?

As usual, circumstances of exceptional hardship pursued her on her way to Meaux in the winter of 1695 when she was escaping from Harlay's ordinances in Paris. The winter was one of the worst in contemporary memory. Her carriage was snowed up, and she and her servant had to be dragged out of the drift. For hours they sat in the snow before rescue came. Not surprisingly, her health at Meaux was even worse than usual.

Bossuet suggested that she should change her name so that her enemies should lose track of her and tire of maligning her. " A splendid idea," she commented, " if only he had been able to keep a secret. But he told everyone he met that I was in a certain convent under a certain name. Immediately libellous writings about me were sent to the Mother Superior and the other nuns." Complaints about Bossuet's indiscretions are constant in her story, and in the end the great man was to show that he had no idea whatever of keeping secret even from the world at large matters confided to him on condition that he should treat them " with the secrecy of the confessional."

The Bishop, still busied with the Issy Conferences and his usual heavy timetable, did not visit Meaux until Easter. It was then that he obtained Mme. Guyon's adhesion to the Issy Articles. His next visit was on the feast of the Annunciation, kept that year in Paschaltime. Here is her story briefly summarised. She was ill and confined to her room. But the community were with her singing a hymn in honour of the Incarnate Word. Bossuet suddenly appeared. As soon as the nuns left the room, he whipped out a paper and asked her to sign it. It was a confession that she did not believe in the Incarnation. One may reasonably suppose that there is a muddle in the account here, for Bossuet was surely trying to get her signature to a confession that she *had* denied the Incarnation. Anything else would be too fantastic. His request, either way incredible to her, she, of course, refused, and Bossuet, according to her account, tried to make her change her mind by promising to tell everyone how good she was, if only she would sign. Naturally, she was not moved by this bribe.

A few days later, he returned, bringing two documents. One was a profession of faith which Mme. Guyon tells us she would have been ready to sign without even being asked to do so. The second was a certificate of her orthodoxy. She signed the profession of faith, but Bossuet, instead of giving her the certificate, took it away, explaining that he wanted to improve the wording. But next day he returned, snatched up the profession of faith which was on her bed, and told her that she could not have his certificate until she had signed many other things, including the confession about not believing in the Incarnate Word.

So the torment continued, Bossuet always trying to force her to sign the confessions he needed. But she does say that his attitude varied. He was always at his worst, she said, when he had just come from Versailles—where, no doubt, Mme. de Maintenon had warmed him up to his work. She also says that he confessed that it was her enemies who were urging him to carry on the horrible business. As for himself, he was personally satisfied with her attitude.

A letter from Mme. Guyon to Chevreuse tells us how Bossuet treated her on 10th June when he threatened her with every possible dire penalty, calling her contumacious and a Lucifer in her presumption. When she refused once more to sign papers against her conscience, he threatened to tell the world all he knew about her private life. " My Lord," she answered, " you know that I entrusted all that to you through excess of good faith and confidence and under the seal of confession."

It is interesting to note that in the same month Mme. de Maintenon complained bitterly about the Fénelonistes in a letter to Noailles. " My love and esteem for M. le Duc de Beauvilliers makes me undertake impossible things. . . . We do not know what we are doing now, and our only excuse is our friendship for a man who well deserves that we should not easily give up on his account. But what can we hope for ? . . . Does all this change his heart or his feelings for a woman whom he described to the King a few days ago as inspired in an extraordinary way? And on the other hand, M. de Chevreuse treats us as calumniators, and talks to the King about the latest rumours regarding his esteem for Mme. Guyon. He laughs at her extravagances in the freest way though we know him to believe that he has received a communication of grace through her. I no longer know where I stand. Mme. Guyon may be deluded; M. de Cambrai may have given too much rein to his imagination; but that Messieurs de Beauvilliers and Chevreuse deny facts they know surprises me so much that I feel 1 can count on no one."

A fortnight after that letter, Bossuet returned, his mood utterly changed. He preached a sermon for the feast of the Visitation which astonished even Mme. Guyon for its defence of the ways of interior prayer, of all things, and he finally gave her his certificate of orthodoxy without demanding any confession of past heresies.

The only way to account for Bossuet's astonishingly inconsistent conduct is to suppose that he disliked the orders he was receiving from the Pantocrat of Versailles and which he dared not disobey. Mme. de Maintenon, for her part, as the above letter indicates, had reached a point where she hardly knew where she stood and what to do for the best—*her* best. Nothing could be got out of the widow. Fénelon stood firm, even to the point of speaking to the King in praise of her. Meanwhile, the enemies were mobilising outside, ready perhaps to bring down the whole house of illusions and she herself with it.

Bossuet, in his full account given later to the world, during his battle with Fénelon, passed very quickly over the events of these six months in Meaux. In it he praises Mère Picard "the very wise Superior of the convent," and we know what she thought of her guest. He goes on: "As all her [Mme. Guyon's] letters and all her words breathed only submission and blind submission, she could not be refused the Sacraments. I instructed her with care; she subscribed to the Articles in which she saw the entire destruction of her teaching "—did she? Père La Combe's letters to her suggest the contrary and they also suggest that she was sending him very much the same account as she gave the world in her life-story. Bossuet goes on: "I received the declaration which she made for me against the abominations of which she was accused, and, presumed her innocent so long as she was not convicted by a legitimate examination into which matter I did not enter. She asked my permission to leave in order to go to the Eaux de Bourbon. After her submission, she was free."

"She was free"; it was Bossuet who admitted the fact, even when he was stretching every possible point in his favour in order to destroy Fénelon. And why should she not be free, seeing that she had voluntarily taken refuge in the Meaux convent, had not made any subsequent promises and had been arrested by no one? Her own account is: "As I had been six months at Meaux, and I had only arranged to stay there for three, and moreover, my health was very poor, I asked M. de Meaux if he was content or if he wanted anything else. He said no. I therefore told him that I felt the need to go to Bourbon. . . . He turned to the Superior, and said: ' Mother, I beg you to welcome those who come to fetch Madame, whether her daughter or some of her friends.' "

The Duchess of Mortemart came to fetch her, and she left with the blessings of the community. Within a few days, Mère Picard was writing to say that " nothing will break the bond which unites us in God's love. . . . My dearest, I am yours as God wills, full of confidence that His goodness will accomplish what it has begun." Such was the heretical Quietist of history in the eyes of an excellent Visitation nun who had lived with her in the closest intimacy for six months. If she was only playing a part, what an actress she must have been!

She had her certificate from Bossuet with its statement that she had had nothing to do with " the abominations of Molinos " in her pocket, as well as the community's testimonial from which we quoted earlier.

Then suddenly the whole picture changes, this time more dramatically than ever. But let Mme. Guyon once again tell her own story.

" Hardly had I arrived [at Vaux-le-Vicomte, where her daughter, once trailed across the Continent by her spiritually adventurous mother, lived as the wife of Fouquet's nephew, the Marquis de Vaux] than M. de Meaux repented of having allowed me to leave his diocese." Even she seemed to have accepted the idea of the Bishop's right to hold her prisoner, a point that at least suggests her submissiveness.

Bossuet had completely changed his mind because Mme. de Maintenon was furious with him for having given the certificate and furious with his view that the whole affair was now finished. " She said," Mme. Guyon continues, " that it would finish nothing at all. On the contrary its effect would militate against their plans which were to open the eyes of people prejudiced in my favour. He [Bossuet] saw that in losing hold of me, he had lost all that he had been hoping for. So he wrote telling me to return to his diocese. The Superior warned me in a letter that he was more resolved than ever to torment me. However much she herself would have liked to have me back, she felt obliged to warn me that M. de Meaux's feelings were as I had suspected. I had in fact suspected that he had set the highest hopes on the policy of per-secuting me. [This suspicion, whether well based or not, could only have referred to the See of Paris, which was to become vacant in three weeks through Harlay's death]; and as he had his knife in a person far above me [presumably Fénelon whom Bossuet was at the moment consecrating] he thought that in letting me go, he had let everything slip out of his hands. Mother Picard enclosed with the letter I have just mentioned a new certificate from M. de Meaux so different from the first, which I was to return to him, that I at once realised that I had no further hope of justice from that prelate."

This second certificate, issued a week late, was predated to the same day as the first. In it all mention of her clearance from having anything to do with " the abominations of Molinos " was omitted.

Instead, she was to agree never " to write, to teach, to dogmatise in the Church, nor to spread printed or manuscript writings, nor to guide souls in the ways of prayer nor in any other way."

Mme. Guyon had wisely taken the precaution of handing over the first certificate to her family for safe-keeping. " After what had happened my family had the highest interest in a document of this kind, a document which was my justification, and which it would not be likely to give up." Spiritedly, she goes on: " We can judge by M. de Meaux's excitement and the hopes he was nursing, of the effect on him of my refusal to return. He said I had jumped over the convent walls in order to escape. Apart from the fact that I happen to be an exceedingly bad jumper, the whole Community was witness to the contrary. However the story spread so rapidly that many people believe it."

Such is her story, and in view of the appalling consequences it stands as a terrible indictment of the most eminent churchman of his day. But was it true?

Everything is in favour of Mme. Guyon's version of the events; little or nothing in favour of Bossuet's.

Bossuet must have known that she had immediately left Meaux after obtaining his first certificate. Meaux, Vaux-le-Vicomte and Paris are close together. Yet it was only eight days later that he wrote a letter giving her permission to go to Bourbon, and asking her to avoid Paris. By doing this, he was creating evidence to suggest that she had " leapt over the wall " earlier without his permission. In his later account, in which he admitted that " she was free," he suggests that she had promised to return to the convent, which is not quite the same thing as not leaving it, and he mentions only one certificate, the one " of which her friends are so proud, but which they never dared show." Yet in a letter to his nephew at the time, he speaks of a " copy of the certificates which Mme. Guyon received from me." He also speaks of her being received back at the convent " where her room was kept for her when she returned from the watering-place." Why not? She loved the community and wanted to return—but with the first certificate that cleared her, not the second that left her where she had been. And if she was free, what crime did she commit in changing her mind and not returning? But perhaps the strongest point of all is that the nuns must have been apprised of their bishop's orders in regard to so important a guest. If her freedom to go did not apply until the second certificate was issued, they would not have let her go without protest. And they would certainly, for their own sake, have immediately informed him of any disobedience to his orders on her part. Instead, according to Mme. Guyon, they went out of their way to praise and thank her and to express how close their spiritual link with her was. Mme. Guyon's version was certainly spread abroad by her friends, yet Bossuet did not trouble to get the evidence of his community of nuns to refute that version of the affair.

There is no escaping the fact that Bossuet's account is a jumble of contradictions and improbabilities forced on him by the trick he played on his victim.

It is possible that there may have been a genuine misunderstanding somewhere, and one shared apparently by the community, but even so there is no pardoning Bossuet for the way he must have taken advantage of the misunderstanding to spread about the story that Mme. Guyon had leapt over the walls of his convent in order to escape from his rightful ecclesiastical authority.

This puzzling affair may be taken as the first step on Mme. Guyon's way to the Bastille and it prepared the way for the open struggle on Fénelon's part to justify his own teaching and the teaching he believed to be hers, while she was lying unjustly in prison. This was what caused the immense scandal to the world of two great churchmen fighting in public—the battle which led to Fénelon's "disgrace." We have heard much of the sexual abominations that Molinos and other Quietists were supposed to have practised and may have done; but one asks oneself whether in the final tally of evil these would weigh as heavily as this trick which the Eagle of Meaux played on the Dove and through her on the Swan—if indeed he did play it, for there can, of course, be no certainty in the reconstruction of disputed points in the small amount of historical testimony which posterity possesses.

In Bossuet's favour it can at least be said—and all his behaviour shows it—that he was acting under the strongest possible pressure from above. Left to himself, he wanted to be fair and kind—at least until the fury of public polemic took hold of him. As Mère Picard

wrote to Mme. Guyon: his very softness emboldened him to ill-
treat her, because his character was such that he acted thus with
amenable people, while bending before strong characters. Mme.
Guyon herself, writing a few months later when she was hiding
from the police, said: " Since that time, I have realised that this ·
prelate, filled with good qualities, far from relying on his own
inspirations about which I have no complaint, has been acting
against his own feelings through the instigation of ill-intentioned
people, so that despite the consistent satisfactoriness of more and
more examinations, the same strange impressions persisted."

Bossuet gained nothing from his subservience. Harlay died on
6th August, 1695, apparently unregretted by anyone. False rumours
of unsavoury details of his end were spread about, and it was said
that only two bagatelles made it difficult for his panegyric to be
written: one was his life, the other his death.

The great ecclesiastical prize of Paris was in the hands of Mme.
de Maintenon. Fénelon's friends still desperately hoped that he
would get it despite his so recent consecration to Cambrai. Mme.
Guyon held it " as a great secret that Mme. de Maintenon pretended
to wish to promote Fénelon, while acting so as to prevent the
nomination." Bossuet, though nearing seventy, was still the obvious
choice. But if he had any expectations, he was soon undeceived for
he was writing within a fortnight of Harlay's death that he expected
" to be buried at the feet of my saintly predecessors, working for
the salvation of the flock entrusted to me." Earthly patrons, and
especially patronesses, do not always play the game. The story
goes that Mme. de Maintenon consulted the influential Curé of
Versailles who told her that everyone was hoping for Fénelon.
" You know," she answered, " what prevents us from proposing
him. But we still have M. de Meaux and M. de Châlons [Noailles];
which of them would you choose ? " "The one who would refuse,"
wisely answered the Curé, " and certainly M. de Châlons will
refuse." Mme. de Maintenon's niece was engaged to Noailles'
nephew—an alliance between the humble d'Aubignés and the great
Noailles which filled the King's wife with pleasure—and the Bishop
of Châlons was persuaded not to refuse.

PART TWO

The Battle of the Giants

CHAPTER ONE

ONE BOOK AFTER ANOTHER

BOSSUET'S CONTENTION that Mme. Guyon had leapt over the walls in defiance of his ecclesiastical authority was to prove fatal to her. It gave the State the excuse it needed to pursue and arrest her. She had become a criminal evading examination and justice. The matter had become a public affair, and all the enemies seeking their chance of downing the mystical revival and influence at Court and pursuing heresy could breathe the fresh and welcome scent. By this time Mme. de Maintenon was beginning to realise that her hope of saving Fénelon from his attachment to Mme. Guyon and from his now dangerous views was fading. As for Bossuet, the affair of Mme. Guyon and soon the affair of his episcopal colleague and former friend and disciple were becoming something of a personal vendetta. His bad conscience needed to be justified and nothing so easily causes stubbornness and anger. In fact, the whole tactic had to be changed. It was no longer a question of saving the Court cenacle and the pietist group from itself; it was a question of detaching from it anyone who wished to evade the royal anger when the whole story of heresy in and around the royal household came to light.

Mme. Guyon, realising the line that was to be taken over her decision to leave Meaux, had no option but to disappear. The police in every age have taken the view that the most dangerous course for anyone suspected of crime is to take refuge in flight. They said it 250 years ago to Mme. Guyon. "I thought it best," she wrote in a letter, "to keep silence and to retire to a hidden place, but not in order to shun the light, as people try to persuade him [Bossuet]. Have I ever shunned the light [indeed not]? Have I not always presented myself when it was a question of answering for the purity of my faith which I have ever been ready to defend with my life? It is true that, realising the feeling against me, I have retired into a profound solitude, away from all the world, where I see no one. If I am dangerous, could I have chosen better to avoid all suspicion, especially as I have only done so after having witnessed to my faith until the end? I have retired to solitude and have no relations with men; and they are saying that I seek the darkness in order to do evil! When I appeared, they accused me of trying to seduce people! What step can I take without being condemned? If I speak, my words are blasphemies; if I am silent, my silence causes indignation."

She put it more simply when she wrote that it would have been hell if she had given herself up to Bossuet again.

Bossuet's version given to the world was: "I will not tell the story of how she put forward the day I had fixed for her departure, nor how she hid herself afterwards; how she was caught and convicted of many contraventions of the things she had signed. But what I cannot hide is that she still behaves as a prophetess." Yet it took six months for the police to unearth a woman who, according to Bossuet, was still supposed to be actively proselytising and prophesying! Nor were the police themselves ever able to convict her of any heresy or crime. M. Tronson, who always tried to be fair and sensible, advised her to go on committing the crime of evading Bossuet and the police: "Madame, I think you have every reason to remain in peace in your solitude, abandoned to Divine Providence and carrying the cross which His love lays on you."

At any rate, she possessed the instinct of the intelligent criminal. She did not try to fly the country or bury herself in some remote country place. She just remained quietly in Paris, another grain in the sand of the capital's densely living population. Using false names, she changed her address three times: "I passed the days alone reading, praying, working," she tells us. But towards the end of the year 1695 [actually two days after the feast of good-will towards men, 27th December] I was arrested."

The King wrote next day to the new archbishop, de Noailles: "She will be kept where she is until to-morrow morning when I shall be happy to see you at Marly if your duties allow."

According to Mme. Guyon, the King had been deceived by "the strongest calumnies," and when she was finally taken, he and Mme. de Maintenon had sufficient scruples to wonder whether a convent, rather than prison, would not be the right place in which to detain her. But Bossuet's influence prevailed. "He wrote to me to say he was delighted and that this mystery has hidden many evils in the Church" Mme. de Maintenon at once reported to Noailles. So despite the fact that Louis "was quite scandalised by the conduct of M. de Meaux," the prisoner was taken to the State fortress-prison of Vincennes—Vincennes, where Saint-Louis had once administered true justice under the oaks, where now the greatest of the sons of Saint-Louis held this woman prisoner without real charge or trial, at the instance of the greatest of French bishops.

At once, the Lieutenant [Chief] of Police got down to his inter-rogations. De La Reynie, accustomed to deal with conspirators against the State, poisoners and every other kind of criminal in the news, now took Bossuet's place with his own practised "third degree" methods. In the usual police way, charges, great and petty, were thrown at her, from having in her possession at home such dangerous books as *Don Quixote* and Molière's plays and of writing to La Combe, to accusations of heresy and having taken in people of good faith.

Mme. de Maintenon complained to Noailles that the long reports of the examinations revealed nothing. Portchartrain, the Secretary of State, promised her, as Ministers will, that they would be getting results soon. But she did not believe a word of it. So the prisoner was taken backwards and forwards from her cell where she was "severely kept" (padlocked doors, thick walls, little light, the dampness and cold of winter, even if she had her own furniture and her own attendant) to the interrogation room where, as Mme. de Maintenon pointed out to Noailles, M. de La Reynie would omit none of the usual "customs."

Where the Chief of Police failed, the official theologian of the Sorbonne, Dr. Pirot, together with the Curé of Saint-Sulpice tried their hands—but without any better success. Bravely, she stuck to her guns. She had never believed in any false doctrines; she had used wrong expressions and her books had been condemned in the end because of this, though they had originally been approved;

she did not need to make any fresh personal retractation, seeing that the Bishop of Meaux himself, having heard her explanations, had given her a certificate approving of her conduct and her faith.

Though she made efforts a few months later to be sent to Blois to live there under her son's responsibility, she was in fact to remain in prison, uncharged and untried, for eight and a half years—and a strange prisoner she must have made: "While I was at Vincennes and interrogated by M. de La Reynie, I remained in great peace, very happy thus to pass my life, if it were God's will. I made up hymns which the girl who looked after me learnt by heart as I composed them. Thus we sang your praises, O Lord. . . . The depths of my heart were full of that joy which you give to those who love you in the midst of their worst misfortunes." The reality of her life always partly remained in a dimension other than that of actuality.

What had happened to the Archbishop of Cambrai during the winter of 1695 to 1696 when his friend was first in hiding and then in prison?

To us who know so much more than the world then knew about the fervent spiritual intimacy between priest and prophetess there must seem to be something rather cowardly in Fénelon's reactions to the treatment of Mme. Guyon. Indeed, we have become so conditioned in any civilised country to independence and free speech, not least in matters of religion, that it is hard to understand a caution that was, we must remember, very much part of his character. Why, we ask, was he not actively defending an intimate friend of whose personal innocence he had no doubt? Why was he writing jolly letters from Cambrai to Mme. de Maintenon about the pleasant manners of the Flanders peasants who " despite their rough freedom live as nuns in a delightful innocence, without any refinements of piety or of anything else; where virtue is as rough as are outward manners, but where the heart is excellent." Mme. de Maintenon was quick to pass on such a letter to Saint-Cyr for the edification of the Canoness and the hot-house Quietist *dévotes* who stubbornly stood their ground through all the troubles.

To understand Fénelon's behaviour we have to remember certain facts.

As an archbishop, his position had become specially difficult.

To this day Catholic bishops are always terrified of any outward suspicion of differences between them. The reason is their fear of causing scandal to the faithful through any open acknowledgment of division and even, it sometimes seems, of any open acknowledgment that they could make any mistakes at all or suffer normal human emotions. If this fear was less strong in Gallican France in the seventeenth century, it was one which Fénelon in particular would have understood both because of his extreme sensitivity and because of his Ultramontane sense of the unity and holiness of the Catholic Church in the face of the behaviour of too many of its members. But where to-day tolerance of errors, deviations and heresies is accepted because it is recognised that only spiritual weapons can be used against them, in Gallican France it was the intolerant State-Church which dealt with the evil. If we think of Quietists and Quietism in the France of the day in something of the same way as Americans have been thinking of Communists and Communism, we shall not be very far off the mark where feelings and reactions generally are concerned. For an archbishop, Preceptor to the second heir to the throne, to be the open champion of a Mme. Guyon must have been a position analogous to that of a highly-placed leader of the Republican Party secretly backing a prominent fellow-traveller. The circumstances of the comparison are, moreover, exact, for Fénelon, an expert about right-thinking and wrong-thinking in the State-Church, did not deny that his friend had said and written many things smacking of this Quietist monstrosity with its danger to souls and bodies of decent people. What he did believe, however, was that she herself had never been proved to be, so to speak, a member of the Party or one who wanted to achieve its evil purposes. Hers was an innocent fault due to muddle and excess of zeal for the public good.

It was a delicate position to maintain in the face of public opinion, led by his *confrère*, that born demagogue of the ecclesiastical pen, the Eagle of Meaux—and a most dangerous one.

We need to appreciate the situation if we are to understand both the narrow limits of his championing of his old friend and the astonishing courage he was to show within those limits. Mme. de Maintenon herself had already acknowledged that she believed that " he would rather be martyred than confess that he has been mistaken about her." She, too, was constantly expressing her awareness of the dangers surrounding them all: "We are spied upon from all sides, and if God did not sustain me, I should be in despair to be where I am."

On the other side, the cool Beauvilliers, a man not given to exaggerations and imaginary fears, was writing to Tronson: "I must tell you, and I am absolutely sincere in all this, that an exceedingly strong and lively cabal is forming against the Archbishop of Cambrai. M. de Chartres [Godet] is too honest to belong to it; but underhand ways of prejudicing and arousing his mind are being used. As for Mme. de Maintenon, she completely falls for what she is told, and thinks she gives glory to God by going to any lengths against M. de Cambrai. I fear we may be about to see him deprived of his duties with the Princes on the grounds of being able to harm them through his bad doctrine. If they try this and succeed, my turn may come." And to reassure Tronson, he added: "Besides, as I have already said to M. de Chartres, there is no need to be anxious about the Princes; none of them even knows that there exists in the world a woman called Mme. Guyon, nor a book called the *Moyen Court.*"

What Bremond calls "an obscure force" seemed to be fatally driving the various actors towards a catastrophe which could profit none of them. "An invisible personage controls the plot, makes useless all attempts to come to terms, tears up each treaty of peace, and breathes an ever fresh ardour into the protagonists."

The truth was that behind them all was the King. He was now nearing sixty, touchy, suspicious, his affairs going badly, and quite out of his depths in this religious business that was beginning to set all tongues wagging. "This opposition," wrote his wife to Noailles, "has not been inspired by me; it is in the heart of the King about all novelties. I see that I shall be blamed; but I owe you the truth and I tell it you." As yet Louis did not understand, but the picture we have to bear in mind is that of many people having direct or indirect access to him and thus determining his changing moods and views, while those who acted in his name had nervously to guess which way he would jump and adjust their behaviour in accordance with their guesses. No wonder the story is full of puzzles and unresolved contradictions.

Fénelon's line of action in face of his friend's unjust imprisonment
and the mounting denunciations of her writings and conduct, under
the inspiration of Mme. de Maintenon and Bossuet, was clear and
consistent.

Throughout, his defence of Mme. Guyon was not primarily the
defence of a persecuted woman for whom, as we have seen, he felt
no particularly strong natural affection, but rather the defence of
the most important element in her teaching, namely, the possibility
of personal access to God, who dwells at the " fine-point " of each
human spirit—a possibility which can be realised only through the
killing of self-love that commonly obscures the Divine within us.
He believed that this view was entirely Catholic and that it had been
continuously experienced and taught by the mystical saints and
doctors, even though the spiritual technique required for full
realisation was very difficult and suited only to a few, who were
given special graces. But its existence threw light on the spiritual
direction generally of all people seriously interested in spiritual
values. Spiritual progress depends not on fear and conformism, but
on love. He was convinced that Mme. Guyon with all her apparent
absurdities was someone who had hit the right trail and progressed
far along it. Consequently, unless the Church itself ordered him to
do so, he would absolutely refuse to join in the almost universal
condemnation of his friend, however much else about her and her
writing he could be persuaded privately to criticise. In fact, to make
sure that there could be no misunderstanding about his position,
his motives and his aims, he would go out of his way *not* to work
for her liberation and the justice she could rightfully claim. To do
this, he thought, would be to invite the retort that it was the woman,
the friend, that he was concerned about, when it was in fact the
supremely important matter of her essential witness to the truth.
If once it was thought that he was only really interested in a woman's
fate and her questionable history and writings, his real purpose
would inevitably be compromised.

His second line of action would be to write a book proving
from the witness of the saints of the Church that his cause was fully
justified.

In February, two months after her imprisonment, Fénelon wrote
to Tronson:

" As for her person, they want me to condemn it together with her writings. If the Church issues a formulary on the subject, I shall be the first to sign it with my blood; apart from that, I neither can nor ought to do it. I have myself witnessed certain facts which have greatly edified me; why do they want me to condemn her about certain facts which I have not seen and which prove nothing in themselves without hearing her to know how she would answer. . . . As for the writings . . . let us suppose them far worse than they say; have they not been condemned by dozens of ordinances which no one has contradicted, and to which her friends, and she herself, have submitted ? . . . They are trying to force me step by step, without my noting it, by a kind of secret arrangement.

" It is M. de Meaux who acts as the *primum mobile*; M. de Chartres acts through zeal and friendship; Mme. de M. worries herself and gets irritated with us with every fresh impression made on her. Thousands at the Court maliciously remind her of poisoned words against us. The Bishop of Chartres and she are persuaded that nothing has been gained unless I condemn the person and the writings. Even the Inquisition would not ask me so much. . . . What would it matter that I believe Mme. G. neither bad nor mad, if in fact I abandon her in a profound silence and let her die in prison without bothering about her and all that concerns her, either directly or indirectly ? . . . All the mystery reduces itself to my unwillingness to speak against my conscience."

To Mme. de Maintenon herself he wrote a few days later, on 7th March, that he knew Mme. Guyon's true sentiments " better than all who had examined her in order to condemn her, since she has spoken to me more openly than to them. I have examined her most strictly, and perhaps gone too far in opposing her. I have never had a natural feeling for her, nor for her writings. I have never experienced anything extraordinary in her, prejudicing me in her favour." He then told the King's wife that he could guarantee to get Mme. Guyon to explain her true doctrine satisfactorily. " Maybe, you think, Madame, that I only make this offer to get her out of prison ? No, I promise to make her give this precise explanation and this refutation of all her errors without thinking of getting her liberated. . . . After it all, let her die in prison. I am content that she should die there, that we should never see her again, nor hear tell of her." We may charitably suppose that these expressions were part of Fénelon's rhetoric rather than true feelings, and intended to drive his point home to the prejudiced mind he was addressing.

Then assuring her that he was neither a rascal, nor a liar, nor a traitor, nor a hypocrite, nor a rebel against the Church, he tried to plead with the woman who had attracted him, perhaps more than Mme. Guyon, as he had so greatly attracted her: "Why do you close you heart to us, Madame, as though we belonged to different religions? Why fear to talk about God to me as though your conscience told you to avoid being seduced? Why believe that your heart may not rest at one with us? Why destroy what God has so clearly built? I leave with the hope that God who sees into hearts will unite them again; but I leave too with an inconsolable sorrow at having become your Cross." But his feelings were not inconsistent with a somewhat acid reminder that her views about Mme. Guyon owed not a little to the fact that " M. de Meaux has reported to you as impieties things which she had confided to him with a submissive heart and in the secret of the confessional."

" I have had great dealings with M. de Cambrai which always concern Mme. Guyon," she reported to Noailles, " but we cannot persuade one another." It was not surprising, because so long as the learned, influential and, above all, deeply devout Archbishop of Cambrai refused to join in the condemnation of Mme. Guyon, the latter remained undefeated and Mme. de Maintenon, her pious persecutor, had to go on suffering, like Bossuet, from a bad conscience. Indeed, she was to make another effort to get Mme. Guyon out of prison to be more decently guarded, but Bossuet stood firm.

Through the early months of 1696, Fénelon, Chevreuse, Beauvilliers and Tronson laboured to fulfil the promise made to Mme. de Maintenon—to work out yet another " precise explanation and refutation of her errors," which the prisoner could sign with sincerity. This would be laid before the Archbishop of Paris who was the final authority now that she was imprisoned in his diocese. All this was to be done in great secrecy so that no one could say that the motive was her liberation. But the attempt came to nothing. The forces round the Throne and the servile bishops, pious as they might be and subjectively assured of their good intentions in destroying Quietism through the *cas Guyon*, had only one object: this was to make Fénelon himself condemn her. If they failed in this, it was inevitable that a tremendous and public row would break out, for Fénelon was the peer of the other bishops and the strongest personality among the clergy of France, save for the Eagle of Meaux to whom all eyes must look if the issue was to be decided before the world.

2

Before describing the way in which Bossuet tackled his problem, let us take another look at him, for in some ways he remains the most puzzling character of all in this story. It would be so much easier if he were the villain whom a defender of Fénelon is apt to see or the fine old warrior of the Church *sans peur* and *sans reproche*, dear to the French tradition. The trouble is that he seems to have managed to be both at different times, and even together.

Bausset comments that Bossuet had on many occasions a capacity to see the tree in the acorn—had he not foreseen that all the sects were rushing towards Socinianism, did he not in 1689 predict that the principle of the sovereignty of the people would overthrow the strongest monarchies? In a system of spirituality which viewed perfection as seeing God only under abstract relations and apart from the precepts which He imposed on men, he no doubt believed that he recognised a point of view which little by little might lead a number of people to complete indifference in religious matters.

We know how well founded were Bossuet's fears about the onrush of rationalism, free thought, sentimental romanticism and political revolution, with which in fact the name of Fénelon was to be so often associated in the future, however little Fénelon himself could have foreseen this and however horrified he would have been had he foreseen it. Indeed, Bossuet's fears about the new spirituality, as he saw it, were by no means without subtlety or insight.

The difference on paper between mysticism and agnosticism can be made to appear very small, though worlds divide them. Both mystic and agnostic conceive of an unknown or unknowable God. The *mystics* contemplates an unknowable God, whose omnipresent, intimate, superior Reality, intimately experienced or sensed, threatens to deny full reality to the world of appearances, of human reasoning, of utilitarian values. The *rationalist agnostic* thinks of a God who, being unknown, if He exists at all, may be disregarded in favour of the only reality: the experience and laws of the universe which our senses perceive and our reason understands in terms of unchanging patterns or laws which, properly applied, bring know-ledge and progress to human life. If Bossuet's fears of the de-structive effects of Guyonist mysticism were much less well based than his fears of Socinianism and political revolution, this was due to the fact that it is very much easier to be an agnostic than a mystic, though the pseudo-mysticism of the romantic and revolutionary movements have played a great part in the formation of the disorder which has followed the collapse of the *ancien régime*.

True mysticism, a severe and difficult discipline, requiring the solid structure of divine revelation, was in fact to be by-passed in later history, thanks in part to Bossuet's attack on it. Bossuet hated it because he underrated human motives and even the importance of man, and consequently overrated the importance of State and institutional Church.

Where Fénelon, throughout the battle, pinned his faith on Mme. Guyon as a *person*, who, he believed, had experienced the true God of Catholicism, and was therefore, spiritually and morally, above suspicion, Bossuet was only interested in the possible theological and practical moral deductions from her teaching. Bossuet, in fact, possessed far less real faith in the Church than did Fénelon, because Bossuet's practical conception of the Church was something, as it were, semi-detached from God and semi-attached to passing human institutions. Fénelon's instinct was to see the Church as God's instrument, God's help *for men* rather than as an end-in-itself. He therefore saw no difficulty in the chosen mystic and saint in personal touch with the unknowable God *within* the revealed doctrine, pattern and praxis of the Catholic Church. And because of this, the aim of his teaching and pastoral work was to help individual *souls* to God *through* the Church rather than to fit the mass of the faithful mechanically into the order and discipline of the Church. To suggest to him that there could be any possible resemblance between the truly Catholic mystic in the line of the great mystical tradition and the agnostic disrupter of the Church's authority and discipline would have seemed to him an absurdity; but to Bossuet the possibility, though never formulated in those terms, was a subconscious haunting fear, as indeed similar haunting fears have always disturbed the ultra-clericalists whose working beliefs are in the institutional Church with its apparatus of divine doctrine rather than in Christ in and through the Church which He founded as the normal channel of His grace to men.

These subconscious dreads of the future, the fruits of fundamental uncertainties and too strong superficial certainties behind the mind of a genius, were the motives which really led Bossuet to oscillate between his natural humanity, piety and indeed strong appetite for the divine, felt with all his emotions, and his deeper faith in the primacy of system and order, divine and human, but insufficiently related to their end, man's realisation of Reality itself, which is God.

The fiercest enemy of the Protestant heresy stood out in his times for his wisdom and kindness in dealing with the individual, erring Huguenot for whom he had perhaps more human sympathy than Fénelon. The servant and adulator of the *Roi Soleil* was haunted by a sense of guilt about his own priestly life. The hater of Quietism within the bosom of the Church made immense efforts, given his prejudices, again and again to find the best in Mme. Guyon until he thought it hopeless for a variety of not very edifying reasons. And, most surprisingly of all, the flayer of mysticism, so that it almost disappeared for generations after him, came to be fascinated by the object of his attack so that he reached a point where the differences between himself and his great opponent seemed hardly more than verbal, though the resemblance was, in fact, superficial.

To return then to our story. Immediately after the Issy Conferences, in the course of which Bossuet learned so much about the nature, doctrine and tradition of the Catholic mysticism as taught even in recent years by Saint Francis of Sales, Saint Jeanne de Chantal, Saint Teresa and Saint John of the Cross, he conceived the idea of resolving the conflict with Fénelon in a way that appeals to all born writers: he himself, with his astonishing power of rapid assimilation and learning by writing, would produce a full-length treatise on Mystical Prayer.

It was both a labour of love, for the subject was now an en-thralling one to him, and a conscientiously-approached apostolic work for the fuller guidance of the Church in France, increasingly disturbed by the Quietists on the one side and the Jansenists on the other. Never for a moment did the great man doubt that his findings would gain universal approval. But how would Fénelon take such a book? Bossuet's self-confidence and his firm belief that Fénelon was on the side of the angels, however mysteriously deluded by the matriarch of Quietism, as people called Mme. Guyon, made him sure that the Archbishop of Cambrai would allow himself to be guided by so clear and full a light. Had they not both signed the Issy Articles, despite those unnecessary Fénelonian variations of a draft that owed all to himself? And had he not himself, the great Bossuet, agreed that there was much more to be said for Fénelon's witness from the contemplative saints than he had realised before applying his brain to this new subject? This new work would, anyway, be based on Issy, and it would finally make clear what was permissible and what was dangerous in the whole subject-matter. He did not realise that only his lack of understanding could explain such confidence in judging the rights and wrongs of God's intimacy with His friends.

In fact, a week or two before the wretched Mme. Guyon had been ferreted out and clapped into prison, Bossuet and Fénelon had had a friendly correspondence on the subject of prayer, and Bossuet took the opportunity of inviting Fénelon to discuss with him what he had been writing. Fénelon, insisting on his own desire to expose false mysticism, agreed: "When you please I shall go either to Meaux or to Germigny to pass a few days with you and to associate myself with your work according to your desire." But he added, cautiously: "Meanwhile let me ask you, in the name of Our Lord who has afforded you so much light on the matter, to listen to Him from within yourself, to suffer what the little ones tell you, and to be on your guard against all prejudice." Fénelon's sigh of warning shows that he was not too confident of Bossuet's success in a subject-matter which has deceived so many by the complexity underlying an apparent simplicity. He did not, however, suspect what to-day we might call " double-think " in Bossuet's invitation.

Six months later, when the first part of *Instruction on the Different*

States of Prayer, as Bossuet called his book, was finished, Fénelon still declared himself ready to read and approve it.

Now it was Bossuet who began to have a guilty conscience, expressed in his usual unctuous way: " I am one with you at bottom, with a wish to be so and the respect which God knows. But all the same, I think I feel a something I do not understand which still separates us a little, and this I cannot bear. My book will help you to enter into our mutual thoughts. I shall only rest when I am one with you in mind as I am in heart."

Bossuet's work, though never completed according to the author's initial plan, was sufficiently valuable and well done to be used some fifty years later by no less an authority than Père de Caussade S. J. as the basis of his own treatise on Prayer. De Caussade, who to-day enjoys a considerable vogue as a mystical authority and a devotional writer, seems to have used Bossuet mainly as a form of self-protection, for in mid-eighteenth century the reaction against Quietism and the influence of Jansenism had rendered the whole subject dangerous. The Jesuit could hardly be attacked if he flew under the shadow of the Eagle's wings. Allowing for this, it still remains true that Bossuet, despite his initial prejudice, could write a book on the subject which de Caussade (whom Mme. Guyon, one feels, would have taken to her heart) could popularise.

What then of Fénelon's reaction? The trouble here was that Bossuet had approached his subject by concentrating on Mme. Guyon and the Quietists and demonstrating the errors of their ways. Whether Bossuet did this without any *arrière-pensée* about Fénelon's infatuation or whether he did it to hurt or indirectly attack Fénelon we do not know. But for the sensitive Fénelon there was no doubt about the matter. The book was a "trap," as he later bluntly called it, an attempt to force out of him a " retractation " of his whole position under the " specious pretext " of the teaching agreed on at Issy, but with the little accidental detail that the greater part of it involved the utter condemnation of his friend.

Fénelon's reaction is best expressed in the letter he wrote to Chevreuse in July, 1696. " I saw, as soon as I opened M. de Meaux's pages, even without reading them, marginal quotations from the *Moyen Court*. This convinces me that the work attacks, at least indirectly, that little book. This makes it impossible for me to approve it; and as I do not want to read it and then refuse to approve it, I am determined to read nothing of it and to return it as soon as possible. The least I can do for one of my friends who is in an unhappy position and whom I still esteem and who has always edified me, is to keep silent when others condemn. . . . M. de Meaux has no need of an approval as feeble as mine. He only asks for it to prove to the public that I agree with him, and I am much obliged to him for his so charitable care. But such an approval would simply look like a disguised abjuration forced out of me, and I hope God will never allow me to fall into such cowardice. . . . Had it only been a question of a book containing all the systems of the inner ways, I am certain that he and I would have been in agreement, because I feel sure that I only believe what he himself has confessed to be his beliefs."

Fénelon's habit of not reading what he did not want to read we already know, and his touchiness at this point may well seem somewhat excessive, though it shows how infinitely more delicate were his reactions than those of his ecclesiastical *confrères*. In fact, as with Mme. Guyon's writings, it is evident that he did read some of Bossuet's book, since he was able to draw up into propositions Bossuet's attack on Mme. Guyon. And in a polite letter he told Bossuet that Chevreuse would explain his reasons for being unable to give the book his approval when returning the manuscript to him.

Bossuet was, or professed himself to be, dumbfounded, scandalised and shocked by Fénelon's refusal. It was a case of openly driving a wedge within the episcopate itself, he protested. It was a case of Fénelon openly cutting himself off from his own consecrators in the chapel of Saint-Cyr, and all this for the sake of that wretched woman! His vanity, both as the chief ecclesiastic of France and as a brilliant amateur in the subject he had just taken up, was touched to the quick. And if, in fact, he had deliberately laid a trap, Fénelon's courage must have baffled and frustrated him. He even asserted that he was prepared to modify his book according to Fénelon's criticisms rather than be denied the approval. But of course no modification could possibly meet the point of Fénelon's criticism. It would have needed a new book. So long as Mme. Guyon was in question, with Bossuet determined to condemn her

and Fénelon equally determined to defend her, every step taken
could only divide the two bishops and precipitate the open rupture
with its momentous consequences for the unity of the Church in
France.

Within a few days Fénelon had prepared a long memorandum
on the reasons why he could not approve his colleague's work—
what workers these men were!—the Pope later was to wring his
hands in despair at the amount those " Frenchmen " wrote—which
he read to Archbishop de Noailles, Godet (both rather nervously
siding with Bossuet) and Tronson, Beauvilliers and Chevreuse (these
sympathising with Fénelon) before forwarding it to Mme. de
Maintenon.

His argument is simple. If Bossuet's accusations against his
friend were true, she must have been from the beginning a monster
of iniquity. If so, what of his own position, a priest chosen to
control the education of the Princes, made an Archbishop and
consecrated at Bossuet's own hands? " I have often seen her;
everyone knows it. I have esteemed her. I have let her be esteemed
by illustrious people who believed in me. . . . Not only have I
approved the basis of her teaching, but my esteem for her and all
our relations have turned on this condemnable spirituality. . . .
That is what I must swallow in the face of the whole Church, if
I approve the book." And what of those who appointed and
promoted him, the defender of " such a monster " ? What of
Bossuet himself who consecrated him, who with his own hand
gave Holy Communion to the authoress of such impieties, who
allowed her the regular use of the Church's sacraments and who
twice certified her personal orthodoxy?

To Mme. de Maintenon, already reporting to Noailles how
strong the feeling at Court about Quietism was becoming, he wrote:
" I have told Messieurs de Paris and Chartres, and M. Tronson,
that I see no shadow of difficulty between M. de Meaux and myself
about the basis of the doctrine, but if he wanted to attack Mme.
Guyon personally in his book, I could not approve it." Of Mme.
Guyon he wrote: " There is no rough village girl who would not
have been horrified by what they pretend she taught." They were
imputing to her " a devilish design, a monstrous system." According
to them, she denies " explicit faith in the attributes of the divine

Persons, the mysteries of Jesus Christ and of His humanity. She
wishes to dispense Christians from all outward worship. . . . She
holds that once an act of faith and love have been made, that act
continues always in life without ever having to be renewed. . . .
She only leaves Christians with an impious and brutal indifference
as to vice and virtue, as to God's eternal hatred and His eternal love.
. . . She forbids as an infidelity any real resistance to the most
abominable temptations. . . . That is what they say. I maintain that
no ignorance could be so gross as to excuse a person putting forward
such monstrous maxims. . . . What is more worthy of the fire than
a monster who, under the appearances of piety, only furthers
fanaticism and impurity ? . . . Let others who only know her writings
take them in so rigorous a sense and condemn them. I leave them
to it. I neither defend nor excuse her person nor her writings.
Knowing what I do, is not that to do much ? But for myself, I must
in justice judge the meaning of her writings by her sentiments which
I know thoroughly, and not judge her sentiments by the rigorous
interpretation put upon her expressions—things she had never
thought. Which is better—either to awaken memories in the world
of my attachment to her in the past, which would mean avowing
myself either the insanest of men for having failed to detect such
obvious infamies, or the most execrable one for having tolerated
them; or to keep a profound silence on the writings and person of
Mme. Guyon, as a man who excuses her in her conscience in that
she did not sufficiently understand the theological value of each
expression, nor the severity with which the language of the mystics
was later to be examined in view of the way in which a few hypocrites have abused it ? That the mystics, even the most approved,
have greatly exaggerated is the common talk to-day. Even Saint
Clement and many Fathers of the Church, it is held, have spoken in
terms requiring much correction. How then do they expect a
woman to be the only one not to exaggerate ? Why must it be
thought that all she has said goes to make up a system fit to make
one's flesh creep ? " Fénelon then demonstrated to the King's wife
how he had held fast to true doctrine—the same doctrine as Bossuet
had defended and expounded. But since " this is not enough to
dissipate the umbrage taken, I believe it to be necessary for me to
declare myself in a more authentic manner. I have written a book

in which I thoroughly explain the whole system of the inner ways and in which I distinguish, on the one hand, all that conforms to faith and is founded on the tradition of the Saints, and, on the other, all that goes beyond it and must be rigorously censured."

After this letter, Mme. de Maintenon and Fénelon met again, but apparently without finding any common ground. "I have seen our friend," she wrote to Noailles. "We have argued hard, but very quietly. I should like to be as faithful and as attached to my duties as he is to his friend. He never loses sight of her and nothing touches him on that subject." A fine tribute dragged from the woman who had been so attached to both of them and had then grown so jealous of the woman in whom she discerned a rival to herself.

Posterity cannot but judge that, in the light of all that had taken place, Fénelon's argument was very strong. Mme. Guyon's published books had passed the censors at the time they were published—a point, strangely enough, never underlined. Bossuet, it is true, had read her manuscript writings, while Fénelon had refused to read them, but those papers were private and only handed over as to a private confessor in the confessional. They were the unguarded, unedited secrets of an over-full, spiritually romantic heart. Besides, Bossuet, even if through kindness, had given her the sacraments and witnessed to her good faith *after* his detailed study of them. As for the others, they had all encouraged or at least accepted her. How could it be that the logical French mind should at one moment treat Mme. Guyon as a woman of deep and inspiring spirituality and at the next as a heretical impostor? How could Fénelon, for his part, now condemn the woman he had recommended to the whole circle of Court *dévots* without making a fool of himself and of them? Above all, how could he do it at the bidding of Bossuet whom he knew to be quite inexperienced in the discernment of spirits in this difficult subject and to be determined to do Mme. de Maintenon's bidding in killing or curing him of the friendship which that powerful woman could no longer stand?

But it seemed to some of Fénelon's friends that if he could not condemn Mme. Guyon's life and motives and therefore, as he saw it, approve of Bossuet's book on that account, he could at least follow the lead of so many bishops and condemn her writings as such, quite apart from what her motives might have been. Tronson, for example, wrote to him: " I cannot, My Lord, help thinking, after considering the matter at length, that there is no reason why you should not take that line." Fénelon's answer amounted to saying that he never really thought that even her published writings deserved to be officially condemned. In other words, he took the same view as the ecclesiastical censors had originally done before the Quietist scare had been fanned in France by Mme. de Maintenon and Bossuet. This was certainly his real view though he hedged at times. Such a condemnation, he pointed out to Tronson, would imply that he really thought that Mme. Guyon had intended the false and evil interpretations of her teaching which was now being given to it. In other words, whatever he might be led to say in letters about refusing to condemn his friend's motives, he also believed in that part of her teaching at least which he knew so well by his personal contact with her. Had not Tronson himself admitted that if you took her views on balance, the apparent exaggerations were balanced by orthodox qualifications? We can understand now why he always believed in her orthodoxy, but to Bossuet who concentrated on her manuscripts and knew nothing of the spiritual intimacy between them for many years, his stand was incomprehensible and sinister.

It is unlikely that Bossuet at this stage could have been persuaded to give up his campaign against Fénelon. It was intolerable that this stubborn bishop should remain powerful at Court and should have in his care a future king of France. It was beyond all decency that his friends, the dukes and duchesses and especially the powerful friend of the King, Beauvilliers, should continue to believe in him.

But as events turned out, it was not Bossuet, but Fénelon himself, who had taken the final step leading to open warfare.

As Fénelon had told Mme. de Maintenon, he had long made up his mind to an entirely fresh line of action. He had adopted Bossuet's own weapon, and written a book: the book, which, like Bossuet's, would once and for all make clear the difference between true mysticism and false, but this time, not on the basis of an ignorant woman's writings, but on the evidence of the saints of the Church themselves.

As early as February, 1696, he had written to Tronson: " Would it not be a good thing if I wrote a work in which I loudly condemn and with all severity the false maxims which are imputed to that person? In this way the public will know my true feelings. There is no need to fear that I will cause bad blood by contradicting M. de Meaux's book, now in preparation. On the contrary, I want to conform entirely to the 34 Propositions, and only to refer to him as my master. My book will be ready very shortly."

Thus, well before he had set eyes on Bossuet's manuscripts, he had already hit on the word " maxims " in connection with the book which was to become so famous and, alas, so notorious under the title *The Maxims of the Saints*.

CHAPTER TWO

THE MAXIMS OF THE SAINTS

THE MOUNTING tension between the two prelates who were being driven, as Mme. de Maintenon herself put it, "to extremities," augured no good for the imprisoned Mme. Guyon.

If Bossuet was right, the prophetess, according to the customs of the time, was justly left in prison as a danger to Church and State. But if Fénelon was right, there was no excuse, even in those times, for holding her as a common criminal, though she might have been detained under a kind of house-arrest until the whole matter was cleared up. For Bossuet, it was essential that she should not be freed or treated with any indulgence. Yet he was apprehensive: "You would not credit," he wrote to a fellow-bishop, "all that is being done in secret in favour of that woman. . . . But I must tell you that if I yielded an inch, all would be lost. They have not as yet made any headway against me, and I do not think they will gain anything whilst I live."

Mme. de Maintenon herself had a bad conscience about the woman whom she once introduced into her beloved Saint-Cyr. "The stubbornness of our friends," she wrote to Noailles, "gives me a real heartache. Yet I cannot think the less of them. All our relations now seem no more than a dissimulation. I find myself in a country utterly strange to me. Everything in it is unpleasing to me. There is no one with whom I can open my heart." The roles were being reversed. While she at the start had driven a hesitant Bossuet, now it was an irate and scandalised Bossuet who was driving her. She was a good woman, pulled in opposite ways and out of her depths in this confusion of personal tensions, fear for the King and the State, and a doctrinal dispute in which all her sym-

pathies were really with Fénelon. Even a year later she was writing
to a Dame of Saint-Cyr: "I return to you M. de Fénelon's letters;
I can see in them nothing but good, and, even if I am wrong, nothing
is dangerous to a nun who is ready to give up anything at the bidding
of her superiors." If only Mme. Guyon had never existed, she must
have many times sighed.

Archbishop de Noailles, the only competent authority in Mme.
Guyon's case, hesitated as usual and tried to please all parties. At
one moment, he was persuaded that Bossuet's book should not be
published. Bossuet brushed him aside. Peace, perhaps, could be
re-established, he thought, if only the prisoner could be got to
inculpate herself, so he had yet another shot at the old technique
which had so often failed.

This time, Mme. Guyon's examiners baited their hook more
cleverly. They tried to make use of the double meaning of the word
"retractation." It could be used to mean either a personal retractation
of a false doctrine which had been knowingly propagated as such,
or a retractation of errors to be found in her books, without reference
to her subjective intentions. But Mme. Guyon was too old a hand
to be taken in. She would sign a retractation of the second kind, but
not one which she could be understood in the first sense. But the
cautious and troubled Beauvilliers pointed out to the Archbishop
that it was now more and more essential to distinguish the *cas Guyon*
from the wider implications of the growing quarrel between
Bossuet and Fénelon. He had never quite shared his friends' faith
in Mme. Guyon. "Heated spirits," he wrote to Noailles, "insist
on muddling them together, and this will result in the end in very
serious troubles, if you in your wisdom do not prevent it in the
ways you have in hand and which depend entirely on you." To keep
the two issues distinct was also Fénelon's aim in his book, but they
could not be kept distinct, unless it could be widely published that
Mme. Guyon had signed an official act of submission acceptable to
the Archbishop of Paris. There seemed to be only one man who
could obtain an act of submission universally acceptable, and this,
of course, was Fénelon himself in whom she fully trusted. She was
also prepared to trust Tronson who had on so many occasions stood
by her, despite his having no particular reason for being prejudiced
in her favour. On the contrary, as a very old and tired man, of

clericalist stamp, and anxious about his old pupil's future, his natural feelings would have been against the prophetess.

So the complex negotiations continued between the Dukes, Tronson and Fénelon himself to draft a formula of submission which seemed honest to them and which would be acceptable to Noailles. At last on 28th August, 1696, a draft satisfactory to all was given to the prisoner. She only took the precaution of asking Tronson whether she could sign in conscience. On his assurance to this effect, she unhesitatingly did so. This formula did not differ in essence from the previous ones at Meaux, and it contained the declaration: " I owe, before God and men, this witness to the truth that I have never sought to insinuate, through any of these expressions, any of the errors they contain; I have never understood how anyone could have got these wrong meanings into their heads."

It was a final vindication before the highest authority of the position she had substantially held throughout those years of suffering and persecution in the face of the immensely imposing ecclesiastical forces arrayed against her. But even if her highly-placed friends had not stood by her through thick and thin, one feels certain that this remarkable woman would never have yielded on the point that she had never *intended* to teach error. She was of the mettle that prefers to be burnt to the stake to speaking against her conscience, and few in those times would have been capable of distinguishing as delicately as she did between the rights of the Church in declaring what was objectively false and the rights of the individual in judging of his own subjective intentions of mind and heart. In the roll of woman heroes she ought to have a much higher place.

In a letter to Noailles, in which she expressed the sincerity of her submission under " the seal and gage " of the Blessed Sacrament she had received that very day, she asked to be allowed to live in a more suitable place. She made a similar request to the King, asking him specifically to let her live near Blois in her son-in-law's property. " M. de Portchartrain yesterday evening read to the King a long letter of Mme. Guyon's asking that she might be allowed to retire to a property near Blois, belonging, I believe, to her son-in-law." Mme. de Maintenon reported to Noailles, and a few days later told him that she had persuaded the King not to press matters against

Quietism, but to leave it all as much as possible to him, the Arch-bishop.

There was, of course, no intention of giving the prisoner her freedom. The Archbishop of Paris was probably expressing the general feeling when he asked Tronson to explain to her that her detention was " a necessary means of dissipating the suspicions of the past and those that might be formed in the future," suspicions that would help to injure her own friends. Fénelon's hands were tied because he had deliberately chosen to fight for her reputation without arousing the smallest suspicion that his real interest might be in her temporal fate.

However, it was decided by Noailles, over Bossuet's head, to have Mme. Guyon removed from Vincennes in October to a house in Vaugirard where nuns would be her gaolers. She was soon writing to Chevreuse to say that of the two she preferred the gaolers of the prison. Another point she deplored was that she had to pay for her own keep at Vaugirard, whereas at Vincennes she had been the " guest of the King."

" At any rate, she is shut up," said Bossuet, making the best of it. She was also shut up spiritually, since she was entirely in the hands of La Chétardie, the Curé of Saint-Sulpice, of whom Bossuet said: " Now *there* is a man! They could not have done better than to put her in his hands." Though a certain tolerance had dictated the transfer to Vaugirard, she was, in fact, far unhappier there than in the honest roughness of the State prison.

Mme. Guyon's signature to a retractation agreed upon by all except Bossuet had, as before, gained nothing whatever. She was not even liberated, and Fénelon and Bossuet were left facing one another. In fact, from Vincennes, Vaugirard and, soon, the notorious Bastille her personality was to achieve its greatest triumph. For it was over her imprisoned spirit and body that the two most eminent Church personalities in France were to engage in fratricidal strife. " Two illustrious opponents, equal rather than alike, entered the lists," Chancellor d'Aguesseau wrote. " The one, long-since a past-master in ecclesiastical science and covered with the laurels gained in fighting heretics . . . the other, still young and in the prime of life, less known for his writings, but famous for the power of his eloquence and the height of his genius, a master of the subject-matter in dispute . . . both long-since friends, both becoming as famous for their rivalry."

"A Court intrigue," D'Aguesseau and many others called it. Were the Dukes and Fénelon, inspired by a crazy, illuminist woman to control the moral tone of France, especially when the King came to die? In that issue, the King's wife would have liked to be on their side, for she in that sense was wholly on the side of the angels. But personal jealousies and fears had put her, together with the prelates, on the wrong side. Much more important was the element which really drove Bossuet on. He wrote, in connection with his work on mysticism: "If we do not once and for all dominate the mystics, even the good ones, not to condemn them, but to prevent their inexact and usually *outré* sayings from being taken as the rule, all is lost. It is a dangerous illusion to take literally those who have said, in their excitement, that they had no care for their salvation, nor for their perfection, but only for God's grace."

For Bossuet, mysticism was essentially a lamentable extravagance, a kind of spiritual failing tempting the odder saints, which threatened reason and history and consequently the primacy of ecclesiastical and secular institutions for the good government of mankind.

For Fénelon, it was the heart, the goal, of all true religion. For him mysticism was the touch of God directly experienced in the human spirit. It was "the drift of pinions" beating "at our own clay-shutted doors." It was truth itself reached intuitively by a kind of second sight, a God-given sight, truth far deeper and more important to the human spirit than any logical and utilitarian conclusion, than any historical testimony, save only the divine revelation on which the Church of God itself was founded.

This deluded Fénelon, Bossuet held, had been perverted like Adam himself by the voice of a woman.

When Bossuet first heard from Pirot about the book Fénelon was writing, he exclaimed: "Well, sir, let him write it! But tell him to beware of leaving the path of truth; tell him to beware, of hedging. He will find *me* everywhere along his way. I shall raise my voice and carry my grievances to Rome itself, if need be." Nevertheless, the first round caught Bossuet on the wrong foot, for Fénelon's book beat his for publication by a few days. Fénelon was a very quick worker, and by the end of the year 1696 he had completed his short and dry *Explanation of the Maxims of the Saints*. It contained forty-five articles, each divided into two parts. The first stated what was right teaching on that particular article; the second what was wrong. His object in treating the matter in this academic way was two-fold. It would make the issue crystal-clear—a difficult and, as we shall see, dangerous way of dealing with so delicate and and easily misunderstood a subject; and it would avoid the slightest suspicion of personalities, thus contrasting with Bossuet's book. No doubt, he was also anxious to be as unlike Mme. Guyon as possible in his approach to the topic on which she had poured herself out.

Well knowing the danger of his position and the difficulty of his task, Fénelon had taken every possible precaution, short of the suicidal step of asking for Bossuet's approval. He warned Mme. de Maintenon, telling her that the things they called " subtleties " were only what the saints and the Catholic schools had long taught. " I do not stand by any particular language [an important point in view of the later condemnation of the language], and I abandon all expressions that people want to condemn so long as the heart of the matter is safeguarded and the workings of divine grace are not destroyed." She commented to Noailles that she was not seeking any condemnation of his views, " but the truth expounded by the Church." He then submitted his manuscript to his own friends, and to the official theologian, Dr. Pirot of the Sorbonne. Pirot was no friend of Mme. Guyon; indeed, he ardently admired Bossuet, and was in fact also reading his manuscript. Together Fénelon and Pirot worked on the draft for many hours with two manuscript copies. When the task was finished, Pirot exclaimed that the book was " *tout d'or*," " sterling throughout," as we might say. Later, he was to deny that he had ever said anything of the sort. The manuscript went also to Noailles himself, the highest ecclesiastical authority by his rank, and Mme. de Maintenon's almost daily Church contact. The Archbishop advised Fénelon to shorten it still further, and then marked with a pencil places where he thought the wording might be revised. Together, the two men worked to reach perfection, and Noailles even teased him for his readiness to accept corrections with so little fuss. Finally, it went to Tronson who pronounced it " correct and useful." Few prelates in history, surely, have ever taken more trouble to ensure exactitude and correctness of doctrine. They are, as successors of the Apostles, teachers in their own right!

Chevreuse, who advised his friend to write the *Maximes*, was in charge of the publication arrangements. While Fénelon was in Cambrai, the Duke rushed the book through printing, proof-correcting and publication, lest Bossuet find means of stopping it. Unfortunately, in doing this, he allowed printers' errors to pass, which caused Fénelon trouble later. Before Fénelon himself expected it, the *Maximes* had appeared—27th January, 1697, six weeks ahead of Bossuet's *Instruction*.

Bossuet was livid. He knew that Fénelon's book was being written, though later he called "heaven and earth to witness that I knew nothing of the plot and that my hands are guiltless of the scandalous divisions which have resulted." The low cunning of his rival in beating the Father of the Church in the work he had undertaken to write for the enlightenment of the faithful, was more than he could bear.

When Beauvilliers presented him with a copy, he wrote: " He has caused a book on spirituality to be printed two days ago. In it everything is directed towards the justification of Mme. Guyon without naming her. He is trying to put himself at the head of the dispute. The book itself is nothing much—only alembicated pro-positions and verbiage." Later, he wrote: " The whole style of the book is of an unsurpassed arrogance, and it is all so complex that most people cannot understand a word." He took it away for a fortnight's examination of the content. With his secretary, he studied for two hours each morning, furiously annotating the pages with his thick pencil.

To Godet of Chartres he was writing on 13th February: " The book is causing much talk. Some say it is badly written, others that it is full of very daring things, others still that some cannot be defended. Some think it is written with all the delicacy and care imaginable, but that at bottom it is not good; and others that at a time when false mysticism is doing so much harm, no one should write on the subject except to condemn and leave true mysticism to God. They add that true mysticism is so rare and so unnecessary, while false mysticism is so common and so dangerous, that it cannot be too much opposed." This last was certainly his own view.

Later, Bossuet was to describe the reaction to the book in the following terms: " All Paris, the Court, the Sorbonne, the communities, the learned, the ignorant, men and women, all the Orders, they were without exception indignant." Even allowing for Bossuet's genius in avoiding understatement, everything suggests that this reaction was unnatural. How was it that everyone was discussing it? How was it that Paris and France itself deemed the whole world to be menaced by a book that few can have taken the trouble to read—and could not have understood, had they taken the trouble? Despite the fact that Noailles, Pirot and Tronson had carefully examined it, this dry, specialised text-book on an obscure subject was, within a matter of days, the talk of the town with a wave of indignation mounting against it. When later Bossuet accused Fénelon of spreading the story that Bossuet's " imperceptible springs " had caused the surprising excitement, Fénelon's dry retort was that at any rate "nothing was less imperceptible than the springs which in fact were moved."

The storm, the effect of which was to make headline news, as it were, of the fact that an imprisoned heretic was being championed by a great prelate of the Court in whose charge lay the upbringing of the Princes themselves, drove all the chief actors to seek shelter before the lightning struck and the thunder roared. They were all running to exculpate themselves in the eyes of the monarch who had been apprised of the scandal by Bossuet on his knees and with tears in his eyes to beg the royal pardon for not having given earlier warning of his fellow-Bishop's outrageous conduct. " The King is moved beyond what we had thought possible," Bossuet wrote. " M. de Cambrai is deeply depressed, but no less proud for all that. I am his *bête noire*. He is proud and stunned. Mme. de Maintenon only supports me because of M. de Paris."

On 21st February, the King's wife wrote to Noailles to say how embarrassed she felt at meeting Fénelon and his friends. " He knows the bad effect of his book, but defends it with reasons which more and more persuade me that God wishes to humiliate that great mind who perhaps has counted too much on his own inspirations." Père de La Chaise, the Jesuit—the Jesuits, in France and Rome, were to defend Fénelon as bravely as they dared—tried to calm the royal anger for Fénelon's sake, but, said Mme. de Maintenon, " in view of the dispositions I see in the King, M. de Cambrai will derive little satisfaction from this clarification. . . . I have done what I could to make sure he is warned. This opposition has not been inspired by me; it is in the heart of the King himself in regard to all novelties. I know they will accuse me, but I owe you the truth, My Lord, and I am giving it to you."

Louis, it is said, was moaning: "What will become of my children? In whose hands have I put them?"

Once again, let us pause to consider that the arch-heretic who had arisen in the bosom of the Eldest Daughter of the Church had not published his book until the Archbishop of Paris, the theologian of the Sorbonne and the venerable Superior of Saint-Sulpice, the home of sound clerical training, had declared themselves satisfied with it. "God sees and will judge those who use two weights and two measures," wrote poor Fénelon. "The whole of my system reduces itself to a simple and indivisible point: it is that of dis-interested love. The tradition of the Fathers is clear; even the Schools have made this sentiment prevail everywhere. Examine the works of canonised saints and you will find them full of this teaching. . . . Town and Court cabals, doctrinal and political cabals, are moving heaven and earth against me. If my book teaches error, I am ready to make reparation before the Church. But if its doctrine is sound, I hope that God will repress men of evil intention and enlighten those who are alarmed through that kind of zeal."

Meanwhile, Bossuet's own book had appeared. Filled, as it was, with denunciations of Mme. Guyon and the " new mysticism," it fanned the flames of anti-Fénelonism. Fénelon complained of Bossuet's claim to judge the issue before telling the reader what the Church's tradition and doctrine in the subject-matter were. "What is false," he insisted, " cannot be refuted save in the light of what is true, thoroughly considered." And he concentrated his attack on what he believed to be the key of the controversy—whether man is capable of loving God for Himself alone, as Mme. Guyon had long ago put it, whether in fact man could love God with a touch of the pure, divine love itself, or whether he was always bound to corrupt, self-interested love? He believed that on this clear point Bossuet had not only virtually repudiated the Issy Articles, but the weight of theological teaching.

The act of love of God, argued Bossuet, is inevitably bound up with the reward and happiness which will be given to the man who loves God—it is servile love. Man cannot but seek happiness—to say otherwise is equivalent to equating the love of God, that is, the supreme end of all religion, with a spiritually suicidal despair for the alternative to happiness is final despair. Fénelon, holding the view which Godet himself acknowledged to be correct, that reward is the specific object of the virtue of *hope* (not love), while God in and for himself alone is the specific object of the virtue of *love* or *charity*, readily acknowledged that psychologically we cannot but desire the happiness that God intends for those who love Him. But just as a man cannot wish to live and yet may nevertheless prefer death, so the Christian, without ceasing to hope for reward and to expect it, can with God's grace in his deliberate acts choose God *for Himself alone, apart from all considerations of personal happiness otherwise than in accomplishing God's will.* To this Bossuet triumphantly retorted: " We can very well sacrifice our mortal life for something better, namely, the life of the blessed; but when you pretend that we can sacrifice the life of the blessed, you must offer something even better'in exchange. But in fact man must either be happy in possessing eternal life or unhappy in losing it." To which Fénelon answered: " God's glory *is* the more excellent thing to which we can sacrifice our own happiness, even though the two are in fact inseparable because God willed it so. To say otherwise would be tantamount to saying that there is no difference between God's glory and man's eternal happiness—in other words to make man the equal of God, which is blasphemy."

But Bossuet was not really concerned with these philosophical distinctions. " I stand by the point," he wrote, " because it is decisive. It is the desire to separate motives which God has united which makes you seek all the strange things which you alone discover within your impossible hypotheses." In other words, believe in such a thing as the possibility of perfectly disinterested love, and a man can transcend and justify anything in its name, not least indifference towards the whole regular system of Christian teaching on man and society whose basic force and sanction lies in the hope of eternal reward. Is man a creature capable of finding self-realisation in a higher, timeless and spaceless order of reality, in God the all-real, the all-good; or is he only capable of a basically self-regarding choice between reward and punishment in a kind of spiritual-utilitarianism? Bossuet did not really believe in the crudity of the second alternative, else he could never have written the *Instruction*, but his fear for the whole clerico-social system of his day as against individual inspiration and revolution was so strong that he distorted his mind when it was a question of destroying a man who seemed to be opening a door to the inrush of individualism, romanticism and anarchy. Knowing subsequent history, one cannot but sympathise to some extent with a fear which echoed Pascal's warning that if man seeks to become an angel of light he will fall lower than the beasts. But Christ's injunction "Be ye perfect" and the lives of the saints attest that Pascal and Bossuet had reached at best half-truths.

So certain of his ground did Fénelon feel on the doctrine of pure love that he considered turning the tables on his opponent by denouncing him to the Holy See. He was more than once advised to do so. He even recalled how in the famous controversy between the Dominicans and the Jesuits about reconciling man's free-will with the efficacy of divine grace, the latter when facing apparent defeat retrieved the situation by taking the offensive against the Dominicans. Thus they secured a perpetual truce which was in effect a victory for them since they were the challenged party.

Had he done so, he might have won the battle, for there is no doubt that on the technical issue of pure love, he had the great majority of theologians with him, since pure love is the heart and meaning of religion itself and, as Fénelon maintained and Mme. Guyon believed, pure love was sustained by and entirely compatible with the Christian and Catholic revelation necessary for fallen man. It was the distant, but only, goal, but to be normally sought by mankind through an arduous and untiring co-operation with the grace which Christ offered through the channels of the Church which He founded and in which He mystically lived after His earthly life.

But Fénelon, fearing to exacerbate the quarrel and create greater scandal, chose the other way. He would submit his own cause and his book, over the head of the Gallican Church where the King and the Eagle of Meaux reigned, to the judgment of the Pope himself. If it was the less wise choice in terms of earthly tactics, it was far more consonant with the spiritual quality of the cause he was pleading and the standards by which posterity would judge.

CHAPTER THREE

"DISGRACE"

DESPITE THE way in which Bossuet had inflamed public opinion against Fénelon, the hope still remained that the issue could be quietly settled and the full scandal prevented. Bossuet's attack on pure love had been a mistake in the eyes of the better-balanced bishops like Noailles and Godet. They realised, like Fénelon, that to deny to man the possibility of loving God because God *is* love was tantamount to saying, as Fénelon contended, that man would have to cease to be man if he wanted to be perfect, as Christ bade him be. They realised that to condemn disinterested love amounted to putting Christianity below the moral level of pagan religions and philosophies in which far higher ideals than crude spiritual and temporal hedonism had been put before man and enthusiastically followed. If Bossuet was right, then the life and death of Christ, so far from dividing history between times of darkness and times of spiritual light, brought greater darkness and corruption than ever. On all such points which Fénelon tirelessly put forward there could be no answer.

But Noailles and Godet had better arguments when they pressed the practical point that Fénelon's attitude opened the way to the danger of *false* mysticism, of Guyonism and Quietism running amok. Were not Protestants and strange Northern sects like the Shakers greeting the Catholic Quietists driven from Italy? Had they but known it, would not the Protestants of England and Holland prove to be the most determined disciples of Mme. Guyon, little as they understood her real mind? Noailles, seeing how things had gone, was irritated with Fénelon for quoting him as having approved the *Maximes*. His approval had been unofficial, he maintained, and not for publication. There were serious errors in the printed book (though these, Fénelon attributed to faulty proof-reading by Chevreuse). It was not a very brave excuse, but the Archbishop of Paris and Mme. de Maintenon's spiritual director could not afford to be brave just then.

Writing on indefatigably, Fénelon dealt with each of his critics, and did so brilliantly, but without ever satisfying anyone but his friends on the question of prudence. Let the book be examined again, he asked; but not if His Lordship of Meaux was to be on the board of examiners. Let Bossuet, if he must, hand over to the examiners the grounds of his condemnation, but let the decision rest with others. But before he knew where he was, Bossuet was already dictating to Noailles and to Godet, in the Archbishop's own house, a condemnation of the *Maximes* and a demand for a re-tractation on the part of his fellow-Bishop. To his unfortunate colleagues, vainly endeavouring to gain some time, the Eagle said: " I hold you responsible for this division that you are causing in the episcopate. Do what you like! But, for my part, I will raise my voice to high heaven against these errors which you can no longer overlook."

It was then that Fénelon decided to appeal to Rome.

In his letter of 27th April, 1697, he first explained why he had written the book. " I had noted that some people were abusing the maxims of the saints, so often approved by the Holy See, and trying to insinuate little by little pernicious errors, while others who knew nothing about spiritual matters were turning those maxims into derision." He then reminded the Pope that some mystical writers, innocent in their own consciences, had made theological mistakes in their " pardonable ignorance." It was this which " had inflamed the zeal of several illustrious bishops and caused them to draw up 34 Articles in which they deigned to agree with me." Referring to Mme. Guyon's books, he went on: " This is what has caused them to censure certain little books, some parts of which, taken in their natural sense, deserved condemnation." Then, referring to Bossuet, he wrote: " But, Holy Father, men rarely recoil from one extreme without falling into the opposite one. Some people have taken all this as an excuse, and against our intention, of turning into derision, as an extravagant chimera, the pure love of contemplative life." He then explained how he had sought to distinguish the true from the false in his own book; for the true he had relied on the writings of canonised saints and for the false on the decrees of the condemnation of Molinos. Under seven heads he enumerated the points for which he had stood.

(1) The condemnation of the "single act" of attending to God which could be made once and for all and never needed to be made again or varied and complemented by other spiritual acts.

(2) The insistence on the indispensable necessity of exercising every Christian virtue.

(3) The condemnation of the possibility of perpetual and un-interrupted contemplation entirely free from venial sin, distractions and the distinction between the virtues of faith, hope, etc.

(4) The condemnation of the idea of a passive prayer incom-patible with any free and meritorious acts.

(5) "I have admitted no other quietude in prayer and other exercises of the spiritual life, except that of the peace of the Holy Spirit within which the purest souls can make acts of prayer in so uniform a way that they appear to uninstructed people to be, not distinct acts, but a simple and permanent union with God." [The possibility of reconciling such a simple and unvaried state of prayer with a will, that is active and embraces the normal and varied types of prayer, is much easier for us to appreciate to-day than it was then, since the relationship between the conscious and subconscious activities of the human being is far better understood. Much of Fénelon's teaching and practical spiritual direction intuitively anti-cipates the findings of modern psychology.]

(6) "Lest the doctrine of pure love, authorised by so many Fathers of the Church and so many saints, be made to serve as a refuge for Quietists, my principal aim has been to show that no matter in what degree of perfection one may be and with what purity of love one may be filled, the *hope* by which we are saved must always be kept in one's heart. We must always hope, desire and ask for our salvation even in so far as it is our salvation, since God wills it and wills it for His glory. Thus hope lives in the exercising of it, not only by infused habit, but also by its proper acts, which, commanded and ennobled by charity, are perfectly simply related to the sublime end of charity itself, which is the pure

glory of God." [Here, too, modern psychology helps us to understand an inner complexity of motivation within which the human
being can act for different and independent motives with priorities
often distinct from surface feelings.]

(7) " This state of pure love is restricted to very few perfect souls,
and in them it is only habitual, that is, a habit still subject to daily
faults and, still more, to a variety of acts which are no less good and
meritorious, even though a little less pure and disinterested."

Strange as it seems to us to-day, the Archbishop of Cambrai could
not send this letter to the Head of the Catholic Church without first
obtaining the permission of the King of France. Nor was Louis's
" Very Christian " permission easily obtained. It was for Louis to
detect heresy in his kingdom, not the Ultramontane Pope.

" The King," Mme. de Maintenon had written to Noailles a
month earlier, " has found M. de Cambrai's book very bad. . . .
The cabal daily becomes stronger and bolder. I see in it neither
simplicity nor passivity. It is up to you, My Lord, to sustain the
cause of the Church, and up to M. de Meaux whom the Père de
La Chaise attacks when he sees the King." The *Maximes* was already
running into a third edition, and Bossuet was busy making sure
that Louis's anger would not melt away. Was he not " the best-
intentioned Prince in the world in matters of religion? " It was
in fact in an interval when the King seemed to hesitate about what
to do that Bossuet's guarantee that Fénelon's condemnation in
Rome was certain persuaded Louis to allow Fénelon's letter to be
handed over by Beauvilliers to the Nuncio in Paris.

Fénelon's reference of the *Maximes* to the judgment of the Holy
See would in our day bring all discussion and argument among
good Catholics, and especially bishops, to an end. There would be
silence until the Pope had pronounced judgment. Nothing remotely
like that happened in those times. The endlessly complex manœuvres
went on unabated in France, while Fénelon knew well that Bossuet
would go to any lengths to ensure that the Pope's advisers in Rome
would persuade the old Pontiff to pronounce in his favour. In
France, royal action was being taken. At length, Saint-Cyr itself
was reformed and the Canoness Mme. de La Maisonfort, together
with others, were expelled and sent to Bossuet's care in Meaux.
Beauvilliers himself. the closest to the King in the Fénelon circle,

was watched and controlled. In May, Fénelon had to answer the King's own remonstrances, and he insisted that his appeal to Rome had been too long delayed. " A Bishop cannot allow his faith to be held suspect without rendering an account of the situation to the Holy See as soon as possible." And he went on meaningly: " I had in fact pressing reasons for not allowing my cause to be prejudiced in advance by people who have powerful contacts in Rome "—in others words, Bossuet and the King's diplomats. In the same letter, he assured the King how ready he had been, and remained, to come to an agreement with the Archbishop of Paris, " who only has powers of persuasion over me," that is, no ecclesiastical authority, and with Tronson and Pirot about amplifications and corrections to his book to meet all serious difficulties.

But Bossuet, despite Mme. de Maintenon's admission that he had no right whatever to judge Fénelon, swept all before him as one sweeps a cobweb out of a room, to use Fénelon's own words. Later, he would plead before the world that his fellow-bishop would not trust him. At the time, he was denouncing his fellow-bishop as an already condemned heretic in bad faith and smacking his lips at the prospect of his removal from Court.

Meanwhile Fénelon himself, in all humility, seeing that he had referred the matter to Rome, and in further endeavours to come to terms with Noailles and Godet, was ready to pursue any line he was asked to. He would redraft the book, have it examined again, discuss it at any length. He was even in the end to agree to Bossuet's presence at an episcopal conference. He undertook, in fact, the work of revision so as to make any further misunderstandings impossible. But the manuscript, with the corrections, ends abruptly on page 57. He had received that day a letter from Godet, clearly the frightened spokesman of the dominant Bossuet, saying: " The credit which your book gives, in spite of your intentions, to the Quietism of our days, frightens and worries me more than I can say. . . . If you defend your book with explanations, it will be held to be good, useful and doctrinally sound. It will be reprinted. All who condemn it will be accused of stupidity and lack of brains. It will help to do infinite harm. . . . I pray the Lord that you will do what the Holy Spirit inspires you to do, and that you will thoroughly realise the difference between voluntarily retracting, simply, humbly, courageously, or having a book that cannot possibly be approved censured in Rome." It was an attack on Fénelon himself rather than on his book—a suggestion that the greater the truth, the greater the danger. A case was surely never so completely prejudged and an appeal to its author never so ingenuously expressed. Even self-defence and correction were denied him even by a sincere friend, like the Bishop of Chartres.

Even when Fénelon agreed to Bossuet's presence at an episcopal examination, subject to the final judgment being reserved to Noailles, Tronson and Pirot, Bossuet refused the terms. Despite all his protestations of friendship for his old disciple, he was making it clear once and for all that he had only one concern and purpose —to condemn the *Maximes* finally and publicly with the unofficial, but overriding theological authority that was his in France, the other Bishops concurring with and countersigning such a condemnation. The mere signature of other Bishops would mean little, he thought, so long as the real weight behind it was not the judgment of Jacques Bénigne, Bishop of Meaux.

Mme. de Maintenon once again expressed to Noailles that regard for Fénelon which her intrigues against him, too well pursued, could never completely kill in her. " As for M. de Cambrai's conversion, only God can achieve it, and I am sure you cannot believe him to be as imbued with his maxims as in fact he is. His heart is filled with it all, and he believes himself to be upholding religion in spirit and in truth. . . . I believe him prejudiced in good faith and therefore he will not come back. I know the whole affair so well and have known it for such a long time, that I can speak of it more frankly than any other."

Fénelon's stubborn fight, so strangely similar, given the difference of degree and experience between the two friends, to Mme. Guyon's, at least gave sufficient heart to Noailles and Godet to force on Bossuet a condemnation in August by the three bishops of the *Maximes* in moderate language and terms. This condemnation, of course, prejudged the only decision that would now really count, that of the Holy See. But it was enough to ostracise Fénelon himself and his courageous friends, Beauvilliers, Chevreuse and the others. Only his high rank and his great responsibilities, so soon to be taken from him, as well as his appeal to the Holy See, can have saved him from a fate comparable to those of La Combe and the hidden, but by no means forgotten, prisoner of Vaugirard.

2

The hour had come for Fénelon's famous " disgrace." The word " disgrace " sounds to us a strange word to use in connection with an order to a bishop to remain in his own diocese, but the situation has to be understood in the light of the customs of the day and of Fénelon's distinguished position at Court, with the household of the Princes and among the Clergy of France. In particular, we must remember his own delicate sensibilities and subtle ambitions. Though these were held in check by the quality of the spirituality which had caused him to grow in the always difficult pursuit of the way of self-abnegation and abandonment to God's providence, a decree of banishment even to his own diocese, where in fact, he worked the greater part of the year, was like the flick of the royal whip in his face.

Fénelon himself precipitated the royal decision to exile him to Cambrai by asking the King's permission to leave the country and go to Rome, there to defend his book in person. In Rome he would live in complete retirement and return to France, he told the King, the moment the Papal verdict had been pronounced.

He tried to see Mme. de Maintenon in order to enlist her help with the King, but she did not have the courage to meet him face to face. " Nothing of this really concerns me, and I know not why I mix myself up with it," she wrote to Godet. So he had to write to her: " Nothing is left to me now, Madame, but to seek the liberty to start from Rome. Only with great regret do I ask this; but everything has been done to force me, against my will, to this last resort. I cannot but go on making the most humble, the most respectful, the strongest requests to the King for this leave. I shall travel on guard against myself, in no spirit of contention, to un-deceive myself if I am wrong, and to seek what I cannot find in France: I mean someone with whom the matter can be ended. It is not only a question of my book; it is a question of myself, since I must be thoroughly undeceived about my book, if I am wrong. . . . If they intend to maintain, without any proof, that my teaching is nothing but novelty and error, before the rightful authority has decided the question, then they are presupposing the question at issue in order to persuade the King into action and to overcome me. In that case, there is nothing more for me to do but to adore God and carry my cross. But those who are trying to put a term to this business by sheer act of authority are in fact beginning, not ending, the affair. As for myself, Madame, I hope, not in my own powers, but in God's grace, that I shall only show, whatever happens, patience and strength in regard to those who attack me, docility and unreserved submission to the Church, zeal and attachment to the King, and gratitude and respect for you until my last breath."

As for Noailles on whose benevolent, but vacillating, policy the King's anxious wife was now entirely relying, Fénelon neatly said in his letter: " *Loin de me plaindre de lui, je le plains* "—" far from feeling pity for myself in regard to him, I pity him."

There could, of course, be no question of Louis or Bossuet allowing the Archbishop to plead his own case with the Pope. The personal esteem in which he was held by the Pope together with many of the Cardinals, as well as the support of the Jesuits and other Orders, would weigh the balance too heavily against the unpopular Gallicans.

Louis had, in fact, already decided. He had caused an account of the *Maximes* to be drafted by the Bishops, and after some hesitation had had it delivered to the Nuncio. On 1st August, he refused Fénelon's permission to go to Rome and ordered him to live in his diocese, there to remain without returning to Paris and to the Court.

That same day, Fénelon wrote to Mme. de Maintenon: " I shall leave here to-morrow, Friday, to obey the King. I would not even pass through Paris, but for the need to find a person ready to go to Rome and willing to make this journey. I return to Cambrai, my heart filled with submission, zeal, thanksgiving and boundless attachment to the King. My greatest sorrow is to have caused him all this worry and to have displeased him. . . . I am willing to be ever more crushed. I ask His Majesty only one thing. It is that the diocese of Cambrai, which is innocent, shall not suffer from the faults imputed to me. . . . All that is left to me, Madame, is to ask your forgiveness for all the trouble I have caused you. God alone knows how much I feel this. I shall never cease to pray that He Himself will entirely fill your heart. All my life I shall deeply feel your kindnesses to me of old—as deeply as though I had never lost them. My respectful attachment to you, Madame, will never lessen."

Beneath the courtly language, Fénelon was surely expressing in this letter a real feeling of personal affection for one of the two women who had so profoundly affected his destiny. Mme. de Maintenon persuaded herself that all she had done had been done in kindness. "I have always believed that kindness helps the cause of truth. . . . M. de Cambrai will be better off in his diocese than he would have been at Rome. . . . It would be disagreeable if the Pope, causing the book to be examined, called its author to Rome to explain himself; this is not according to our customs, and the King would not stand for it." But her conscience pricked her so badly that her health was affected. Even her tactless husband laughed at her for being apparently ready to die over the business. Louis had, no doubt, been already sufficiently annoyed by his grandson throwing himself on his knees before him to beg his beloved master be spared this disgrace. "The purity of the Faith is at stake," his grandfather sententiously told him. "It is not a matter about which I can dispense favours."

The storm threatened Beauvilliers and the whole of the young Prince's household which had remained faithful to Fénelon, who still nominally retained his position in it. But for the moment they, together with Fénelon's friends at Court were spared, despite the King's severe warning to the Duke who in fact, while defending Fénelon, had taken the personal resolution not to read Fénelon's now censured books—a resolution which immensely edified Mme. de Maintenon so that she gave it to Saint-Cyr as an example for the community there. Writing to Beauvilliers from Cambrai, Fénelon said: "What afflicts me most is displeasing the King and exposing you to losing his favour. Sacrifice me, and remember that my own interests are of no account compared with yours. . . . I will try to do my duty, even though the injuries done to me spoil the good that I could do in a place where the needs of religion are great. I pray that God will forgive those who have made it so hard for me to carry out my tasks with profit."

The King in the end had written to the Pope directly. The relevant papers on both sides were despatched to Rome, and each party was arranging for its agents to act on behalf of the principals in France. With the situation as it was, it might have been expected that at long last an armed truce would have been declared between the two great prelates mobilised for the solemn and final test. But not a bit of it. The last vestige of discretion in managing this scandalous business was thrown off, and the final rounds were to be fought in the fullest glare of publicity.

CHAPTER FOUR

APPEAL TO ROME

INNOCENT XII, a wise, pacific and reforming Pontiff, over eighty years of age, would gladly have been spared the task forced on to him by Fénelon, Bossuet and Louis XIV. Seeing that the argument continued between the great prelates of France, the Pope had hoped against hope that the issue would be conveniently settled there. But once it became clear that matters were going from bad to worse, he made up his mind to have the whole question examined with the thoroughness and impartiality suited to the highest traditions of the Holy See, whatever this might cost in delays and in French anger.

Bossuet took it for granted that there would be a quick, snap judgment which, naturally, would be a resounding condemnation of his enemy—was not Fénelon considered a heretic even in his own diocese, he pointed out. Fénelon, too, naturally wished for an early decision, though Bossuet accused him, in the face of the evidence, of trying to delay proceedings. The Pope, undeterred by these manœuvres, appointed eight theological consultors in September, 1697. It was believed that the original division of opinion favoured Bossuet, but when the Pope decided to add two more consultors, Cardinal Fabroni, who favoured Fénelon, managed to secure that the two new nominations should be favourable to Fénelon. The ten consultors were to examine the propositions taken from the *Maximes*, without reference to any further explanations from the contending parties. In due course, they would report their findings to the Cardinals of the Congregation of the Holy Office.

But though the final decision seemed now to be safely in the keeping of men who would not be browbeaten by the furies of Bossuet, nor, for that matter, enchanted by the subtle reasonings of

Fénelon, tremendous campaigns were set in motion in France and Rome to influence public opinion and, if possible, those in whose hands Roman judgment lay.

In his determination to use any means to force an early and final triumph, the Eagle of Meaux appointed two agents to act for him in Rome, the Abbé Phelippeaux, a priest of Jansenist tendencies, and the Abbé Bossuet, nephew of the Bishop and pupil of Phelippeaux. The Abbé Bossuet, we shall see, was perhaps the strangest of all the personalities to play their part in this story. On his side, Fénelon used a relation of his own and his Vicar-General in Cambrai, the Abbé de Chanterac, a priest of the highest integrity and extremely like his master in disposition and piety. If there is a judgment in these matters, nothing could prove it better than the way in which the majestically but ruthlessly sweeping Bossuet was served in Rome by an unprincipled ecclesiastical intriguer, while the gentle, if increasingly strained, Fénelon was served by a servant of God schooled in his own idealism.

But the struggle to bring pressure on the Roman judges, and to resist that pressure, was not enacted behind the scenes in Rome only; it was openly fought, with the world as judge, in France, in the form of a veritable and mounting flood of polemical writings, launched by Bossuet and answered by Fénelon. It has to be read to be believed. Bossuet attacked with all his fury in grand, rounded, rhetorical prose, while Fénelon answered with subtlety and finesse, but also with the sting and vehemence that never work in so deadly a fashion than when a delicate sensitivity, master of the written word, finds itself at bay. It was the bludgeon, handled by a master of timing, and the frail, but lightning-quick, rapier once again. Everything, but truth and fairness, were on Bossuet's side. He was the aggressor. He did not scruple to make public papers and letters confided to him on terms of "confessional secrecy" by Mme. Guyon or sent privately to Mme. de Maintenon when Fénelon was pouring his heart out to her. Behind him were the Court, the ministers and the police of France ensuring that his every word had its fullest effect on public opinion. Fénelon was not only defending himself against avalanches of accusations—and defence takes up much more space and labour than attack—but he had to face every obstacle that could be put in his way, the authorities endeavouring to censor his writings, to prevent their circulation and even to forbid their being printed in France.

It is impossible here to quote at length from these endless polemics, while to summarise them would kill the palpitating life within them. But here we may give an early instance of Fénelon's manner.

"Would to God, My Lord, that you had not forced me out of the silence I have kept so long as I possibly could. God, who searches hearts, knows with what docility I wished to keep silence until the common Father had spoken—how I was ready to condemn my book at the first sign from him. Suppose, My Lord, as much as you please that you are called to be the defender of the Church against me, as Saint Augustine was in his time against the heretics of the day. But a bishop who submits his work and keeps silent after that submission is no Pelagius, no Julian." Or again: "You say ' this new spirituality burdens the Church with dazzling letters, pastoral instructions, replies filled with errors.' What right have you to call yourself the Church? The Church has not spoken; it is you who speak before the Church. . . . It is not the new spirituality, but the old, that I wish to support. I do not fear to say to you what you have said against me in your first book, ' the Church is watching,' watching to make sure that the doctrine you spread does not prevail. You openly attack the pre-eminence of love over hope. You treat as ' pious excess ' against the essence of love the aspirations of Saint Paul and of Moses. You call extravagances of love the conditional sacrifices made by all who were greatest and most saintly in the Church. You destroy acts of perfect contrition, that is when we are sorry for our sins, not just because of the happiness we hope for, but because of the justice we love for its own sake. You leave no real middle way between the supernatural virtues and vicious acts. Between your love mixed with hope and vicious culpability no innocent action is possible. . . . What may be thought of your motives? I am ' that dear author whom I carry in my bosom '—yes, but only to throw him with Molinos into the abyss of Quietism. You go about shedding tears for me everywhere, and you rend me as you shed them."

Fénelon's writings, surreptitiously despatched to Rome to avoid the police, were copied and printed in Italy and Rome with

increasing effect on public opinion, the more so in that the Eagle
of Meaux, so long accustomed to soar unchallenged over the length
and breadth of France, was for the first time finding his match and
being driven to evasive action so as to avoid his opponent's surer,
straighter flight. Bossuet was no longer dominant when he was
forced to write: "After this, My Lord, I have no more to say to
you. If there is anything in your writings of importance which I
have not yet answered, I shall do so by other means. As for letters,
write as many as you please; keep Court and town amused; let
your spirit and your eloquence be admired, and bring back the
graces of the *Lettres Provinciales*. I can no longer be a party to the
show you seem to wish to make before the world." From the
proud Bossuet there came the admission that "M. de Cambrai has
spirit enough to terrify." But it was a different spirit which
prompted Fénelon's lament: "Both of us, you and I, have become
the object of the mockery of the impious. We are causing anguish
among the good. God will judge the true author of these evils. . . .
Let others be men; this will not be a matter of surprise; but that
the ministers of Jesus Christ, these angels of the Churches, should
play such scenes before a profane and incredulous world, this it is
which calls for tears of blood. Much happier would we have been
had we, instead of waging these wars of words, been ever catechising in our dioceses and teaching the poor villagers to fear and
to love God."

Meanwhile in Rome, Nephew Bossuet (who had not as yet
been ordained priest, though later he was to become a bishop) was
bribing all and sundry and pulling every string in his uncle's favour
in a milieu described by himself as follows: "I believe that no
doctrinal matter should be brought up here; they are too ignorant
and too much sold to favour and intrigue . . . all questions of dogma
embarrass them, given the ignorance in which they find themselves.
. . . All is ignorance or politics." Even of the Pope, Nephew Bossuet
wrote, after the verdict, that it was a miracle that anything was
achieved with him. "But for him Fénelon would have been condemned as strongly as Molinos." With so low opinion of ecclesiastical affairs in the entourage of an excellent and well-governing
Pontiff, it was hardly surprising that the nephew drove the uncle
to measures which cannot but for ever soil the reputation of so

great a churchman. For the moment the uncle was urging the King to take what opportunity there was to press his views on Rome, to hint that time was up and that the royal pleasure would not stand for delay, and even to catechise the Pope himself through the Nuncio on the evil of Fénelon's book. How surprised Innocent must have been to find that Louis XIV had suddenly developed a talent for advanced theological learning and language—and how grimly amused by the thought.

But Rome stood firm in face of all the pressure. Week by week, the Consultors studied the questions before them for up to six or seven hours at a time. It took them four months, from September, 1697, to January, 1698, to reach the stage for a vote. The Consultors found themselves equally divided, five for and five against the *Maximes*. The famous work which Bossuet had denounced as heretical and endangering the very Church itself turned out after prolonged examination by the Pope's closest advisers to be impossible to condemn at all, since on an equal division by the Consultors the matter would be normally dropped. But the case was considered so important and French pressure so strong that Innocent decided to nominate two Cardinals to preside at further examinations in the hope of coming to a positive decision. All efforts were in vain. The equal division remained, even though the five unfavourable to Fénelon changed and narrowed the grounds on which they based their opposition.

Nephew Bossuet was forced to report to his uncle that the Pope was saying that the matter was by no means clear after all. It was a terrible blow. Bossuet had been playing for the full stakes. His whole prestige, authority and, to do him justice, his passionate zeal to root out danger and heresy from the fixed, classical pattern of the Church as he saw it, had been wholly committed.

Something must be done to terminate these intolerable delays and vacillations at the Court of Rome.

2

Gesta Dei per Francos might have been Bossuet's cry at this moment when Rome seemed to be faltering in the crusade for right thinking; and he did in fact write to his nephew: " It is

God's cause; I have truth only in mind." The great purpose of saving the Church of France from the enemy within, all the more sinister and dangerous because so subtle and so holy, surely now justified any means to achieve the end—and with the two Bossuets "any means" carried far.

Nephew Bossuet thought he knew the way. Let Fénelon's personal reputation be attacked and openly besmirched. The way did not seem difficult. "You must not hesitate to send me everything that will show the attachment of M. de Cambrai for Mme. Guyon and Père La Combe, as well as their teaching on moral questions."

We have seen that always lurking at the back of the attack on Quietism was the thought that the teaching was the cover for impure conduct. But it was a daring conception indeed to bring —even indirectly—the Archbishop of Cambrai, the Preceptor of the Princes, the pious, sweet, mortified, delicate nature of Fénelon, who, as a priest, said that his temptations were anything but those of the flesh, within the range of such scandal. And yet if it came off, not only would Fénelon, but the whole Court cenacle, the whole conspiracy, be utterly ruined. The nightmare of a France of the future in the hands of the spiritual revivalists would be dissipated.

But to ruin the moral reputation of a Fénelon was not quite as easy as to ruin that of a Molinos or even a Mme. Guyon. If Nephew Bossuet was too coarse-grained to see this, the great Bossuet who knew all the facts and who had intimately known Fénelon all his life as friend, disciple and fellow-bishop was inexcusable for allowing his agents to go forward with such dirty work.

La Combe was still languishing in the prison-castle of Lourdes where his treatment seems to have varied, though any seventeenth-century French prison would never err on the side of comfort. A 1693 letter to Mme. Guyon tells us enough about his fate: "The violin and the harp, the drum and the flute are silent. Such instruments for fine concerts hang on the willow trees of my exile, where I am condemned to the mines, for I am reduced by an admirable providence to work in the gardens from morning till night, having no other study than the cultivation of the earth, nor ordinary meditation but that of plants. Apart from this, everything is reduced to the life of a brute." He had fellow-Quietists with him in gaol, and the little community had, it seems, the opportunity of following from afar the struggle and faith of their prophetess, Mme. Guyon.

It was time to wake the prisoner up from such rude peace as his melancholy lot afforded him. Into his cell came new examiners to bully a mind already gravely weakened by suffering and captivity. We do not know what exactly happened, but out of it all one piece of evidence was extracted from him, a letter dated January, 1698, and addressed to the local bishop. " As for my morals, in confusion I have worked things here in such a way as to give spiritual advice, though to few people, but to some of the other sex. . . . I have said that good and saintly souls are sometimes delivered to the trials of impurities. . . . I have fallen into excesses and miseries of the kind mentioned above. I confess it with sorrow and tears."

Did this uncompromising idealist write it? It expressly contradicts his previously stated sentiments about Mme. Guyon. Did he write it freely? Was it a forgery? We do not know. But what does it matter? Even if it had been freely written and sincerely meant, of what value was it as evidence, save of the weakness of a maltreated, half-mad prisoner in a distant castle, who had not seen Mme. Guyon for eleven years and never seen or communicated with Fénelon? What possible bearing could it have on the great issues staged in Paris and Rome?

But the Eagle of Meaux pounced on it as a rare prize. He wrote to his nephew: " Something new will soon be out. It is a piece of writing of Père La Combe, in which he confesses his impure illusions. The liaison between Mme. Guyon with this priest who was her director will be shown, as also his liaison with M. de Cambrai. M. de Paris is sending Père Rollet the declaration of Père La Combe, a horrifying one." It is incredible! La Combe's sins in prison (if the confession is to be trusted—and this is hardly the case) are referred back more than a decade to Mme. Guyon; and, in the context of a poor prisoner whom Fénelon had never even seen, Mme. Guyon is associated with the defendant in the case! La Combe—Guyon—Fénelon; Fénelon—Guyon—La Combe; what does the order matter? Why bother to establish the nature of the link? Under the putrid cloud of moral suspicion, any association was good enough to damn one's rival.

La Combe, having yielded this evidence to his enemies, was taken from Lourdes castle and brought to Vincennes. There he wrote—or was made to write—a letter to Mme. Guyon, dated 25th April, 1698, telling her " I recognise with sincerity that there was illusion, error and sin in certain things that with too much freedom happened between us; and I reject and detest all views and all behaviour which are not in keeping with the commandments of God and of the Church. . . . Once again I beg you, for the love of Jesus Christ, to have recourse with me to the one remedy of penance and to wipe away, by a truly repentant and regular life in all things, the evil impressions caused in the Church by our wrongful steps. Let us humbly confess our sins together before heaven and earth; let us blush only for having committed them and not for confessing them."

Copies of this letter were circulated for the edification of the public, and Mme. Guyon in Vaugirard knew of it. She wrote to the Duchess of Beauvilliers: " Prison must have turned his head; for how can one do such things, and, supposing they had been true, confess them? I presume the letter is false. . . . Letters like this are not circulated when the crimes are true; it is enough to authentify them and thus put them beyond dispute."

The Curé of Saint-Sulpice, against whose spiritual services Mme. Guyon had more than once protested, has given an account of the interview at Vaugirard when he and Noailles (the latter surely rather uncomfortable) brought the letter to the prisoner. The Archbishop, it seems, began by trying to get a confession out of the prisoner. Failing, as many tougher men than he had failed, he faced her with La Combe's letter. " She changed colour," the Curé reports. Why should she have changed colour, if she already knew all about the letter, as we know she did? She was well up to the trick of forgery. Is the Curé an accurate reporter? It hardly looks like it. Anyway, he goes on to tell us that Mme. Guyon confessed to having "embraced" La Combe when he returned from travelling. Possibly; but also possibly not. " Having changed colour," he tells us, " she examined the letter closely and with care. She suggested that the priest's writing might have been forged. She said two things: one, that perhaps the letter had been drawn from him by torture; two, that his head had possibly been turned." All attempts to make her confess more than the above " embracing " were, according to this report, fruitless.

Both letters of Père La Combe were duly sent to Rome and duly presented to Innocent XII in an Italian translation by Nephew Bossuet who was in the habit of catechising the old man who was Supreme Pontiff. Abbé Bossuet had written in delight to his uncle: " These two pieces of evidence will make more impression than twenty theological demonstrations. That's the sort of argument we most need." But it is interesting that the Bishop of Meaux who did not hesitate to use this kind of evidence in Rome never dared mention it in his famous and formidable *Relation on Quietism* in which every possible accusation, including much taken from material entrusted to him " under confessional secrecy," as Mme. Guyon called it, was used. Did he recoil from underlining the link between Fénelon and a woman accused by her closest priest-friend, before she met Fénelon, of misdemeanours? Did he for a moment believe it?

Happily, good Popes know too much about the strange and devious ways of mankind to be unduly impressed by evidence of this kind. In Rome they were saying that it needed seventy-two sound witnesses to condemn a bishop, and Chanterac, Fénelon's agent, complained that the Romans knew a good deal more about the intrigues of the French Court than he could possibly know himself. But in France the fresh scandal had a double effect—on Mme. Guyon and on Fénelon.

For Mme. Guyon it meant what she called " her last extremities " —imprisonment in the redoubtable Bastille where she was placed in the second room of the Tower of the Treasury. She was, of course, a prisoner drawn from the ranks of the Court and nobility, but the cold, the thick damp walls, the lack of light and the heavily padlocked doors are no pleasanter even if the room is a little larger and a cartful of one's own furniture has been placed in it. It is doubtful if these amenities greatly softened her sense of " the outcry and horrible unleashing of feelings against me," but " if, O Lord, you wish to make me a fresh spectacle before men and angels, may your holy Will be done! " Again, she was dragged down for examinations by the police, this time to worm out of her more details of the dark intimacies between herself and La Combe. She stood firm, as she had always done. " Mme. Guyon is stubborn," complained Bossuet. The fact did not, of course, prevent stories of her confessions from spreading as far as Rome. It was given out there, as Chanterac wrote to Fénelon, that " La Combe has deposed that he misbehaved with her, and that she herself now admits dishonest things taking place between them, at least kisses and embraces, and people do not doubt that all the rest will soon follow." A month later, it had reached the rumour that " La Combe had committed the worst crimes with her, and already she is confessing a part, even the grossest things against purity." On his side, La Combe, under police pressure, had confessed sleeping with Mme. Guyon for fifteen nights, and even Mme. de Maintenon, moved by the hysteria for which she had her share of responsibility, apparently took this seriously enough to suggest to Noailles that Mme. Guyon should be confronted with him, " since it is he himself who says that he had passed fifteen nights with her."

Poor La Combe! The long captivity of this highly sensitive and emotional priest was already driving him to complete madness and to the lunatic asylum where he lingered on for twenty years. Perhaps his excitable nature with its burning idealism accounts in part for this fate, though when he and Mme. Guyon were free, it was La Combe who was the less bizarre and the better balanced. At any rate, posterity owes him the acknowledgment that he was always deeply faithful to his spiritual vocation, that no one would have thought him mad had he not finally gone mad under persecution, and that few men have suffered more distressingly in the name of religion, for so little advantage or profit to themselves, whether at the time or in the eyes of posterity. His is certainly the saddest case in this story—sad until the end, for his enemies took care to keep secret the news of his madness so that his final " confessions " might not be discredited.

For Fénelon the suspicions raised against his association with the supposedly guilty couple led to him being hit where he would feel it most—by injuring those he loved dearest. It was Mme. de Maintenon, stabilised against Fénelon at last, it seems, by the stories of La Combe and Mme. Guyon and the publication of Bossuet's *Relation*, which we reserve for the next chapter, who pressed for action. " Yesterday," she wrote to Noailles on 24th May, 1698,

" I spoke to the King on the great affair. He wants to remove M. de Cambrai and all who are around the Princes; but he is trying to put it off, and this because of hurting M. de Beauvilliers. I said all I could to push him on, without however showing a keenness on the subject that might have scandalised him." And a few days later: " Every day I see more and more how I have been tricked by those people to whom I gave all my confidence without gaining theirs." And here perhaps she touched the core of the matter for her: " If they had been acting with simplicity, why did they not let me in on all their mysteries? If they feared to tell me, is it not a proof that they had a firm plan and that they were making use of my friendship and my credit in order to establish this novelty at Court?" She was seeing it all in terms of wounded feminine vanity.

The King's wife had no need to worry. Louis made a clean sweep at the end of the month of Fénelon's intimate relations and friends in the Princes' Household, de Langeron, his greatest friend (known as the " little Abbé "), de Beaumont, his nephew (the " big Abbé "), the Père de Valois, the Jesuit confessor, Fénelon's brother, of the Guards, Dupuy (known as the " bon Put "), and the under-governors. Though they all depended on their salaries and the King was asked to leave them their nominal appointments carrying the salaries ; he refused.

Thus ended one of the most interesting pedagogical experiments in history. From the spoilt, bad-tempered little Prince, Fénelon and his friends had made a now sixteen-year-old second heir to the throne whose virtues were contemporarily described as universally admired and included " chastity, charity and simplicity." Neither he nor his brothers had ever heard of Quietism and the affairs of Mme. Guyon, and no one thought that Fénelon and those who worked with him had done anything but conscientiously devote themselves to their duties. But all this was disregarded; and, out of Fénelon's hands, the Prince's character deteriorated, for Beauvilliers lacked Fénelon's subtlety.

Fénelon himself was nominally spared for the time being, a matter which greatly annoyed Bossuet, though of course he could no longer exercise his functions. The Eagle had his own plans for giving Fénelon's job to his friend, the Bishop of Mirepoix. " I know nothing as yet about the principal position," he wrote to him. " You know my views and the steps I have taken. I am keeping on at it, and nothing would give me greater pleasure. A hundred times a day I wish you were here so as to help us in a matter which demands so much attention and thought." :" As thunder follows lightning, there will be a new preceptor," he had also written. And he consoled himself with the thought " At any rate, the King has certainly declared that M. de Cambrai will not return," and then reported that Fénelon's friends still believed that they would return " more glorious than ever: they count on the death of three or four persons, and among them they place me." One somehow wishes that history might have spared us this further evidence of Bossuet pulling strings for his friends from the spoils of his enemy: surely the least delicate of sanctimonious minds would have avoided forwarding personal interests through a quarrel ostensibly based on such great issues.

What of the Duc de Beauvilliers himself at the summit of the ladder of honour and responsibility in the Kingdom, the one just man, the King's friend and the person Mme. de Maintenon could no longer pardon? He, like Chevreuse and the others of the Court cenacle, had remained true to Fénelon, though he was shaken about Fénelon's judgment and wisdom, though not about his goodness.

The way of the world was going against him, and the climbers were thinking it well to avoid such falling stars. In their isolation the dukes and duchesses remained as dignified as they had been in their hour of splendour. Beauvilliers's place was coveted by the Duc de Noailles, the Archbishop's brother and the father-in-law of Mme. de Maintenon's niece who had just married the Comte d'Ayen, Noailles's eldest son. Mme. de Maintenon pressed for Beauvilliers's dismissal in favour of her powerful connection—we know how much she valued the high ennoblement of her own family, for her secret marriage to the King (Fénelon was among those who advised against its ever being made public) was more of a moral accident than a cementing of family greatness. For once the blood royal showed itself nobler than the *parvenu* blood of the d'Aubignés. Louis, in distress at the thought of losing so good a servant, had recourse to the doubtful advice of the Archbishop whose own interests were so bound up with the fall of Beauvilliers. And it is a pleasure to set against the smallness of a Bossuet the integrity of Archbishop de Noailles who, despite all temptation and many specious excuses, insisted on Beauvilliers's integrity and advised the King that the recent dismissals were enough to protect the Princes from the Quietist danger. Louis was genuinely glad to be able to keep his best servant and Noailles kept his honesty dark from Bossuet. The King's grandson, to remain under the " good Duke's " care, would at least continue to be formed in the school of Fénelon.

In Rome itself, the superficial reaction, at any rate, to the stories propagated by Fénelon's enemies was typically Italian. Chanterac's letters showed that they were causing more amusement than indignation. The story, for example, that Fénelon had called Mme. Guyon " *mon amie* " worried Fénelon who warned Chanterac to remember the usual Italian meaning of the word *amica*. Cardinal Ferrari, to whom the point was passed on, laughed at the idea that the Italians did not understand the French language, and added that anyway these were paltry matters of little relevance to the *Maximes* with which alone Rome was concerned.

There was much more indignation about the persecution of Fénelon's friends. " There is no wrath like that of a woman," they were saying in reference to Mme. de Maintenon. Such efforts to prejudge Rome's decisions " do not give a very fine idea of the submission to be rendered to the Holy See." When Chanterac saw the Pope himself in June and told His Holiness that his master was ready to resign his Archbishopric and do penance for the rest of his life if anything could be proved against his faith and morals, Innocent held up both hands in protest and with great solemnity insisted that the Holy See would only act according to the inspiration of the Holy Spirit. In another audience, Innocent muttered aloud: " They have expelled his nephew," and later, " they have expelled his kin," and later still, " they have expelled his friends," as though the old man could not believe it possible.

But below the gay Italian surface there is seriousness, and these good signs did not blind Fénelon's agent to the dangers of the French campaign in building up a picture of a great churchman with a questionable past where a *dévote* woman was concerned. Fénelon, the bishop, was less vulnerable than the priest Molinos had been, but Molinos, the favourite of the Pope himself at the time, had been crushed by his enemies from one day to the next. It was imperative, thought Chanterac, that Fénelon should defend himself by an absolute condemnation of everything for which Mme. Guyon had stood. Stories of all kinds were current and worse was expected to come, whether from Mme. Guyon, other imprisoned Quietists in France, and, maybe, from Fénelon himself.

But Fénelon had never been ready to denounce his friend and he would not do anything now without drawing careful distinctions about what might have been wrong with her and what he knew was not wrong.

"Will they say *anathema Guyoniae* as they said *anathema Nestorio*?" he wrote to Chanterac. "Is this the way to talk about a person who has submitted? Do they insist on this from me in order to brand me and satisfy the ambitions of those against me? I have declared that I would do in this matter whatever the Pope, my superior, requires. Can one be more submissive, more remote from all stubbornness. . . . If they condemn me, their force will crush, especially in France, all who stand by the true meaning of that virtue [love or charity]. All good mystics will be decried, and the Schools themselves will be changed. If only Rome would make a decision, or impose silence, all would be finished in eight days." Mme. Guyon, he insisted, was simply an excuse for throwing dust in people's eyes about the real issue which was " pure love."

His cross, as he called it, must have been appalling to bear. He was outstanding for the spiritual idealism of his life which had been marked by a conduct as priest and bishop far above what was customary even among the better clergy of his time. He was the champion of the Holy See. His delicacy of nature made him especially sensitive about anything that smacked of the coarse, let alone of the kind of stories being spread about. Yet he could not but observe the limitless malice among the small men and the thwarted righteousness among the great. The persecution he was suffering could only strengthen his conviction about the real cause and nature of the persecution Mme. Guyon and others had suffered. And from this distance in time one cannot help reflecting on the strange way in which those who had accepted the spiritual path of

self-abnegation and abandonment to the will of God had been led
to practise their teaching to the last drop.

However, the intrigues of the King's supporters under Bossuet's
lead had not deflected in any way the patient labours of those
officially responsible for the examination of the *Maximes*. Chanterac
filled his letters to Fénelon with the latest news of the proceedings.
The consultors remained equally divided in their views, and those
favourable to the prelate were engaged in trying to narrow and
clarify the points which troubled the other five, it being generally
agreed that all depended on the way " pure love " was explained,
since the whole of Fénelon's doctrine flowed from this. Twice a
week, they reported to the Cardinals of the Holy Office in session
at the Minerva and once a week to the Pope himself. Chanterac
reported that matters were going well. He told how the Pope and
the Cardinals showed marked attention to the argument when
Fénelon's defenders were speaking. But constantly raised hopes of
a final vote and a decision by the Holy See were frustrated by the
impossibility of breaking down the equal division of opinion among
the experts.

The affair dragged on through 1698, and no one could say how
far the delays favoured either side, for if time allowed further spread
to the calumnies about Fénelon, it also allowed Rome to grow
more irritated by the French semi-political pressure and the pre-
judgments of a cause which, once referred to Rome, should not
have been publicly discussed either in Church or Catholic State.

CHAPTER FIVE

ODIUM THEOLOGICUM

THE LONG delays with the tale they told of the uncertainty of an issue which to Bossuet had been crystal-clear from the beginning, had led the great man in mid-1698 not only to try to ferret out scandals about Fénelon, but to make the mistake for which posterity can least easily forgive him.

Nephew Bossuet had not missed any chance of driving him into a kind of kill-or-cure action. He had cleverly played on his weakness, by hinting, for example, that Fénelon's genius as a writer added to his reputation and was said to have inspired his uncle's jealousy. Yet how easily the friend of Mme. Guyon could be crushed, how vulnerable he was! A little detail—and Bossuet had been told so much about the true history!

Under this kind of pressure for the whole truth, Bossuet had, towards the end of 1697, worked on a book in Latin, as one might a book to be kept from the public, because of its confidential material *De Quietismo in Gallia Refutato*, "Quietism refuted in France." The manuscript was not to be circulated except privately and to those whom it concerned. Copies were not to be made. Nephew Bossuet had not paid much attention to such instructions, and had had the copies he needed made. Even so, it was not good enough ammunition for his purpose, and, with affairs in Rome not improving, what was needed was a French version of the substance of that Latin monograph, to be given to the whole world. Those facts, cunningly inter-knit with artfully suggested insinuations and all expressed with that oratorical righteousness that a great preacher knew so well how to make telling, would do the trick. Bossuet, whose early precautions show that he understood well enough what he was doing, could not resist the suggestion. On 26th June, 1698, he published the famous *Relation on Quietism*, which the indulgent Cardinal de Bausset described as " the most afflicting monument of the controversy."

The facts on which this public attack by one Catholic bishop on another (under judgment, but not judged) was based, were Mme. Guyon's autobiography and other manuscript writings, delivered in her innocence to a would-be friend and judge under what she called " confessional secrecy "; the letters which Fénelon had written to Bossuet when, as a trusting disciple dealing with a father-in-God and a friend, he could still open his heart to him; and the long letter written to Mme. de Maintenon to explain, almost in despair, why he could not approve Bossuet's attack in the name of mysticism on Mme. Guyon—a private letter handed over to Bossuet by Godet, with its owner's consent, at the price, literally of damnation with which Bossuet threatened her if she did not consent.

We know the nature of Mme. Guyon's early outpourings, damnable evidence against her in the hands of an enemy, matter for gross laughter if put before a hostile world. We have seen, too, that Fénelon's mind was of that dialectical type which instinctively makes out the worst case against himself the more impressively to refute it. In his spirituality, too, his instinct, especially when he felt certain of his ground, was to say and to protest too much, to express his readiness to change, apologise, submit, do penance, with an over-heated flamboyance. In private letters to those he most fully trusted he was of course least on his guard and most apt to gesticulate with words and emotions. Apart, therefore, from the propriety of using this private correspondence and the secret spiritual papers in a work destined for the general public, such material could be made in Bossuet's supremely able hands to sound damning.

Bossuet did not fail. The story he had to tell the world was of the way in which an otherwise great and irreproachable Churchman had been bewitched by a dangerous and heretical woman, caught out in her folly by instance after instance in her own writings. Having been thus bewitched, that prelate was prepared to defy his fellow-bishops and divide the Church and episcopacy of France.

Anyone could make fun of poor Mme. Guyon, untutored and

emotional as she was, if they overlooked her goodness, misunderstood the stark and traditional lines of a contemplative spirituality marred by the extravagance of language and imageries faithfully confessed because she had been told under obedience to omit nothing, and judged her sufferings and persecutions as partly morbid and mostly well deserved. One needed only to string together, with the appropriate horrified comments, the stories of blasphemous analogies and dark possibilities, the whole ending with the sinister suggestion in regard to Père La Combe's mad revelations, and say: "The time has come when God wills that this union be entirely revealed; I need say no more." Anyone could have made a good job of ridiculing this woman on the basis of her own writings, but as it happened Bossuet, to whom she had entrusted those writings in the highest confidence and who had himself examined her again and again, given her the sacraments and found her guiltless of ill-intention in faith and morals, was the last man with the right to do it.

But Bossuet, who in private called Mme. Guyon Héloise and Fénelon Abelard and in his book called her a new Priscilla and him a new Montanus, had to use a little more ingenuity, but not very much more, to tell a story of Fénelonian inconsistency, hesitation, evasion, bad faith, from the private letters of a man of dual nature. How many others would stand the test of seeing their own most private letters raised in their own lifetime to the one-sided judgment of a genius in the course of a bitter controversy on the most delicate and personal of subjects? Pure love, like carnal, we repeat, has its privacies and its secrets. How easy for Bossuet to pose as the simple, innocent man, utterly incapable of guile or faction, finding himself, quite against his will, of course, the blunt champion of the imperilled Church in the face of the delusions of a woman and of the subtlety and less than candour of her highly-placed priest-protector. From the *Moyen Court* and worse to the *Maximes des Saints* the path was deadly straight.

Bossuet, foiled where it was a question of abstract doctrine, had chosen to fight on the much more hopeful issue of facts and personalities. His nephew had told him that one piece of dirt was worth twenty theological propositions in this business. He, with an air of innocence, had gathered the dirt together, carefully sieved it from its context, complexity and character, dressed it with his incomparable gift of eloquence and style, and exposed it to the truly innocent: the public, from the King himself who believed every word of it and ordered it to be read for the edification of his grandson, to every man and woman able to read. In the circumstances, the book was only too easy to believe.

Mme. de Maintenon, who had once carried the *Moyen Court* in her pocket and introduced the good widow to her beloved convent-school, wrote to Noailles: " M. de Meaux's book makes a great noise here. People can talk of nothing else. The whole world now knows the truth. Mme. Guyon's follies keep them amused. The book is short, lively and well done. People lend it to one another, snatch it from one another, and devour it. It has awoken the anger of the King because we let him make an archbishop like that. He is reproaching me bitterly. The whole trouble of this business will fall on me. . . . Our Court Quietists are abjuring Mme. Guyon almost as awkwardly as they had supported her. They are saying that M. de Meaux's book has opened their eyes, and that there is nothing in the book which does not come from them." In fact, much of it came from her, though she had no right to reveal it.

The publication of the *Relation*, together with the evidence given by La Combe in prison, had led, as we have seen, to the dismissal of Fénelon's friends from Court. In Bossuet's eyes, Fénelon was finished. " If he replies," he muttered, " I shall grind him to dust." We shall see.

2

When Bossuet threatened to grind Fénelon into dust, he may well have felt confident that his boast would never have to be put to the test. He could not have been so foolish as to suppose that his rival was incapable of an effective reply, for he must have realised that the forensic brilliance of his book laid it wide open to rebuttal when the whole truth was revealed; but he had good reason for hoping that no reply would be made.

The attempts to prevent Fénelon from printing and distributing his writings were being more effectively realised. The King's officers were mobilised for the purpose and the difficulties were

becoming unsurmountable. It was rumoured that the King insisted
on forbidding both Bossuet and Fénelon from adding further to the
episcopal scandal by further publications. Such an edict, given
immediately after the appearance of Bossuet's *Relation* would have
been fatally unfair to Fénelon, but, even so, Bossuet, hearing of the
rumour, grumbled angrily at the idea of both prelates being treated
in the same way. " All Paris felt scandalised yesterday," he wrote,
" about the prohibition against such writing which was said to be
applicable to both parties without distinguishing between us who
write to make the truth clear and those who only write to muddle
truth and fight it." A foretaste of the new model democracy of
our times!

But such physical difficulties did not trouble Fénelon half so
much as his conscience was doing. He believed that any further
public step he might now take in France would complete the ruin
of his friends at the Court and in the country. " The rest of my
friends," he wrote to Chanterac, " and they are my most precious
possession in the world, now only hold on by a hair—that was the
term used when I was assured that they would be lost if I continued
to write publicly in reply to M. de Paris." To the Pope himself
he wrote: " Most unhappy and unheard of is this kind of controversy, Most Holy Father. Bishops now join hands in mutual
destruction. Not a word can be uttered without its turning to
scandal. To gain the day or to be defeated are equally a matter
for mourning."

Such was Fénelon's state of mind when Chanterac began to send
back news of the effect produced in Rome by Bossuet's book. He
reported " the terrible impression even on people best disposed to
you. The moment your sincerity and piety can be questioned, your
teaching, yesterday viewed as the teaching of the saints, finds itself
enveloped in certain expressions that your enemies hold to be too
favourable to Quietist maxims so that it must become little by little
suspect and doubtful and your book will only find few and feeble
defenders."

" Every day," Chanterac wrote in another letter, " they add to
it all the new stories about Père La Combe and Mme. Guyon. He
has confessed having committed with her the worst crimes, and
already she has in part confessed even the grossest crimes against

purity." Rumours were put about in Rome that compromising letters between Fénelon and Mme. Guyon were being held back to use as a last resort—a would-be parallel, no doubt, with the Molinos case. But beyond this kind of story which might or might not be dangerous there were two points which even Chanterac and his best friends found it hard to answer. One was that, whatever the detailed rights and wrongs, Fénelon had behaved throughout in such a way as to find himself compromised in his personal reputation —and this was an impossible position for a great Bishop. The point was a source of extreme anguish for Chanterac himself who complained, not without justice, that Fénelon had not been frank with him. The undeniable parts of the *Relation*, which even so, as we now know, did not tell the whole story of the spiritual intimacy with Mme. Guyon, were strange news for Chanterac who had in fact been telling people in Rome that " M. de Cambrai had only seen Mme. Guyon three times in his life "—or so Nephew Bossuet said. Nor in his answers did Fénelon explain away his " hiding the heart of the affair " from his own agent. There is no doubt that there is something odd and left unexplained in what looked like a " bad conscience " in regard to his personal association with Mme. Guyon which runs through the whole story. Yet a " bad conscience " in the ordinary sense is impossible to square with Fénelon's moral integrity. It seems more like a kind of *pudeur*, very characteristic of the man, which throughout made him shy of publicly, or even privately, acknowledging an association which meant so much to him but could so easily be misunderstood and lead to trouble for both parties. If so, it had been an error of judgment for which he had to pay heavily.

The second point was the idea that Fénelon's *Maximes* was not really an honest investigation into mystical theology, but a veiled defence of Mme. Guyon whose writings Fénelon had never condemned. Chanterac kept harping on this and Fénelon kept on answering that he had always believed her books to be censurable in the natural meaning of their language: " Only that person's intention I excused—and then only in a secret memorandum which no one would have known anything about, had it not been published to cause scandal. Excusing her intentions alone, was that a crime ? If she seriously meant the visions and prophecies imputed to her, she is mad and her head is turned; in all this I see no trace of what I thought I saw in her; but whatever her extravagances, be she a devil incarnate, none of this touches me. My business is not with her person which I do not judge, but leave to the judgment of my superiors; nor with her printed books which I have always thought censurable in the true, proper, natural and only sense of the text; nor of her manuscripts which I have not read; nor of the monstrous visions attributed to her which no one can show me to have approved. I only defend my book, that is I submit it rather than defend it."

It was, in part, the old contradiction between the Mme. Guyon whom Fénelon had trained by Fénelon's presence and authority, and the Mme. Guyon known to Bossuet through her earlier writings. But Fénelon, having taken his line of loyalty at all costs to the woman he had known, was forced into a good deal of less than candour, a good deal of hedging, to maintain it.

Only at the centre of judgment was full objectivity being maintained. Chanterac saw the Pope again, and he seemed disinterested in the Guyon angle, indicating with a weary gesture towards Bossuet's book that he was growing tired of this long dispute. He did not think it necessary for Fénelon to be fetched to Rome, against the King's will, to explain himself further. Cardinal Casanate assured Chanterac once more that the Holy See was only dealing with the *Maximes* as a book to be judged for its doctrine, and once judgment had been pronounced the Pope could take action in France to settle the war of words and restore the Archbishop's credit in everything.

But whatever Fénelon's scruples, he really had no choice but to answer Bossuet's deadly attack, and Bossuet meanwhile had become so sure of himself that he did not object to the order given by the King on 8th July that Fénelon was not to be prevented from writing and publishing since it was unfair that he should be silenced while his enemies were able openly to attack him.

Practised now in the art of swift polemical controversy—he must have written about half a million words in the course of two years —Fénelon produced his *Réponse à l'écrit intitulé Relation sur le Quietisme* ("Answer to the Relation on Quietism") after only three weeks of work. In fact, it appeared so rapidly that in many parts of

Europe the answer forestalled the attack. Even so, it was a substantial work of some 50,000 words.

Fénelon's defence was really based on a turning of the tables
against Bossuet because if Bossuet had really believed during all
these years what he claimed to believe now, then he was proved
out of his own mouth to have been far more guilty than Fénelon.
For it was Bossuet, not he, who had studied Mme. Guyon's books
and her manuscripts, who had examined her, who had given her
certificates of good faith and good intentions, who had admitted
her to the sacraments, who had possessed all the evidence he had
now thought it fit to give to the world, even though it had all been
entrusted to him in " the most sacred secret after that of the confessional itself." If Bossuet had then believed what he now professed
to believe about Mme. Guyon and himself, how could he have
defended Fénelon's appointment with the Princes, above all, how
could he have consecrated him bishop? " Here are the hands which
will consecrate you," he had said after Fénelon's nomination. For
his part, he, Fénelon, had never done more than maintain the distinction between the intention of Mme. Guyon and the objective
errors and extravagances which she had written, a distinction on
which alone Bossuet's own conduct towards her could have been
defended—how else could he have admitted her to the sacraments,
while condemning what she had written?

But was not Fénelon's whole conduct at Issy and later a massive
defence of Guyonism, Bossuet had asked? Was it? retorted Fénelon.
Who was it who had asked for enlightenment on mystical theology,
confessing never to have read a word of Saint Francis of Sales, Bd.
John of the Cross, Ruysbroek, Harphius, Tauler, Saint Catherine of
Genoa, Suso, Balthazar Alvarez, Teresa of Avila, Mme. de Chantal?
To judge a mystic, Bossuet had realised that he needed to make up
for his ignorance of the subject, and Fénelon had helped to enlighten
him.

What had happened since? Fénelon had not approved Bossuet's
book on mysticism. Why not? Because he could not believe that
Bossuet's description of the monstrosities and iniquities of Mme.
Guyon's teaching were, if true, consistent with an innocent Mme.
Guyon's refusal to admit bad faith on her part. If she had really
believed the abominations described by Bossuet, then she was,

anyway, a guilty woman. Not believing in her bad faith, he could not approve of accusations that involved such bad faith. Only a Bossuet, it seemed, was able to persuade himself that subjective honesty could go hand in hand with a belief in outrageous teaching. Meanwhile, Bossuet had been promising everyone to get a re-tractation of such infamies out of Fénelon himself in order to save the Church itself by forcing the new Montanus to abjure the new Priscilla. And all, just because he had been forced to refuse—entirely in private—to approve Bossuet's book. Because of a refusal forced on him by Bossuet's sharp tactics, he had been accused of trying to create a schism and to divide the hierarchy of France!

As for the last few months, Fénelon was on impregnable ground because of his appeal to Rome. Even admitting all the evil that had been spread about him and his book, was the Church to be saved from the consequences by Bossuet's *ipse dixit*, or was it to be saved by the judgment of the Pope? Had he, an exile in his study in Cambrai, been responsible for the scandal and the clamour? " I am alone and deprived of all human help. Anyone who has any care for his own interests dare not know me any longer. . . . Where are those ' great bodies,' those ' great forces ' whose favour supports me against the manifest truth? That prelate tries to discover cabals, factions, great bodies who support the impiety of Quietism and who divide minds even to the very sanctuary of the Roman Church, even to the Holy Office. Thus he writes: ' Eloquence baffles simple minds; dialectic entangles them with its threads; metaphysic going beyond all limits drives minds into unknown countries.' The threads of my dialectic do no more than clearly demonstrate the paralogisms of this prelate. They simply re-establish the text of my main arguments, which he has altered in his quotations. This metaphysic which goes beyond all limits only says: God is to be loved for Himself, independently of an eternal reward which is not due to us and which He might not have given us. Those unknown countries are the aspirations of St. Paul and of Moses."

And with a final flourish, he begs his opponent to publish the whole truth openly, not to make a half-secret of it which is so much worse. Let all the truth be sent to Rome. " But if, on the other hand, nothing more can be said to brand my person, let us return without a moment's delay, to the question of my teaching, on which

I demand a decision. He himself [Bossuet] has reduced it to ' one point ' which he calls ' decisive,' to ' a single point in which the decision of all is contained.' This point, decisive to the whole system, is, according to him, that I have taught ' a love separated from the essential motive of beatitude.' This is the point on which we can ask for the Pope's early judgment. On it M. de Meaux should be as ready to submit as I am. . . ."

The skill was mainly in the clear arrangement of facts accumulated to grind to dust Bossuet's allegations. And that, oddly enough was precisely the Bossuetist expression used by a Cardinal in conversation with Chanterac: " Nothing more could be wanted for your justification; you are grinding M. de Meaux to powder."

In Rome, according to Chanterac, the excitement was terrific. " All Rome echoes it, and all who have read the book seem so moved and persuaded by it that they cannot but praise and admire it." And in a further letter: " Your *Réponse* could not have been more warmly applauded nor have enjoyed a greater success. Those most deeply engaged against us and even those most prejudiced in good faith are simply obliged to confess that this *Réponse* is invincible, so long as the facts you give are true; and when it is pointed out to them that those facts are nearly all taken from M. de Meaux's own *Relation*, they hang their heads." Innocent himself was delighted with a defence that re-established in the eyes of the world the spiritual and moral status of a great bishop of the Church.

In Paris, the effect was similar, people noting especially the brilliant way in which Fénelon had defended himself without in any way involving his friends at Court and without attacking the highly-placed supporters of Bossuet, such as Mme. de Maintenon and the Archbishop of Paris.

These great people, who had striven to make the best of both worlds, whether for personal or public reasons, and been driven forward on the Eagle's path by the whirlwind that Bossuet could create almost with a sweep of his light-blue episcopal robes, now began to wonder about the nature of the country into which they had been landed. So private negotiations for peace were started by an agent of Godet, two or three weeks after the publication of the reply. They dragged on slowly and unhopefully. Fénelon was suspicious because he thought, not without reason, that even though negotiations might be started in good faith, Bossuet, now less certain of the issue in Rome, would not fail to turn them to his advantage.   The terms, Fénelon said, were not in themselves impossible and he was interested in so far as all was done with the knowledge and approval of the Pope.   But the more he studied the proposal to publish a fresh edition of the *Maximes*, corrected so that it could be universally approved, the less he liked the idea.   It was suggested, for example, that this new edition should start with a repudiation of Mme. Guyon.

But to the end Fénelon remained as firm as at the start about his attitude to the unwitting cause of all his misfortunes.   Suggesting to Godet's agent that Bossuet needed a confession by hook or by crook in case the *Maximes* was, after all, not condemned in Rome, he wrote: "I cannot speak against the personal intentions or feelings of Mme. Guyon without wounding my own conscience. I never saw anything of what they allege. The things may be true, but I know nothing about them; and if I said anything about them without being certain of my facts, I should be speaking rashly."   Why did they insist on this avowal?   "Simply so that they can charge me with impiety in defending her."

The failure to negotiate a settlement led to the confiscation in Paris of all Fénelon's mail.   "This shows two things," he wrote, "the absolute authority they employ and the bragging way in which M. de Meaux had prided himself on clearing the way for my answers, simply because he was so sure that there was nothing I could answer."

Though Bossuet had told his friends that he had written his last word in this controversy, the war of words was not yet to end.   The Eagle now issued his *Remarques sur la réponse de M. de Cambrai*, "Remarks on M. de Cambrai's Answer," and Fénelon had to reply in a *Réponse aux remarques de Mgr. l'Evêque de Meaux sur la Réponse à la Relation sur le Quietisme*, "Answer to the Remarks of His Lordship the Bishop of Meaux on the Answer to the Relation on Quietism."   It seemed endless; but as the title grew longer, the writings themselves grew shorter.   This time, Fénelon limited himself to 30,000 words.   To write it, he says, was more painful to him than anything else he had done.

Its character may be illustrated by some quotations.   " Your art is to refute what I never said so that you can deny an imagined fact, thus diverting the attention of the reader from the true fact with which I reproach you." A string of false quotations and falsifying summaries from Fénelon's writings are given, for example: *Fénelon's words:* "Pure and direct contemplation is negative in that it does not occupy itself voluntarily with any sensible image, with any distinct and nameable idea" becomes in *Bossuet's version*: "Direct contemplation can only attach itself voluntarily to a limitless and unnameable Being." Another trick, Fénelon charges, is to confuse two entirely separate things, as when Bossuet pretended that Fénelon had said that Mme. Guyon was another Saint Catherine of Genoa, whereas he had only compared them together because both had fallen into illusion. When Fénelon challenged Bossuet to name "the many people" to whom he (Fénelon) had distributed Mme. Guyon's books, the only answer he had got was that these matters were *minutiae* and it was not a question of "manual distribution." "Instead of proofs, you answer with a joke and a mockery." With regard to Bossuet's charge that Mme. Guyon's works were for Fénelon "cherished books," "favourite books," the retort comes: "Let me in this pressing need give things their proper name and unearth your sophisms"; and he proceeds to enumerate and describe seven of such sophisms. A very neat point was made when he dealt with Bossuet's charge that a Protestant writer (Bishop Burnet) had bracketed Quietists with Protestants in wishing to abolish Roman superstitions and quoted from Fénelon's *Education des Filles* to show it. Yes, but, answered Fénelon, "that Protestant writer, according to his purpose, continues to quote French writers who want to reform worship. So he does me the honour of quoting, with me, you, My Lord, Cardinal Le Camus, Abbé Fleury and several others. So I am a Quietist with you. God sees, and all will see one day, to what lengths you need to go in order to blacken me."

Even less defensible was Bossuet's attempt to maintain that an addition to the original draft of the Issy Articles "could not be part of the articles, but at most just a few words—which proves nothing." Answered Fénelon: "You have an original copy: produce it. I am ready to produce mine. It will be clearly seen that the Article, which was not originally with the others, was drawn up on the spot between us in M. Tronson's room in Issy, and added when we were about to sign. Everyone can see by this example how accurate you are when you deny facts."

And so it went on; Fénelon, with the precision of a brilliant surgeon, delicately dissecting truth from error, fact from suggestions, exaggeration, confusion, innuendo, and not fearing, with the art of an equally brilliant advocate, to show up to the public of France and Rome the consequences of this use of evidence. Yet the whole work was begun and ended within eight days!

The book ended with his answer to Bossuet's bold comparison of the *cas* Fénelon-Guyon with the *cas* Montanus-Priscilla. "This comparison seems to you just and moderate; you defend it by saying that it was only a question between Montanus and Priscilla of a commerce of illusion. But your historical comparisons are hardly successful. Just as the docility of Synesius did not resemble mine, so my pretended illusion does not resemble that of Montanus. That fanatic detached from their husbands two wives who followed him. He delivered them over to a false inspiration which was a veritable possession by the evil spirit which he called the spirit of prophecy. He himself was just as much possessed as these women. In a diabolical seizure of fury which he suffered with Maximilla, they both hanged themselves. Such is the man, the horror of all centuries, with whom you compare your fellow-bishop, 'that dear friend of a lifetime whom you carry in your bosom.' Yet you do not like me to complain of such a comparison! No, My Lord, I shall not complain of it any longer. Only for your sake will it afflict me. And who, indeed, is to be pitied, save the one who injures himself so sorely by accusing his brother without proof? You say you do not accuse me when you compare me with Montanus. Who will believe you? Need I reply? Could you do anything better calculated to justify me than to accuse me of falling into such excesses, such palpable contradictions? You do for me more than I could do for myself. But this is a poor consolation when one sees the scandal which vexes God's house and redounds to the triumph of so many heretics and free-thinkers." But Bossuet knew what he was about. The names have stuck and Fénelon's answer is forgotten.

This astonishing book proved to be the final rebuttal of his enemy in the long debate of words. The answer Bossuet was preparing was never published. The French Envoy in Rome thought that this last work of Fénelon in the controversy was " the greatest mental effort of the human mind," an opinion of an admirer which, if exaggerated in one direction, was hardly as exaggerated in the opposite as the scream of fury of Nephew Bossuet. " He is a savage beast who must be hunted for the honour of the episcopate and of truth until he is trampled on and prevented from doing any more mischief. Did not Saint Augustine hunt Julian unto death? The Church must be delivered from the greatest enemy it has ever known." Fénelon, he added, was a " charlatan," a " pretender " and " the most dangerous of all men."

The reply, Chanterac wrote, " completes the entire and evident proof of the perfect innocence of M. de Cambrai, both as regards his morals and as regards his intention in writing his book. . . . The other day at a big gathering, where Abbé Bossuet was present, many were saying, loud enough for him to hear, that all antiquity had never produced anything similar. . . . A saintly religious said that it must have been the spirit of God who inspired him to speak, for the human spirit could not possibly give him such strength and elevation. A man of the world put it more freely when he said that only God or the Devil could write books at such a pace. Copies are in demand everywhere in Italy, in Naples, Florence, and even in other countries; all the libraries are trying to get it."

The great controversy had been so conducted, judged Chancellor d'Aguesseau, that both the parties could not possibly have been speaking the truth, and it certainly looked as though Fénelon was not the one who was lying.

CHAPTER SIX

ROME SPEAKS

FÉNELON WAS bound, when the fury of battle was raging, to his country diocese nearly 200 kilometres from Paris—and 200 kilometres then equalled 1000 kilometres of modern travel. Hampered by the hostile agents of a police-State; flooded by attacks from all quarters "I cannot do all at once," he cried in despair; and deprived of the company—always so precious to him—of those we loved, trusted and wished to consult, he, nevertheless, managed through two long years to return blow for blow in his struggle with a personality whose prestige we in these days find it hard to realise.

Basing himself on two issues, crystal-clear to him: the innocence of Mme. Guyon's intentions and her true Catholic faith, and on her cry that the Christian can and should love God for Himself alone and loving Him can do no other, he stood his ground, never lost courage and, step by step, managed to advance because justice and love were on his side in a struggle with enemies who came to reckon less and less on the means with which they were determined to defend what they believed to be truth, because that truth suited their purposes.

In Rome, Fénelon had been obliged to plead his cause under disadvantages even greater than those he had to contend with in his own country. Bossuet could command the services of the French diplomatic mission with all the resources in the way of spying and propaganda at its disposal. Nor should we underrate the enormous power and prestige of the first Catholic monarch in the world in opposing his own episcopal subject over the issue being fought. Even the Holy See is human, and it was impossible for it in those days when the balance of power in Europe so closely affected the destinies of the Catholic Church, challenged both by Protestantism and the rising movement of free-thought, not to take into consideration the views and policies of the leading Catholic country.

As time went on without a decision, this French pressure increased. In October, 1689, the Curia was "deeply shocked" when Paris adopted the tactless suggestion of Nephew Bossuet to have the *Maximes* formally condemned by the Sorbonne, the seat of French doctrinal judgment, and to have that condemnation supported by the French clergy. Nor was it lost on Rome that one of the chief agents in this condemnation was no other than Dr. Pirot, who had so often examined Mme. Guyon and who had pronounced the *Maximes* to be "*tout d'or.*" Matters were not improved when Louis prompted by his wife, despatched two couriers to the French envoy in Rome to demand once more an early condemnation, a condemnation which, according to a French gossip sheet, must be ruinous for the Holy See because in condemning Fénelon it would have to condemn the Saints whom the Church reveres.

The truth was that the stronger party by far was overplaying its cards as badly in Rome as it had in France. It is unbelievable that the Curia could take Nephew Bossuet very seriously. But this in itself could not decisively counterbalance the immense influence and resources of Versailles still at the height of its European influence.

Meanwhile the lengthy examination of the *Maximes* was drawing to its term.

Fénelon's own feelings are well described in a letter he wrote in December to Mme. de Maintenon. He was looking back in time —if time is measured by the events that fill it rather than the calendar "with something remaining of my faith in your goodness of times gone by."

He wrote: "The one point which I beg you, Madame, to allow me to make is that this book which was, so they said, impossible to explain in any Catholic way and whose impieties my *confrères* thought sufficient reason for pushing me to the last extremes, has seemed to five of the principal theologians chosen by the Pope in the bosom of the Roman Church, not only susceptible of better explanations, but on the contrary so pure and so correct as not to need any explaining at all. True, Madame, five others are against

214 THE BATTLE OF THE GIANTS

it. But the public takes the view that, despite the merits of the latter, they have not the weight of the former. . . . Even more, these theologians agree that my book condemns in a hundred places all the errors that they feared, and they limit themselves to the view that certain passages could support that doctrine—as though the many clear passages ought not to provide an interpretation of those less well unravelled and obviously related to them. . . . The invariable rule of the Holy Office, which is the strictest of all tribunals where faith is concerned, is that a book remains justified so long as a majority of votes does not condemn it. This rule applies decisively in my case. This presumption in my favour justifies me in advance, Madame, in the eyes of all Christianity. Am I called upon to be more opposed to Quietism and a more exact theologian than those five examiners chosen by the Pope? I did not take fifteen months to write my book as these examiners have taken to judge it. I wrote it simply and with confidence, and I could not foresee all the evil interpretations which have been put upon it in spite of me. I thought I was being careful enough when I followed with complete docility and even to the letter the advice of people as alarmed as any about the danger of illusion [Noailles, Tronson, Pirot]. All Christianity now sees that the principal theologians of the Pope justify my book, and that if for extraordinary reasons the constant rule of the Holy Office had not been suspended, the strictest interpretation would give me my case. Indeed, one might have thought that the rules would be, if anything, relaxed to avoid condemning an archbishop who submits and who is innocent in his conduct. Nevertheless, they are demanding that Rome should go beyond all the strictest precedents in order to condemn an archbishop as a Quietist. If the Pope agrees, my duty is to sacrifice myself and obey my superior."

A sense of deepening grievance marks this letter, as it did another which Fénelon wrote to the King, in a rather desperate endeavour to dissuade Louis and his wife from insisting in Rome that the normal procedure of the Holy Office, which would have saved Fénelon's book, was not suited to this special case. In fact, every French endeavour, with the King demanding a " clear and precise " condemnation, was being made to force the Pope to arrange matters to suit the French wishes. Bossuet himself said that anything but a bumper condemnation would cause Rome to rue the day when it spared Fénelon.

As a way of underlining his orders to Rome, the King demanded the official document in which the members of the household of the Princes were registered. He took it up and, with his pen, drew a line through the name of the Archbishop of Cambrai. Fénelon had ceased officially to hold the post which for so long he had only held nominally.

Fénelon's brilliant answers to Bossuet had had no effect in worrying the consciences of the King and his wife who kept a discreet silence about them. They were now committed and meant to see the business through to the end, even though the King understood little and Mme. de Maintenon showed little personal vindictiveness. " The affairs of M. de Cambrai afflict me still, but they no longer worry me. In great peace, I await the Holy See's decision." A form of Quietism, it seems, had at last taken hold of her.

Chanterac reported the effects of all this in Rome. The French pressure was telling in the end. " It is said aloud and without bother," he wrote, " that the King not only demands a prompt decision, but insistently demands a very definite and clear condemnation of your book, as a matter necessary for the peace and health of the State."

Innocent XII, an old man of eighty-four and within months of his own death, had never disguised his personal affection for Fénelon and his high esteem for his piety and talents. Throughout, he had absolutely refused to have the real cause for judgment muddled by extraneous questions about Fénelon's relations with Mme. Guyon or rumours about his moral conduct generally. All the efforts of the two Bossuets to confuse the question with these irrelevancies fell on the deaf ears of a Pope who neatly summed the protagonists in the famous *mot*: *Erravit Cameracensis excessu amoris Dei; peccavit Meldensis defectu amoris proximi* " The Archbishop of Cambrai erred through loving God too much; the Bishop of Meaux sinned through loving his neighbour too little." But at his age it was not to be expected that he could take a final stand against the considered advice of the officials in whose hands the case rested. The Holy See was not in fact to yield to the political and clerical pressure of

France against its better judgment. But that pressure was effective in persuading the Curia to weigh the question as to whether in this case the normal procedure was sufficient. The public controversy between two great bishops was no ordinary event in the life of the Church. The whole affair had been a cause of major scandal in Christendom with half Europe relishing and the other half mourning it. It was reasonable that so unique a case should be uniquely dealt with by the final court by judgment rather than the normal procedure. And this in turn focused attention on a point which came up again and again.

In official Rome there was never any question either of Fénelon's intentions and virtues or of the orthodoxy of his general position as expressed in his many self-justifying writings. But the question here was whether the *Maximes*, written, as Fénelon admitted, somewhat speculatively, hurriedly and without benefit of the endless discussions about the difficult subject since the fatal day when he published the book, was in every respect strictly in accordance in certain particulars with Fénelon's own more fully informed mind and with the general theological sense as it emerged from all this prolonged study in Rome of the delicate problem of passive mystical prayer. As for " pure love " generally, on which Bossuet had rested his case, there was no question that Fénelon was right and Bossuet, an amateur in the subject, wrong. But *how far* and *exactly in what respect* could one say that a Christian might safely go in readiness to sacrifice his salvation for the love of God—how safely, too, could a Christian slip, as it were, into a permanent state of love, in which the virtue of hope seemed to disappear from his consciousness ?

In the exceptional circumstances such matters might require a closer and higher examination so that the equal division of consultors should not lead to the normal judgment of opposing a teaching which subsequent study might cause to be deemed insufficiently precise.

The Pope agreed that the matter should be transferred to the Holy Office cardinals themselves for further examination. Constant expectations of a final judgment were thus disappointed, and 1698 turned 1699 without a decision being reached, despite the fact that the Holy Office sat three times a week with the Pope himself regularly present.

It was during this critical period that the news reached Fénelon in his exile that his old friend, the cause of it all, Mme. Guyon, had died in the Bastille. The news was false; it was the woman who looked after her who had died. But it gives us Fénelon's last words, as it were, on Mme. Guyon, since, despite the fact that they were in-directly always to keep in touch with one another, she in fact survived the Archbishop. "I must say after her death, as I have said through-out her life," he wrote, "that I never saw anything in her which was not a cause of strong edification for me. Had she been a devil incarnate, I could not say that I knew anything about it, but only what I saw in those days. To say anything of an ambiguous nature on that subject to save myself from oppression would be a horrible act of cowardice. Now I need not take special precautions on her behalf: truth alone holds me."

Succinct, but to the point and absolutely consistent. But perhaps even this news of the woman who had played so fateful a part in his life and career could only momentarily distract him from the dreadful preoccupation now at last approaching its climax.

For his position can only be understood if we recall again that here was a man singularly gifted with clarity of judgment and self-knowledge, an archbishop, waiting for months, day by day, week by week, uncertain whether a condemnation would destroy him, not in his worldly position—that, in his suffering, had become his last concern, but in his faith, in his work, in the truth which he knew to be within him. For we must remember that holiness, even great holiness, does not destroy the force of the natural faculties and feelings. On the contrary, it can often strengthen them. His very dedication to God's truth, as his contemplations, meditations, studies, experiences, sufferings had made him see it, strengthened his natural expectation of being justified and it enlarged the im-aginative horror of a condemnation. He could not, after all that he had learnt of his enemies and all he had had to write about them, be in doubt of his judgment that their faith was bad, whether they subjectively realised the fact or not. It had all been his cause to which he had dedicated himself, for which he was ready to die, for which—hardest of all—he was ready, if need be, to submit. He had learnt—and learnt from Mme. Guyon—that in God's providence there is something even deeper than the truth which burns the soul and inflames the feelings: there is the utter childlike abandonment to the sovereignty and will of God which mysteriously moves above the wisest, deepest, holiest counsels of His creatures.

In that *abandon* lies the supreme self-sacrifice which kills the pervasive self-love of the ego and finally opens the gates full wide to the indwelling of a ray of the supreme Spirit of God Himself. Such *abandon* was not a fatalism, an agnosticism, a stoicism. It demanded what Fénelon had tried to give in full measure: the intensest use of the human faculties of seeing, deciding, acting. And because it made these demands, it also demanded an open-eyed self-sacrifice at its most crucial and costly that God's will, not ours, be done. The moment was fast approaching—the moment of test and truth—when the will of God, as Fénelon saw it in this long struggle and suffering, would make its decisive demand in the judgment of the Holy See.

In February, 1699, the Cardinals of the Holy Office reached a final decision. Of the thirty-eight propositions from Fénelon's book which were submitted to their judgment, they found twenty-three reprehensible, though they were divided as to the way in which that reprehensibility should be expressed. No one can judge of the secret motives which led to this last finding; but there is no reason whatever to suggest that it was arrived at otherwise than conscientiously.

Innocent was distressed by these decisions which left him no normal option but to condemn in some way the *Maximes des Saints.* That being so, his sole preoccupation was to find ways and means of softening a blow that would fall on a prelate oustanding in the Church at a time when by no means all its officers were outstanding for their virtues and pastoral zeal. How was the official decree to be drawn up and what class of decree would it be?

The Pope entrusted this task to three cardinals of high standing whom he believed to be likely to deal gently and prudently with a painful office. From the committee he had excluded Cardinal Casanate, suited by seniority and position for the honour, but known to be unfavourable to Fénelon and in close touch with the Abbé Bossuet. Unfortunately, Cardinal Albani, Secretary of the Briefs (or Decrees) believed it to be his duty to represent to His Holiness the unsuitability of Cardinal Casanate's exclusion. Innocent gave way

so reluctantly that he sent a message to the Cardinals asking them to
spare the Archbishop of Cambrai as much as was compatible with
their duty, and he particularly recommended Casanate to consult
his conscience with care—not perhaps the most tactless way of
influencing him in the circumstances.

Before Casanate had been included, the Cardinals, responding to
the Pope's feelings, had agreed that the decree should be in the
form of a Brief, not in that of a Bull. A Brief would be less solemn
and carry less weight than a Bull. Other agreements included the
omission of any condemnation of the explanations of the book
given by the author and the insertion of a statement pointing out
that one of condemned propositions was not Fénelon's at all. It
had in fact been put in through a printing error due to Chevreuse's
misunderstanding. Bossuet had always refused to take any notice
of this fact. But Casanate, after his inclusion in the Commission
negatived these last two arrangements and he could not be persuaded
to change his mind.

So the Brief was finally drawn up in accordance with the last
findings and submitted to the Pope. The question seemed to be at
an end, since a Pope normally accepts such advice. But the old Pope
was not yet beaten.

The Cardinals were called together as usual on 5th March to
meet together in the presence of the Pope, and the sitting began with
the proposition that the Archbishop of Cambrai's book be condemned in the terms agreed upon by the Commission for drafting
the Brief. Then Innocent surprised everyone by something entirely
unexpected. He caused a series of dogmatic propositions or canons,
twelve in number, on the positive teaching of the Church on
mysticism, to be read to those present and a copy circulated to the
Cardinals. Nor did he disguise his personal interest in the matter.
These canons had in fact been drawn up by the examining Cardinals
in the course of their examination of the *Maximes*. Innocent's
purpose in drawing official attention to them now was to side-step
altogether the condemnation of Fénelon's book, and to end the
long dispute with a positive teaching ordinance on the subject in
place of a mere negative condemnation.

News of this dramatic change reached Nephew Bossuet who at
once dispatched a courier to Versailles saying that all was lost

unless the King fought back with all his authority and with suitable
threats. As soon as the courier reached Versailles, the infuriated
Bossuet, seeing the great prize escaping him at the eleventh hour,
set to work. He drafted a most astonishing letter to be dispatched
by the King to the Pope. After the usual injurious remarks about
Fénelon, his books and his machinations, it definitely threatened to
refuse acceptance in France of anything but a condemnation. " It
is easily understood that His Majesty could not receive nor authorise
in his kingdom anything but what he has asked for and has been
promised: to wit, a clear and precise judgment on a book which has
inflamed his kingdom and on a doctrine which divides it. Any
other decision would be useless in bringing to an end an affair of
this importance and which has kept all Christianity waiting for so
long. . . . His Majesty would be saddened to see a new schism born
amidst his subjects, and this at a time when all efforts are being
made to extinguish Calvin's. If this affair which seemed to be
ending is prolonged by precautions which we cannot understand,
His Majesty will know what to do and will take the proper
measures."

As matters turned out, this scarcely veiled threat to the Holy
See reached Rome too late to affect the issue which by then had
been finally decided. One wonders what its effect would have been
had it arrived in time.

The Cardinals had discussed the Pope's new plan, and Casanate
argued strongly against the dangers of further delay, of further
arguments about the mystical canons themselves and, above all, of
retaliations from France which might yet reopen the whole dispute
between that country and the Holy See. He obtained the assent of
his fellow-Cardinals, and the agreement was reported to Innocent.
The latter felt obliged to yield to the now unanimous verdict of his
official advisers. He called an extraordinary meeting for Wednesday,
11th March, 1699, for the reading of the Brief of condemnation.
The next day, Innocent signed the Brief in the chapel of his palace
of Monte-Cavallo. It was at once printed, published and posted in
the Eternal City.

" We, then, after having taken the advice of the same cardinals
and doctors in theology," the Brief stated, " *motu proprio* condemn
and reprove the said book, in that by the reading and use of this

book, the faithful might be insensibly led into errors already
condemned by the Catholic Church; and also as containing propositions which are respectively temerarious, scandalous, evil-
sounding, offensive to pious ears, pernicious in practice and even
erroneous."

"Let us give thanks to God who has led us by the hand,"
exclaimed the incorrigible Abbé Bossuet.

The modern reader, not habituated to the time-honoured
formulæ of the Holy See, may well be surprised to read so weighty
a condemnation of a book which the Pope himself did not wish to
condemn at all and about which learned theologians and cardinals
had been equally divided for so many months. He will not be less
surprised in the circumstances to read Chanterac's report to the
unfortunate Fénelon of the audience with the Pope which he had
been given immediately after the condemnation. The Pope, he says,
" seemed to me at first more overwhelmed and afflicted than you
or I would let ourselves appear to be, or indeed be. He was most
anxious to tell me how angry he was about it, but that he had not
been able to prevent the judgment being given. He covered you
with praise, saying that he deemed you a great archbishop, most
pious, most saintly, most learned, and in fine he promised to do
what I was asking." The request was for a Papal letter praising
Fénelon's submission and recognising his good intentions in writing
the Maximes, as well as recognising that the book had been intended
by Fénelon to bear the meaning later made clear in Fénelon's
letters and defences. In fact, the Pope's promise was never kept,
possibly because of fear created by that final threat from Louis XIV.

The terms of the condemnation were considered to be indulgent
rather than severe. France and Bossuet had wanted the solemn form
of a Bull, not a mere Brief. They wanted the Maximes to be
condemned as " heretical " or, at least, as " leaning towards heresy."
These words were carefully avoided. They were particularly
annoyed at the insertion of the words motu proprio which were
interpreted as an insult to Gallican France to which the great
quarrel belonged. In fact, the adjectives of the Brief leading up to
" even erroneous " were the time-honoured Papal formula for a
book that could mislead the faithful and actually contained some
errors.

Cardinal de Bausset in his biography of Fénelon explains the condemnation as amounting to making clear two main errors which Fénelon had made in the *Maximes*. One concerned Fénelon's wording in connection with the suppression of all acts, apart from that of love, when souls attain a certain degree of perfection. The second referred to the nature of the absolute sacrifice of salvation in the highest possible states of the interior life. As for the other condemnations, the Cardinal quotes the judgment that these were only meant to indicate "the Holy See's intention not to spare anything which *could* have an ambiguous or equivocal meaning, or one susceptible to a false interpretation."

English-speaking readers may well be glad to have the summing-up of the learned and holy Benedictine, Bishop Hedley: "The doctrine intended by Fénelon, in his *Maximes des Saints*, and as explained by him during his controversy with Bossuet, has never been censured, although the opposite party laboured hard for its condemnation. Fifteen years after the condemnation of the book, we find him re-stating to Pope Clement XI (who, as Cardinal, had drawn up the Brief of his condemnations), in careful scholastic language, the doctrine intended by himself, but which he had misstated in his popular treatise. As there were errors, the other side, whatever the crudity or novelty of some of its contentions, whatever its motives or methods—and some of them were far from creditable—was sure in the end to succeed."

Ernest Seillière in his account which has very little sympathy with Mme. Guyon, La Combe and Fénelon, sums up with the view that the condemnation "was extremely moderate in its terms, and, while sensibly wounding the vanquished party, it in no way satisfied the victors who had expected far more. 'Pure love' emerged untouched by the storm and only certain echoes of feminine mysticism, driven off its rails during the seventeenth century by so many exaggerations, were stigmatised in Fénelon's book."

To all this may be added the observation that Fénelon, apart from his *de facto* victory in the cause of "pure love" as the aim and heart of Christian spirituality, was justified all along the line in the cause which really interested contemporaries in France and against which Bossuet was so angrily crusading, namely, the issues for which Mme. Guyon throughout symbolically stood. The first, on which Fénelon never yielded, was the right of a woman to be held guiltless of bad faith or evil intention unless her conduct and her inconsistencies were manifestly inconsistent with any honesty of mind. The second was his own right—and that of anyone else—to stand by his own personal knowledge of the character and spiritual quality of such a woman. The third was the irrelevance, in judging of heresy and false doctrine in a person, of rumour, gossip, untested and false evidence as regards moral conduct, as well as the irrelevance of exaggerations, imagery, subjective impressions natural to the upbringing and psychology of the person concerned, even though the latter were obviously subject to condemnation in themselves. The fourth was the duty to take into account character, the visible " fruits," the inner and fundamental meaning of writings and behaviour as a whole, when seeking to discern personal orthodoxy and good faith, as distinguished from accidental errors. The fifth might be summarised as the iniquity of lying, intriguing, innuendo, calumny, detraction, and all use of force and persecution when seeking to determine truth, and most of all, truth about faith and morals, religious truth.

All this seems obvious enough to us in our day, even though over large tracts of the world political persecution disregards it, while even among us the grounds which distinguish personal guilt and consequently the right to punish, from guiltless error or mis-understanding are by no means always clearly understood and applied. But in Fénelon's day, the reluctant release in the end of Mme. Guyon from prison and a freedom for her that was sub-sequently never molested was a victory for the cause of the freedom of the individual that should not be forgotten. Nor, after all that had happened, should Fénelon's own undiminished prestige as archbishop and a personality of public influence be overlooked in the long struggle for human rights.

CHAPTER SEVEN

VICTORY IN DEFEAT

FENELON'S RECEPTION of the news of his condemnation is one of the classic edifying stories of Catholic moral instruction. The picture of the condemned Archbishop trampling on his spiritual offspring, the *Maximes des Saints*, bracketed in the engravings with the "Institutions of Calvin," associates itself in the mind with the even more famous conversion of King Clovis whom St. Remy bade "burn what you adored and adore what you burnt."

At this distance of time we can, perhaps, take a more realistic, and at bottom, more edifying, view of an episode so dear to the French Catholic heart.

Fénelon, as we have had many occasions of seeing, was a very complex personality. He combined in his make-up a persistence in pursuing what he believed to be right with a constant readiness to express an almost artificial humility and abjection when he instinctively judged the time to be ripe. He had constantly done this in his earlier letters to Bossuet, and Bossuet did not fail in his polemic to make the most of the evidence of such docility to his own greater authority. It would therefore be easy to accuse Fénelon of a certain theatricality, a kind of "double-think," even of hypocrisy—indeed it has often been done. But it was certainly unconscious and in no way deliberate. The truth was surely that he saw clearly and felt intensely, and minds like his, ever on the stretch, ever deeply aware of the present, can welcome as a compensation to the strain under which they always live and as a blessed relief to the quivering of exposed nerves the opportunity of the sudden relaxation of intolerable inner tension. The spirituality, which he had embraced under

Mme. Guyon's influence and which had become so much part of his outlook and spiritual direction to others, corresponded well with his natural disposition. In the intolerably perplexing problems of life seen so deep and from so many conflicting angles, what a happiness, even if also what a sacrifice, to hear the clear voice of God which for the moment at least resolves all dilemmas, all struggles, all self-regarding preoccupations!

It is not therefore hard to imagine what passed through the Archbishop's mind when, on the feast of the Annunciation, 1699, just as he was about to mount the pulpit of his cathedral, his brother brought him the news of his condemnation in Rome. After the long months of struggle, suffering and waiting, was not the bad news as much of a relief as good news would have been a pleasure? And did not his mind instantaneously dwell on that holy indifference, that abandonment to God's will, that killing of self, that Mme. Guyon had so deeply impressed upon him in the old days? Was not, too, his whole cause bound up with the ultramontanism, the appeal to Rome, which had stood in such contrast with the outlook and conduct of his persecutors? Had he not always said that he would submit absolutely to the judgment of the Pope? Could there have been any hesitation? Could there have been a more dramatic opportunity? Pausing but a moment to reflect on what he had to say, the noble, emaciated figure gathered his robes about him and slowly mounted the steps of the pulpit. Taking the text: " Thy Will be Done," he preached his sermon on complete submission to the authority of ecclesiastical superiors who stood in the place of God. And if François de Salignac de la Mothe Fénelon, Archbishop and Duke of Cambrai, Prince of the Holy Roman Empire and Count of Cambresis, is remembered by a distant posterity for one thing only, it will be for that magnificent gesture. The great Bossuet had none comparable.

At the time, he had no idea of the nature and scope of the condemnation, and he referred to the Brief as a Bull. He had yielded utterly. Until the very last moment, he had defended the *Maximes* in the certainty that they were the truth. Until the end, he had expected victory. Now he was saying that if he could undo or retard the verdict by so much as bending to pick up a piece of straw, he would not do it.

But he can scarcely have left his cathedral before his mind was racing feverishly to consider to what exactly a condemnation of the *Maximes* committed him in conscience and in truth? And within two days he was writing to Chanterac a letter which shows how his mind was working.

" I have not yet seen the Bull; but I know that it is as strongly worded against me as if M. de Meaux had drawn it up," he wrote —quite wrongly, as it happened. "We must adore God and keep silent, according to my promise and my submission to my superior. . . . I propose in my episcopal instruction to say only four things, subject to better advice: (1) that I believe myself to have wrongly explained myself, so soon as the head of the Church, enlightened by superior authority, judges that it is so, and that therefore I unrestrictedly condemn my text with the same qualifications as his; (2) that I owe it to myself to declare once again to the whole Church what is in no way contrary to the judgment given, namely, that I have never understood my own text, nor thought it could be understood, save in the only sense which I have always given it in all my defences; (3) that nevertheless I do not pretend that the distinctions between the meaning of the writer and that of the text should trouble the Church over the question of fact, since my meaning and my intention in writing, however pure it may be, do not prevent the text itself from having the natural meaning which the Pope judges it to have. (4) That I submit to the Pope the doctrine of my defences, which is truly mine, and that if it contains errors, then I beg him to have the kindness to make this known to me, since otherwise I would not be able to undeceive myself. . . . The Love of Pure Benevolence [pure or disinterested love] is, owing to the way in which I have been treated, in the utmost danger in France, and becomes so little by little even elsewhere. But now that I have been disarmed, it is no longer for me to fight. I can only edify the Church by my submission and silence. After my Instruction, there will be nothing left for me to do except to catechise the parishes of my diocese. God will take care of His truth; and we must hope that, according to His promises, the Roman Church will, if it be necessary, defend that truth even though at the moment she seems to allow it to be obscured in these most dangerous circumstances."

This letter, written in the face of a condemnation which he thought more severe than it actually was, shows clearly that Fénelon saw no inconsistency in a complete submission combined with the certainty that the teaching he intended was right in itself, but accidentally wrongly worded, and that the denial of his true teaching would gravely endanger the Church, under God. Actually, his attitude appears to coincide with the personal view of the Pope himself, and it corresponds with the spirit of the actual Brief which, in fact, only condemned errors in the *Maximes* itself, not in Fénelon's views on the whole. As such it is an interesting example of the vindication of the view that Christian obedience does not involve any denial or destruction of the judgment of the individual, but the rational submission of that judgment to a higher judgment which, for sufficient reasons, it believes to be more representative of God's authority. Just as he had defended for so long Mme. Guyon's personal innocence and integrity, so, and with far better reason, he would defend his own innocence by asserting that in fact he himself had never believed those things which Rome had solemnly judged to be erroneous. For the same reason he never expressed any sorrow or repentance for the part he had played. For all this his enemies then and his critics since have charged him with lack of humility and obedience. But surely any other attitude would have been really hypocritical and a sin against his own conscience comparable to the sin he would have committed had he weakened over his belief in Mme. Guyon's innocence.

All this was far beyond Bossuet's understanding. " Nowhere does he say that the book is his," Bossuet wrote to his nephew. " He has disappropriated himself of it and he has written somewhere that he took no part in it. Mme. Guyon used to say the same! It is even more astonishing that, despite the way in which he feels his humiliation, he in no way feels his error nor the evil he has wanted to spread. He will say, when he wants to, that he has never admitted having been mistaken and he will find it as easy to excuse himself as Mme. Guyon; for though he can hardly plead ignorance, he will certainly find means, if he wants to, of finding other excuses and such will never fail him. . . . He wants everything forgotten, excepting what is to his credit. . . . The retractations of antiquity, like that of Leporius, dictated by Saint Augustine, are of a very different

character." In Nephew Bossuet's interpretation all this was due to
" the pride and the poison " in Fénelon's character.

It is a relief perhaps to turn to the element of comedy in the
tragedy, for the Papal condemnation, so long and so ill fought for
by Bossuet, Mme. de Maintenon and the King, when it at last came,
put them all into a position of the greatest embarrassment. The
fact was that the Gallican Church then (not unlike the Catholic
Church behind the Iron Curtain now) did not recognise the
juridical acts of the Holy See until they had been approved by the
French King and the *Parlement*. That was why the very term *motu
proprio* was a Papal defiance to France. The consequence of this
situation was that French subjects, even bishops, could not forestall
the royal will in obeying such Roman decrees. Fénelon himself
was debarred from officially submitting to his own condemnation
until the King of France gave him permission to do so. He had, in
fact, to write to Chanterac: " I am not writing to the Pope,
because, according to French usages, I cannot give any sign of
obedience to his judgments until the *Parlement* has accepted it or the
King makes some extraordinary exception for me."

Fearing legal demands on the part of his enemies for some
formula of exaggerated submission, Fénelon went on: " I have
never believed the errors which they impute to me. I can, through
docility towards the Pope, condemn my book as expressing things
I never thought I had said; but I cannot betray my conscience in
order basely to blacken my reputation on account of errors in which
I have never believed. *To lie in order to excuse oneself is a sin which
no power on earth can oblige us to commit* [that was Fénelon's fundamental principle throughout the struggle in regard to himself and
those whom he was defending]; but to lie in order to admit one's
own impiety when one was never guilty is the most horrible of
crimes for a bishop; no power can insist on forcing out of me
such an infamous prevarication. The Pope understands my book
better than I do; and it is on this that I submit."

The King, in fact, was content to give his permission for an
immediate submission with the parting shot that " this unpleasant
business cannot be too soon ended." This expressed his real attitude
throughout. He had never understood what it was all about; it
bored him; but it sounded dangerous to the State, and his wife

assured him that it was very naughty in itself. Fénelon, anyway, had the oddest mind in his kingdom, he thought, and he wished he had never made him tutor to the Princes and an archbishop. They said he had very dangerous ambitions.

On 9th April, Fénelon published his pastoral letter in which he stated that he adhered to the Papal Brief " simply, absolutely and without any shadow of restriction. Thus we condemn both the book and the 23 propositions, precisely in the same form and with the same qualifications, simply, absolutely and without restriction." There was no expression of sorrow or apology.

In his letter to the Pope he allowed his feelings to show much more clearly: " My words are full of pain, but my submission and my obedience are greater than my pain. I speak no more of my innocence, of the outrages done to me, and of so many explanations to justify my teaching. I speak no more of the past."

It is, alas, not possible to counterbalance the scandal of Bossuet's mind and methods in conducting his fight for the truth, as he doubtless sincerely saw it to be, by any generosity or chivalry towards his brother-bishop after he had won his victory. The Brief itself fell far short of the expectations Bossuet had so long awaited; but things had lately been going so badly in Rome for his cause, that Bossuet was in the end happy enough to secure even a moderate Brief in his favour. " It is useless to talk more of the Brief," Bossuet sighed. "We must take it as it comes and make the best of it." Nephew Bossuet echoed angrily with references to those " infernal *Maximes*."

De Noailles, the Archbishop of Paris, remembering perhaps his own personal approval of the manuscript of the *Maximes*, kept silent, except for his duty to the King to publish, as with all the other Archbishops, the Papal Brief. Only Godet, of the three bishops so intimately concerned with the struggle against Fénelon, wrote to him warmly and humanly, expressing his happiness in his colleague's " perfect submission," even though he strangely referred to Fénelon's " sincere return," as though the sinner had been wandering in the outer darkness.

As for Mme. de Maintenon herself, the King, well appreciating the vital role she had played in a business which, on the whole, caused him little satisfaction in the end, kept her posted personally with the news. He sent her the Brief " in a packet so that you can see all the details. It is in Latin; some Father of the Mission will explain it to you. Here now is something ended with. I hope there will be no consequences and that no one will be hurt."

While Nephew Bossuet was busily trying to explain to the Pope how the King's wife had come into the picture, fallen for Fénelon and then turned against him, the Venetian ambassador was telling his Government that if the King were to die " there would be great changes at Court, and that Lady would come out of it all without much satisfaction." Mme. de Maintenon never forgave Fénelon, and some years later she wrote: " Rome condemned the teaching of M. de Cambrai. He accepted. He submitted. But I found myself awkwardly placed. Could I believe such a submission to be sincere while I could not see that prelate becoming, like Saint Paul, a preacher of the faith which he had fought? " She then explains that a " good man " referred her to Saint Augustine. No doubt it was Bossuet himself. " From that moment I was at peace, for I could only believe that a person was truly converted from an error when I could see him attacking that error with as much force as he had used for defending it."

Very different was the reaction in Rome. " It is certain," wrote Chanterac, " that there could not be greater praise and admiration here for your submission, your pastoral letter, your letters to the Pope, and all your conduct. Had your book been approved, it could never have earned you so much glory and esteem. The Cardinals have told me some very private things on the subject that I must keep for when we can talk together." " He was led like a lamb to the slaughter "; " He was delivered over to their will," prelates were whispering to the shocked Chanterac who noted: " We would not dare write or speak like that in France."

Fénelon's enemies in Rome were still, however, not content. Innocent " whose outward behaviour," said Chanterac, " indicates very unsurely what he really thinks in secret," took every opportunity of assuring him of his real feelings: "*Piissimo, santissimo, dottissimo*" (Most pious, most saintly, most learned), he repeated constantly in reference to the man he had had to condemn. But Nephew Bossuet was still hard at work. He wanted the Brief turned into a Bull. He wanted to prevent the Pope from writing to Fénelon in praise

of his submission and making clearer the limits of the condemnation. He even tried to have Fénelon deposed from his See. In all
this he succeeded to the extent of frightening the Pope, who was
actually playing with the idea of nominating Fénelon a cardinal,
into changing the laudatory letter that had already been written
into a cool and formal one. No wonder, Fénelon wrote wearily
to his agent: " Do not seek praises and good offices on my behalf.
The Pope has made it impossible for himself to help me, and he
has done me so much harm that he can no longer do me any
good with the King. The last thing I would do would be to buy
such useless favours with any baseness. As for the praises he
would wish to give me, I have long since told you that they would
be contradicted by the essential facts. If he had thought me *piissimo,
santissimo, dottissimo*, he would have taken care not to brand me
unnecessarily. That is what any sane man would say if he heard
my praises. God forbid that I should buy at such a dear price any
vague words—words contradicted by him who would say them."

This letter certainly reveals the infinite disappointment of the
tired fighter. If this was a spiritual weakness, it must at least console
us to realise that the high standards he set himself in life never
destroyed the lovable humanity which—as also in the case of
Newman—never ceases to attract us as the raw material out of
which sanctity had to be painfully achieved.

Did his thoughts in those dark moments of tragedy move across
the plains of Flanders and Picardy to that fated prison in Paris where
languished the woman who had physically, though hardly mentally,
suffered so much more than he? It is scarcely possible that they did
not. But for that meeting eleven years earlier, Fénelon's career
would certainly have been a primrose path. But for her, honours
of the Court, honours of the Church, would have poured over him
so that the greatness of the ageing Bossuet, to die more than a
decade before him, would make way before a Cardinal-Archbishop
of Paris with a fresh, subtler, more human, more forward-looking
spirit to guide and help the Church of France into the worldly
enlightened days to come, by the light of faith and love instead of
by the Bossuetist legacy of timorous, if noisily majestic, clinging
to the human in the Church rather than the divine.

Yet Mme. Guyon, whose intervention had blotted out a dream

from which Fénelon was never able entirely to avert his eyes, had taught him to judge by deeper values, the value of failure, even though through no fault of his, the value of being mocked, even in his episcopal dignity, by the successful in the world and by the mob, the value of exile and separation from the friends he loved and needed. The struggle within him between an ambition that he knew could have been fulfilled and a degradation he had never merited, but which tested the spiritual ideal which had gripped his inner spirit, had been and was to continue to be the key to his enigmatic personality. He was, in fact, to succeed in and through sheer integrity and charm in a way worthier and deeper than the honours of the Court could ever, of themselves, ensure.

In the bitter hours that followed the apparent failure of his life and work, he cannot have forgotten the fate of the woman who had taught him so much of the truth as he had taught her so much of common sense and sanity in living by that truth. A woman of over fifty now, whose nervous health had always been atrocious, she still lay there, nearly two hundred kilometres distant from Cambrai, in her small, dark cell of the Treasury of the Bastille. Her only company was that of Cathos, her serving-maid. Occasionally, agents of Fénelon's enemies would come again to extract from her avowals and self-inculpations—all to no purpose. For years she had been cut off from her family and her own daughter. When she asked for a prie-dieu and to see her daughter, even though only by sight through the window-bars, the prie-dieu for her prayers was allowed her, the sight of her daughter, whether from near or far, refused. There, as the days, months, seasons, years passed, behind stone walls, ten-foot thick, a sick woman was left to her prayers and her thoughts. She who had written so torrentially, so irresponsibly, about every spiritual detail of her strange life has given us but a page or two about her five years in the Bastille. " During that time I could find no help either in my reason nor in any inner support. I was like those who have never experienced the admirable ways of God's goodness and who have no natural spirit of their own. When I prayed, I only received the answers of death. At that hour, I thought of the words of David 'When they persecuted me, I afflicted my spirit by fasting.' Thus, so long as my health allowed it, I fasted and did heavy penance; but it all seemed to me like burnt straw. One moment of the touch of God's hand is of a thousand times greater help." Desolation of spirit, in other words, went hand in hand with captivity of the body. Yet she has recorded no single word of complaint. No wonder the complex, self-sympathetic Fénelon with his mixture of worldly and spiritual ambitions found in her an inspiration and a guide.

At long last, even Bossuet had to give way about both Fénelon and his friend. At the Assembly of the Bishops in 1700, he acknowledged in formal terms the genuineness of Fénelon's submission, and in regard to Mme. Guyon he more handsomely admitted: " As to the abominations which were thought to follow her principles, there was never any question. She has always testified to the horror with which they inspired her." So much suffering, so many sufferers, Mme. Guyon, La Combe, now completely mad, Fénelon in career and reputation, the Court cenacle of good, pious people whose only sin had been to try to bring a sincere and enlightened service to God in a Court, slipping down the slope that led to the sensual Louis Quinze, the too narrow goodness of Louis Seize and the horrors of the Revolution that would raze to the ground Mme. Guyon's historic prison—and all of that suffering to no apparent purpose, save in the mysteries of Divine providence.

Even Bossuet's admission that the fruits of the heresy which his eagle eyes had discerned everywhere were by no means what he thought they were was not enough to secure the release of Mme. Guyon. Mme. de Maintenon wrote that " he was fully convinced that Mme. Guyon must be left in prison." Not until January, 1703, did the King " find it well that Mme. Guyon should see her children."

After seven years in Vincennes, Vaugirard and the Bastille, they saw their mother again, and in a pitiful condition. Only because she was in danger of dying was it possible to prevail on the King to release her on the strictest conditions for six months. She was to be put under the surveillance of her own son who was to be responsible to the King that " she would have no communication by speech or writing with anyone whatsoever." The slightest breach of this promise and Mme. Guyon would be " incontinently " thrown back into the Bastille.

So on 24th March, 1703, she was taken from the prison in a

litter at four o'clock in the afternoon on what was officially called
a six months' leave " to take the air and be cured." She travelled
to her son's property at Diziers, near Blois, where she was at last
reunited with her family. Even so, Portchartrain, now Chancellor,
wrote personally to the Bishop of Blois to keep a wide eye open
on what might be going on in the Guyon home. Her leave from
prison was later renewed for another six months and then in-
definitely. But she was never again a free woman in the official
eyes of the State, and a nod from the throne would have sent her
back to prison. Nor could she change her abode without the King's
leave.

> *When pure love is fought*
> *They imagine that this ought*
> *To cut off its spreading rays.*
> *But all they can fulfil*
> *With their martyrising ways*
> *Is to make it stronger still.*

So she had sung in her prison cell. So she might well have
sung as they carried her from the Bastille, for, like Fénelon, she
was never to change.

EPILOGUE

Journey's End

It was taken for granted by the earlier ecclesiastical biographers that Fénelon broke off all connection with Mme. Guyon once his relationship with her became public. The condemnation of the *Maximes* naturally meant that his exile in Cambrai was also an escape from his unfortunate associations with a woman who, especially after the death of the great Bossuet in 1704, was not a person to be thus bracketed with an archbishop, now become something of an oracle in his distant diocese.

This view had the authority of the obvious facts and evidence. Fénelon's early correspondence and contacts with Mme. Guyon were not known. There was no other direct correspondence. And after Fénelon's exile in 1697, the two friends were physically separated from one another by long distances. That so much of obstinacy and tragedy should have resulted from a liaison, devoid, apparently, of any visible foundation at all, did not apparently puzzle the writers. Even if the whole business were incomprehensible, it was better for all concerned and for the reputation of the Church that in fact the Archbishop should have had as tenuous a factual relationship as possible with the Lady.

This view overlooked two vital circumstances. The first was the real natures of the two protagonists; the second was the importance of their friends and disciples.

The relationship between Fénelon and Mme. Guyon was in fact something strangely intimate, even if that word "intimate" does not carry in this case its usual associations.

For Fénelon Mme. Guyon was, first and last, a woman who, odd

235

as it might seem, had somehow "contacted" the Divine. Fénelon was a man whose whole complex, cerebral, introspective being cried out for the divine touch which would solve his problems and justify his emotions by transcending them without destroying them. But despite early hopes of that "consolation" or "sweetness" which, according to the commoner spiritual tradition, betrayed the presence of God within the soul, God for him had remained hidden. Sweetness was on the natural plane—in his friends, in his work, in his hopes. The higher and the deeper his spirit stretched, the thicker the cloud of unknowing.

Just at a critical moment in his life when youth had gone and middle life was beginning, he met this woman who had learnt by spiritual experience how and why the true God *must* be a hidden God.

The enjoyment of God he had yearned for was, he now saw, no more than a self-enjoyment. It was, literally, a subtle way of enjoying oneself. It was part and parcel of the whole corruption of fallen man which, but for grace, condemned man to seek *himself* and his pleasure in everything. But God was the exact opposite. God was "pure love," and only if man could love God with a touch of the "pure love" which God granted him was it possible for him to transcend his own fated natural selfishness. Hence, the whole teaching about abandonment to God's will, killing of self, becoming a little child, "knowing and not knowing," "fearing and not fearing," "seeing and not seeing," characteristic of mystical language. Only deep, deep down in the soul, dead to self and all its subtle disguises, could be found a realisation of stillness, of the Infinite, that disappeared—and yet did not disappear—so soon as our space-time air touched it.

In this woman, Fénelon had discovered the reality of the authentic mystical attitude which not only solved his own personal spiritual problem, but coincided with the best mystical traditions of the Saints, not least the later saints of the post-Reformation mystical movement. It furnished him with the clue to the religious philosophy and personal spiritual direction which were his main life's work. In everything else in Mme. Guyon's life and person he was disinterested; but in her as a living, personal witness to the truth he was absorbed.

Such an absorption could not be limited by time. Whether they saw one another or not, whether they corresponded or not, they must remain attached—the more so in that Fénelon, separated physically from his friends for so long, always had an intense awareness of oneness with them in God. His own beautiful description of friendship, when he compares prayer to God with human friendship, emphasises its transcendence of physical accidents: "Everything has been said; but without talking we are happy to be together, to see one another, to feel our closeness, to rest in the savour of a sweet and pure friendship. We do not talk; but in our silence we understand one another, knowing that we are in mutual harmony in everything and that our two hearts are one; the one ceaselessly pours itself into the other." That achieved, it would not be difficult to maintain the contact despite years of separation, though there is reason to think that his friendship with Mme. Guyon was almost wholly spiritual in character—that he had little sensible feeling for her, as compared with his dukes and duchesses, his relations, the household of the Princes, and even Mme. de Maintenon.

In fact, however, these friends saw to it that the two tragic partners would be kept in touch with one another until Fénelon's death.

The inner circle of the Court cenacle never disbanded. The dukes and duchesses and the delightfully intimate group of friends and relations who had become in many cases associated together through the household of the Princes drew even closer together as the years passed. De Beaumont, his nephew, known in the circle as "Panta," Chanterac, Langeron, Dupuy, called "le bon Put," his young great-nephew, the beloved "Fanfan," also called "le Boiteux," because of a wound received in war, together with the endless list of ladies of the highest rank, who sought Fénelon's spiritual direction, meant a constant interchange of views and the passing from one to another of the spiritual messages of N.P. (*notre père*) or N.C.P. (*notre cher papa*) or N.G. (*notre général*) and N.M. (*notre mère*). There is some evidence, too, that Fénelon may have written directly to Mme. Guyon.

But behind this grouping of intimate spiritual friends, deeply attached to both Fénelon and Mme. Guyon, to which we shall have to return in a moment, there remained for many years a matter of very great concern: the future of Fénelon's pupil, the Duc de Bourgogne, to become Dauphin himself in August, 1711, when Louis XIV's son died.

Whatever Fénelon himself may have thought and hoped—and views about this are pure speculation—it would be beyond human nature for Mme. Guyon and the circle of friends not to look forward to the day when Fénelon's pupil should succeed his grandfather as King. We are, we must remember, dealing with men like Beauvilliers and Chevreuse, de Noailles, the Duc de Chaulnes and many others of similar rank—even Mme. Guyon's daughter after the death of the first husband, the Marquis de Vaux, married the Duc de Sully. These were nobles at the foot of the throne itself, and they were fully able to see to it that their spiritual aspirations for a new and better reign under the spiritual ægis of Fénelon would be carried into effect through their own advice and influence.

In 1701 the war of Spanish Succession broke out, and Cambrai found itself for many years in the thick of military preparations and operations.

This had the effect of lifting the weight of Fénelon's exile in that he found himself once again in the midst of the great affairs of the kingdom. In 1708, Bourgogne himself was put at the head of the army assembled at Valenciennes and he was defeated at Oudenarde. Thus Fénelon was relinked with his royal pupil, and was not too happy at his later development under the over-scrupulous and rigid outlook of Beauvilliers, which now seemed to him too pious and negative for a soldier and a future monarch. Fénelon belonged to a family of soldiers, and he could find a place for the military virtues of chivalry within both his spiritual teaching and his forward-looking political views. But whether Fénelon himself was responsible for his pupil's failings or whether, as is much more likely, these were the result of the King's sudden exiling of his preceptor and the longer influence of Beauvilliers, the hopes of a new Fénelonian reign were dashed to the ground when the young Prince who had been strengthened by his latest contacts with his old tutor, died in 1712, a few months after he had become Dauphin.

This apparent calamity was, of course, the bitterest earthly blow to all who had been concerned, from the beginning of the story, with the dreams of a reign of Fénelonianism or Guyonism in France. What importance has to be attached to this aspect of the story is not clear. Certainly the political element in it, suspected by Bossuet and perhaps at times by the King himself, counted for little. If there was anything of a conspiracy in it, then it was thoroughly spiritual. In Mme. Guyon's well-packed and muddled mind it certainly had a part of some importance; but as to Fénelon himself, posterity is left to decide how far secret worldly ambitions, first noted by Saint-Simon, were really part of his make-up; how far they were temptations or velleities he could never entirely destroy in himself. Whatever the truth—and it will never be known unless some new evidence on the subject is discovered,—the unexpected death of the young Prince of spiritual dreams was wholly in its place within the Guyonist ideology. If there had been real ambitions, real hopes, then all the disciples were called upon to accept with a profitable and joyful resignation this supreme abandonment of even the hopes for their country of the spiritual reform for which they had prayed, suffered and worked. Had they been given an insight into the coming reign and the toppling over of the great Catholic monarchy into the Revolution in which a new order for Western civilisation was in gestation, their sacrifice would have been even more painful. Most puzzling of all perhaps for Fénelon would have been a vision of the men of the anti-Catholic Deist Enlightenment and the Romantic movement hailing him as one of their own major prophets, because he so clearly saw through the brittleness and falsity of Church and State under Bossuet and Louis XIV.

The maintenance of this close, if indirect, relationship between the Archbishop and the Lady was all the more remarkable in that time and circumstances had so utterly changed the parts which each of them had to play after the settlement of the great controversy.

Despite the apparent victory gained by Mme. de Maintenon (scarcely heard of again in relation either to Fénelon or Mme. Guyon) and Bossuet (that mystery man who, immediately after his maltreatment of his rival, began to write wonderfully understanding

spiritual letters to our old friend, Mme. de la Maisonfort, the
" Canoness," permanently immured in a convent in Meaux),
Fénelon, in his exile, lost little of personal reputation and he was the
only French bishop of a stamp to inherit the stature of the " Eagle
of Meaux."

His mere presence in the distant frontier town of Cambrai made
of that episcopal city a kind of spiritual Mecca to which visitors of
all kinds and from different countries came to seek his spiritual advice
and share his learning. It is to Bossuet's private secretary, Ledieu,
who visited him in 1704 that we owe a detailed picture of now a
great prelate of the times who lived in a fine style and yet with complete personal simplicity and even austerity. Though tied by the
cares of his great diocese which spread beyond the French frontier and
was so often filled with soldiers of both armies during the war (all
equally cared for by an Archbishop who spent his whole income on
relieving the miseries of war), he made it a rule to hear confessions
in his cathedral every Saturday like any ordinary priest. We have,
too, a picture of him driving out on his pastoral visits in a carriage
with three horses, in his violet robes, golden-trimmed black hat,
white gloves, spectacles on nose, annotating a book with his pencil,
his feet buried in a wolfskin bag.

In Rome, Innocent XII had been succeeded by Fénelon's
supporter in the examination of the *Maximes*, Cardinal Albani,
who became Clement XI. This ensured that the past was past and
that Fénelon's careful submission to the natural sense of the *Maximes*,
but not to any condemnation of the views he was really trying to
express, was permanently ratified by the Church. Fénelon's ultramontane, anti-Gallican and crusading anti-Jansenist zeal, which,
none the less, was doctrinally less rigid than the ultramontanism of
modern times and was consonant with far-reaching plans for the
reform of the Roman court, added to his popularity in Rome and
many sections of the Church, while keeping him bitter enemies in
France itself. Rumours of his nomination to a Cardinalate were
common. This final honour never came, perhaps because it would
have been too much of an insult to Louis XIV so long as he
lived. Had Fénelon survived his king—he was in favour with
Orleans, the future Regent—he would surely have obtained the
Red Hat.

Télémaque, when published through the indiscretion of a copyist, was brushed aside by Bossuet as unworthy of a priest, but it established his immortality both in letters and in political philosophy.

In both of these subjects—in the latter he was engaged in advising the doomed Prince and in studying practical problems of political reform which anticipated many of the demands that preceded the Revolution especially in his defence of human rights and his vision of a universal peace—his special gift was to harmonise idealism and tradition with hard-headed and practical needs of reform. This was also true of his whole spiritual attitude which, while governed by the highest ideal of "pure love" and completely submissive to the tradition of the Catholic Church, was applied in his pastoral work and in his spiritual direction with an extraordinarily modern understanding of the human psychology of the individual and the practical needs of the superstitious and illiterate masses.

In all these matters, Fénelon, the genuine mystic, stood out as compared with the false mystic, Bossuet. The latter was dedicated to grandiose and dated views about the Divine Right of Kings, and the "eternal" Church, and Ciceronian style. Fénelon learnt through "pure love" and perhaps not a little through the strange Mme. Guyon, that the divine had little to do with kings, that the "eternal" Church was also the Church of Christ's living compassion for the ever-changing multitude and each living, unique person in it, that even literature and oratory were made for man, and not man for them.

Thus the great and busy Archbishop and writer, constantly courted by friends, philosophers, statesmen, generals, even rulers, in a provincial city which became something of a centre for the ideas that would mature and grow to giant and, alas, distorted size in the revolutionary century that was beginning, belonged to a world altogether apart from the little homely circle of devotees within which Mme. Guyon passed her last years in Blois.

Yet, apart from their spiritual friendship, which distance could not break, two things, one springing from their common spiritual outlook, the other an accident, still linked them together.

We recall Mme. Guyon's sense of spiritual motherhood and of how she saw the building up of a "little Church of devotees, the childlike 'Michelins' as opposed to the busy, throwing-their-weight-about 'Christophlets'." The Court cenacle had filled the bill during the years of persecution and controversy. But now that she was in fact, if not in theory, a free woman, she busily engaged herself in spreading her mystical teaching by contacts and correspondence, not only in France, but also beyond the French frontiers.

How she managed to do this without getting into trouble is something of a mystery. Her own relations, we are told, were terrified and constantly warned her to be more careful. Happily, the Bishop of Blois was a friend and admirer of Fénelon. But we can hardly be surprised that the widow, now well into her fifties or sixties, who thought little of the years of persecution and prison, remained determined to dedicate her last years to a growing spiritual family. The latter were divided into the *cis* and the *trans*, the *cis* referring to her disciples within France, the *trans* to those in England, Holland, Germany, Italy and elsewhere.

Fénelon's proselytism was of a different order. He did not think in terms of a "little Church," nor did he propagate, as she seemed to, the doctrine of *abandon*, spiritual childhood and "pure love" without reference to denominational distinctions. But the essence of what he had to give people was the same as his old friend's. Moreover, as an international figure in Cambrai, many people from abroad came to Cambrai to meet and consult him specifically on religious problems. Among these was a rather mysterious figure of accidental importance to the Fénelonian legend.

It was a Scotsman called Ramsay, and always known as the Chevalier de Ramsay. The title is authentic in that he was to be made a member of a French order of chivalry, but he was also inclined to pass himself off as a Scottish Baronet of the Ramsay family which had a French as well as a Scottish branch. Actually, it seems, he was the son of a baker. However, he had succeeded in getting a university education, and showed the common intellectual interest at that time in both science and religion. His natural place in the world was to be tutor to children of the nobility. This role he had fulfilled with the children of the Duke of Wemyss and of the Old Pretender and was to fulfil again later. He was involved in the wars of the first years of the century, though it is not very clear on which side or how. As a natural philosopher, interested in religious questions, he went through a period of what to-day we should call scientific humanism. Apparently in this mood he read Fénelon's *Maximes* and *Télemaque*, both of which had been quickly translated into English, and it has been suggested that he may have heard of Mme. Guyon through the English prisoners-of-war in Blois. However this be, he found himself in Holland in about 1708, and there he met the Protestant minister Poiret, a somewhat indiscriminating amateur of spirituality who had founded a pietist circle. " I have dedicated myself," Poiret said, " to the truth and wisdom of God alone, without worrying about the instrument He uses to make Himself known to me, whether a man or a woman, a *savant* or an ignorant person, a Roman Catholic, a Calvinist or a Lutheran or even a Jew or a pagan. I love them all equally if they have the truth with them, and I love and esteem them in so far as they have it and only in so far." Into his pietist net Poiret had drawn the Imitation of Christ, Tauler, Saint Catherine of Genoa, Antoinette Bourgignon (whom Mgr. Knox describes as never having written a sentence " which betrays any marked degree of spiritual insight "), and, of course, the writings of Mme. Guyon. The latter had indeed referred to Poiret as " the man who would publish all my works."

Via Poiret, it would appear, Ramsay went to Cambrai to make the acquaintance of the venerable Archbishop who was far the greatest spiritual figure in the strange world of eclectic pietism which the popularity of religious toleration had brought into being all over Europe. It need hardly be said that Fénelon himself had scant sympathy with such an outlook, and for six months he argued with Ramsay with the happy result that the latter confessed that " M. de Cambrai made me see that we cannot be wisely Deist without becoming Christian, nor philosophically Christian without becoming Catholic." Fénelon, in fact, converted him and in due course passed him on to Mme. Guyon in Blois.

Here then was an intermediary and secretary not so much between Mme. Guyon and Fénelon himself—this, it seems, was avoided on both sides—as between the two circles, Fénelon's " above-board " entourage at Cambrai and Mme. Guyon's rather more peculiar spiritual family in Blois. For while the Archbishop was preoccupied with working out his Catholic philosophy and theology in terms of the spiritual truths for which he had fought, as well as in spiritually directing the men and women who saw in him their spiritual father, Mme. Guyon taught and preached by personal contact and correspondence in France and abroad her spiritual way of *abandon*, naked will and childlikeness to all who wished to profit from it, whatever religious views they might themselves profess.

This was something of a *tour-de-force* since, apart from her own complete loyalty to the Catholic Church, her mystical views had really very little in common with the traditions of Protestant piety. Perhaps this is best brought out by Mgr. Knox when he discusses Thomas C. Upham's translation of Mme. Guyon's autobiography. In this translation Upham managed to convert this " incorrigibly orthodox woman " into an English Evangelical. " The trick of it," writes Mgr. Knox, " is to substitute, at every turn, the jargon of Evangelical piety for the Quietist jargon in which Mme. Guyon wrote. ' Whether we call this state of experience *pure love*, or whether we call it . . . *assurance of faith* is perhaps not very essential ' [quoting Upham]. Perhaps not, except that (as we shall see in a moment) it is just the opposite. . . . It is wonderful what an effect of Protestantism can be managed by merely using ' *the* Lord ' for a translation of ' *notre Seigneur*,' as Upham does throughout. ' The way of forgiveness and salvation by faith in Christ alone,' ' She became truly willing to receive Christ alone as her hope of salvation,' ' Sanctification by faith, words uttered from Mme. Guyon's burdened heart,' ' A heart truly redeemed and sanctified through the blood of Christ '—such phrases as these, by constant repetition, hypnotise the reader into the impression that he is studying the experience of some Evangelical lady in the early nineteenth century. But they are not her phrases, they are the phrases which Upham has considerately lent her." And Mgr. Knox shows how Quietism was accused of making too little of the Sacred Humanity of Christ—the last thing that could be said of the Evangelicals; how the Protestant finds peace after his " conversion," whereas in the Catholic mystical tradition, followed by Mme. Guyon, spiritual trial only really begins after self-surrender to God; how, finally, the converted Protestant feels assured of salvation, whereas, half the trouble over

Mme. Guyon and even Fénelon was over their alleged too great indifference to salvation.

Such considerations, however, did not apparently mar the harmony of the differently-assorted guests, which reigned at Blois under the spiritual motherhood of Mme. Guyon. Comfortably established with a staff of five or six servants—someone complained of a certain lack of " mortification and external rigour "—the now ageir.g lady of more than sixty entertained up to seven people at a time, often English or Scottish Protestants, not to mention the comings and goings of French disciples anxious to imbibe at the spiritual source. Every morning a priest said Mass in a chapel next to the hostess's bedroom, and she herself received Holy Communion later, while her Protestant guests knelt behind a curtain. With Ramsay as her secretary, she attended to a heavy post from France and abroad, " Notre Mère " thus keeping in touch with the Cis and the Trans. Intervals from work and prayer were spent in the amusements and badinages which were part of the spiritual training in simplicity and childlikeness. An alternative was listening to Notre Mère improvising hymns and canticles to the latest air. Very luckily for all of them, the Bishop of Blois was a regular visitor—the last, in this chronicle of the churchmen and dignitaries who saw in this strange woman something that peeps through to posterity only with difficulty.

But bizarre as she may have been, who can help admiring her spirit? It was no mean thing for a delicate lady, even in the tougher life of the seventeenth and eighteenth centuries, to risk the conditions of French prison life, especially after having tasted so many years of them. One of Bossuet's angriest charges against her, unfounded though it was at the time, was that she would not cease to play the role of an active prophetess. Yet here she was at it again after all she had learnt from life, carrying on the dangerous work in close association with heretics and not caring much, it seems, to underline her own Catholic faith save in her practice of it. If her household lacked " mortification and external rigour," this, we must re- member, was in keeping with her spiritual teaching which emphasised inner rather than external mortification. As for herself, " no sooner had I left prison, my spirit at length being able to breathe after so many misfortunes, than my body was overcome by all kinds of infirmities so that I was almost always ill and often near death."

As for her spiritual state in these last years, she describes in 1709 a near-Nirvana of spiritual abandon and detachment. " The basis of this state is a profound annihilation, for I find nothing in me that can be given a name. All I know is that God is infinitely holy, just, good and happy. In Him everything good is to be found; in me nothing but misery. Nothing baser than myself can I see, nothing more worthless. I see that God has given me graces capable of saving a world, and, may be, I have repaid it all with ingratitude. I say ' may be,' for nothing subsists in me, neither good nor bad. The good is in God; my share is only nothing. . . . All disappears in the immensity, and I can neither will nor think. It is like a little drop of water lost and destroyed in the sea; not only is it surrounded; it is absorbed. In that divine immensity, nothing can any longer see itself; objects can only be discerned in God, and this in no other way than by the taste of the heart. All is darkness and obscurity in itself; but all is light from God's side who allows nothing to be unknown, yet without the knowledge of what one does and how one does it and without use of any sense impression. Here there is no clamour, no suffering, no pain, no pleasure, no uncertainty— only a perfect peace, not in oneself, but in God; no interest in self, no remembrance or concern with self. Thus God is in this creature. For her, misery, weakness, poverty, yet without thinking about either misery or dignity. If anyone thinks any good about me, he is wrong—he does God an injustice. All is in Him and for Him. If anything could give me a sense of contentment, oh! it would be because He is what He is, and He always will be what He is. . . . I see all things in God, and I know that He is the principle of everything, while I am but a beast. He gives me an easy disposition, and causes me to entertain people not according to my dispositions, but according to what they are. He even gives me a natural way of dealing with those who share this way, and all this so spontaneously that they are pleased. There are certain pious people whose talk is for me like a defect in their speech; but I do not fear the traps they set for me. I take no precautions, and all goes well. Sometimes people tell me to be careful about what I say to so and so. But I forget at once, and do not bother. I am told from time to time:

you said this or that; those people may misunderstand you. You are too simple! I can believe it. But I can only be simple. O carnal prudence, how I find you opposed to the simplicity of Jesus Christ. I leave you to those who believe in you! For me, my prudence, my wisdom, is Jesus simple and little. . . . Nothing greater than God; nothing smaller than I. He is rich; I am very poor, but I lack nothing and feel no need for anything. Death, life, all is the same: eternity, time—all is eternity, all is God. God is Love, and Love is God, all in God and for God."

Others, orthodox and unorthodox, have said much the same, though not many so well, nor so consistently; and it must surely be admitted that Jeanne Marie Bouvier de la Motte Guyon, saint or not, orthodox or unorthodox, at least managed to live her life in a manner that corresponded astonishingly with the rare faith and experience she professed. God, she had written many years before, must be to us as the very air we breathe; God is not felt any more than we feel the air we breathe. And her life only makes sense, if we suppose that God was thus to her.

There could be no sharper contrast in spiritual entourage and life than between the pietist Guyon group, simple, spontaneous, lay, heedless of theological precisions, and the grand episcopal state maintained, according to the fashion of the times, in his new Cambrai palace by Archbishop Fénelon, the host of so many men of rank and fame, yet combining his public role with simplicity of life, a constant charity to all in need—he was to leave no money, despite a heavy episcopal revenue—the constant letter-writing to his high-born disciples, and his delight in an inner circle of beloved friends and relations. Yet at bottom the same gospel of pure love animated both. Let us look at a letter Fénelon wrote just about the time when Mme. Guyon must have written the last pages of her autobiography. It is a reasonable, practical man's application of the Guyonist inspiration to problems of life. The letter was to the Dowager Duchess of Mortemart, one of the three Colbert daughters with whom he had been so closely linked for more than thirty years.

"I must confess, my good Duchess, that I am delighted to see you overcome by your faults *and* by the way you cannot overcome them. That despair of nature, which means that we can expect nothing of ourselves, and can only look to God in hope, is exactly what God wants. He will correct us just when we have given up hoping that we can correct ourselves. . . . What God demands of you is simply that you will put into practice whatever His grace puts into your hands. It is a matter of being little within since you cannot achieve an externally gentle disposition. It is a matter of allowing your natural pride to fall away as soon as you see it to be such. It is a matter of making-up through littleness what you have spoilt through a sally of pride. It is a matter of littleness being truly and continuously practised on all occasions. It is a matter of sincerely cutting yourself off from your own judgments. . . . Let then your own faults feed your littleness to the same extent as your preoccupation with the faults of others has made you feel big. Become accustomed to see others do without your counsel to them, and you yourself cease to judge them. At least, if you do whisper a word to them, let it be through sheer simplicity—not to decide for them nor to correct them, but only as a suggestion tentatively made, and with the wish that they would warn you as you warn them. In a word, the great thing is to put yourself on the same footing with all the most imperfect little ones. You must allow them a certain freedom with you that will help them to open their hearts. And if you have something to tell them, tell them not so much in the spirit of correcting them, but of consoling and feeding them."

A simple, easy, useful moral, but one springing directly from the sense, common to the Archbishop and the Lady, of man's need to become as a little child in the infinitely loving and powerful hands of God.

Fénelon, as bishop, theologian, philosopher, laboured away to demonstrate how this heart of all true religion was rooted in the tradition and teaching of the Catholic Church, carefully drawing the distinctions needed if his mind and heart were not to carry him into a pantheism and a fatalistic quietism that would eliminate human responsibility, freedom and even individual existence. And the overspill of his contemplation, prayer and study went to the famous letters of practical spiritual advice which in laying bare the many layers of self-love and spiritual pretence in corrupt man cleared the way for the dwelling and inspiration of the Holy Spirit.

Mme. Guyon, content in her own Catholic orthodoxy, saw herself as a channel, cleared by suffering, through which the All-Reality and All-Love of God could pass to anyone, at home or abroad, Catholic or Protestant, so long as they understood and undertook the discipline of killing their self-sufficiency, their sense of their own importance, their pride, their self-love, to become as little children in God's hands.

Those few months of excited correspondence and occasional clandestine meetings in 1688 and 1689 had divided for ever the temporal ways of the two friends in God, driving the one into suffering and imprisonment and placing the other on trial before the whole watching world. But in dividing them on earth, it had united them in spirit. After all the denudation and suffering, these two human beings, so naturally remote from one another, flowed together, equidistantly separated in space from the capital and Court, into calm waters, living and teaching by the same spiritual principles. In the Archbishop, as in the Lady, one discerns in those later years " the last of life for which the first was made." It was not merely a temporal peace and ease, after the days of storm, but a psychological and spiritual *détente* so that Fénelon's inner struggles, sadnesses, self-doubtings seemed moulded into a gentle and admirable harmony, while Mme. Guyon's excited and disordered spiritual cravings melted into that charm, serenity and sensitivity to the spiritual dimension which, even in its earlier and crude explosions, can alone account for the astonishing power she exercised through her life alike on her friends and her foes.

Had there been any substance in the grandiose hopes which seem to have tempted the never overcritical Lady and perhaps at moments crossed the thoughts of the complex Archbishop, hopes of a great spiritual revival in their native land, under a new King and a new Court trained by themselves, such hopes were shattered in the years of trial and apparent defeat and by the early death of the *Petit Prince* of their dreams. But in the peace and fruitfulness of their later years, there was surely a Divine blessing—a Divine blessing, not for crusades and visible religious triumphs, but a blessing for those who know how to gauge the destiny and achievement of the Spirit of Man, namely, by learning in the gentle and yet stern school of Christ that the seed must die before it can spring to new

life, that the Cross must be embraced before its burden can be felt
to be light and sweet, that only in the realisation and love of God
with eyes cleansed and heart purified can man, whom God made
to His own image and likeness, find the Way, the Truth and the
Life. " Unless you become as little children, you cannot enter the
Kingdom of Heaven."

It can be made to sound so easy. If Mme. Guyon suffered
endless persecution for the truth as she saw it, Fénelon never entirely
ceased to be tortured from within by his own failures, even by the
problem of what man really is. Only a few years before his death
he was writing: " I spend my life getting vexed without reason,
speaking indiscreetly, losing patience over disturbing trifles. I dislike
the world; I despise it; and yet I am a little flattered by it. I feel
old age sensibly creeping on me, and I grow used to this without
growing detached from life. I find in myself nothing real, nothing
for my inner and outer life. When I look into myself, I feel I am
dreaming. I see myself as an image in my dream."

The Lady survived the Archbishop by two and a half years.
Fénelon died a peaceful and holy death in January, 1715, his last
prayer being his continual one: " May Thy Will be done, not
mine."

His friend's feelings were expressed by Ramsay in a letter to
" Fanfan ": " Since I have known of his illness I have expected his
death with apprehension. My soul cries after him, 'Abba! Father!';
all my being cried for him; he hears me; he listens; he is in the
bosom of the *p.m.* [*Petit Maître*—the expression used for Our
Lord in the correspondence.] We need not fear for him, but only
for ourselves, for you, but the *p.m.* will take care of you."

At that time Mme. Guyon's health was completely broken, but
she survived her disciple and master until June, 1717, when she also
died piously and in complete resignation to God's will. Only her
heart and her brain were found to be sound when her body was
examined. Certainly by those she had always lived.

It may be well, after all that has been recounted in these pages,
to quote the first lines of her Will: " I protest that I die a daughter
of the Catholic, Apostolic and Roman Church, that I have never
wished for an instant to stray from its sentiments, that since I have
enjoyed perfect use of reason, I have never been a single moment

unready, at least with my will, to spend for the Church up to the last drop of my blood, just as I have always protested, on every occasion and in every meeting, and just as I have always signed and declared, as often as I could, having always and at all times submitted my books to the Church, my Mother, for whom I have always had, and always, with God's grace, will have, an inviolable attachment and a blind obedience, having no other sentiments but hers and never wishing to have any others, condemning without any restriction whatever she condemns, as I have always done."

Here then at the end the Lady, whose life had caused such trouble to the Bossuets and the Mme. de Maintenons of the world and whose fame shone more enduringly with non-Catholics than Catholics, found herself one with the Archbishop, who wrote, " There is but one true religion and one only Church, Spouse of Jesus Christ; He only willed one, and men have no right to make of it many," and whose teaching, though causing such a bother in his life-time, is amply accepted—barring the "natural sense" of certain passages in the *Maximes*—to be Catholic, not Quietist.

It is not to depreciate their Catholicism, but rather to establish its depth and fullness, its spiritual richness and its total Divine inspiration, that we close these pages with two quotations which seem to unite the Archbishop and the Lady in depths beyond the short and troubled range of earthly life.

Mme. Guyon ends her autobiography with the following words: " He who speaks only of the All-ness of God and the nothingness of the creature is in the truth and the truth is in him. For if we drive out of ourselves what has been usurped and we believe to be ours, then truth will necessarily live in us. My children, take this lesson from your Mother; it will afford you life. But though you hear it through her, do not take it as though it came from her or belonged to her; but take it from God and as His truth. Amen, Jesus!"

In his *Treatise on the Existence of God* Fénelon wrote:
" You are *He who Is*. To say of You aught but that is to degrade You. Only those words reflect You. When we add nothing to the word *Being*, we diminish Your grandeur in no way. That word—I dare to say it—is infinitely perfect as You are. Only You can thus speak and hold the Infinite in three such simple words. . . .

"O Being! O Being! Your eternity, which is but You, astonishes me; but it consoles me. Before You I am as though I were not. I plunge into Your infinity. Far from thinking of Your permanence in terms of my continuous flowing, I begin to lose sight of myself, I can no longer find myself, I begin to see in everything that which it really is, I mean Yourself."

THE END

SHORT BIBLIOGRAPHY

Oeuvres de Fénelon and *Correspondence de Fénelon* (35 volumes)
Histoire de Fénelon by Cardinal de Bausset (the official biography)
Fénelon and Mme. Guyon by M. Masson (containing the letters between
  Fenélon and Mme. Guyon, unknown to Bausset and earlier bio-
  graphers)
Apologie pour Fénelon by H. Bremond (the best and most readable book)
Fénelon au XVIIIème Siècle en France by Albert Cherel
Fénelon Inédit by Ernst Jovy
Fénelon et Bossuet by L. Crouslé
Madame Guyon et Fénelon; Précurseurs de Rousseau by Ernest Seillière
Fénelon, l'Homme et L'Oeuvre by Ely Carcasonne (excellent short life)
Fénelon, Oeuvres Spirituelles by F. Varillon, S. J. (long introduction and
  useful anthology)
La Vie de Mme. J. M. B. de la Mothe Guion, Ecrite par elle-meme (1720).
  (The famous autobiography. Upham's *Life of Madame Guyon*, as
  well as some of her other writings, is available in English)
Madame Guyon by L. Guerrier. (A good deal of the truth about Mme.
  Guyon's maltreatment, especially at the hands of Bossuet, revealed
  by a conscientious research-worker who did not mind attacking the
  Bossuet legend)
Mme. de Maintenon: Lettres publiées par Marcel Langlois, (especially
  volumes 4 and 5)
Oeuvres complètes de Bossuet (1840)
Correspondence de Bossuet by Ch. Urbain and E. Levesque
Enthusiasm by R. A. Knox
On Prayer by J. P. de Caussade, S. J.

REFERENCES

Page 16   *Correspondence de Fénelon* (afterwards *Corr.*), II, p. 341

18-21   Masson: *Fénelon & Mme. Guyon*, pp. 3-4

27   *La Vie de Madame J. M. B. de la Mothe Guion, Ecrite par elle-meme*, (afterwards *Vie*), I, p. 51

28   Seillière: *Madame Guyon et Fénelon Précurseurs de Rousseau* (afterwards Seillière), p. 8

28   *Vie*, I, pp. 110, 78, 80, 116

29   *Vie*, I, pp. 80, 116

31   *Vie*, I, p. 148

38   *Vie*, II, p. 161

38   Seillière, p. 33; *Vie*, II, p. 178

39   *Vie*, II, p. 187

40   Seillière, p. 39

43   *Oeuvres de Fénelon* (afterwards *Oeuvres*), VI, p. 391

47   *Madame de Maintenon; Lettres publiées par Marcel Langlois* (afterwards Langlois), IV

48   Guerrier: *Madame Guyon* (afterwards *Guerrier*), p. 155; *Vie*, III, p. 111

49   *Vie*, III, p. 37

50   *Vie*, III, pp. 52, 53

51   *Vie*, III, p. 87

52   Bausset: *Histoire de Fénelon* (afterwards *Bausset*), II, p. 337

54   *Corr.* (1852 edit.), VII, p. 491

59-60   *Masson*, pp. 155, 156, 234, 114, 132, 162

60   Masson, pp. 110, 90

63   Masson, p. 108

63-64   Masson, p. 248

65   Masson, pp. 206, 293

66   Masson, p. 161

67   Masson, pp. 288, 289

69   Langlois, IV, p. 475

71   Guerrier, p. 183; *Vie*, III, p. 10

74   Masson, X

74   Motteville, *Memoires*, V, p. 248;

75   *Corr.*, II, pp. 307, 306; Masson, p. 260

Page 75   Masson, p. 263

79   *Corr.*, I, p. 144

79-80   Langlois, IV, pp. 45, 47

80   Langlois, *Life of Maintenon*, p. 75

82   *Vie*, III, p. 11

89-90   *Vie*, I, p. 234

90-91   Langlois, IV, pp. 79, 135, 93

94   *Corr.*, V. pp. 466-480

95   *Corr.*, VII, pp. 4, 5, 7

95   Guerrier, 202; Bausset, I, p. 357

96   *Corr.*, VII, p. 10

97   Bausset, I, p. 358; Langlois, IV, p. 131

98   *Corr.*, VII, p. 32

98   *Corr.*, VII, p. 38

99   *Vie*, III, Chap. 11

100   *Vie*, III, Chap. 11

101   *Corr.*, VII, pp. 27, 28

101   Seillière, p. 171; *Corr.*, VII, p. 40

104   Bausset, I, p. 131

105   *Corr.*, II, p. 318 (1852 edit.)

106   *Vie*, III, pp. 141, 142

108   Bossuet, *Relation*

108   *Vie*, III, p. 165

109   *Corr.*, VII, p. 46

110   Bossuet, *Relation*; *Corr.*, VII, p. 61

111   Guerrier, p. 243; *Corr.*, VII, pp. 48, 49

113   *Corr.*, VIII, p. 498 (1852 Edit.)

114   *Corr.*, VII, p. 50

115   *Vie*, III, p. 169

115   *Vie*, III, p. 172

116   *Vie*, III, p. 172

118   Bossuet, *Relation*

119   Bossuet, *Relation*; *Corr.*, VII, p. 134

119   *Corr.*, VII, p. 134

120   *Corr.*, VII, p. 137

121   *Corr.*, VII, pp. 148, 98

122   *Corr.*, VII, p. 165

123   *Corr.*, VII, p. 146

126   *Corr.*, VII, p. 150

127   Guerrier, p. 265

Page 128   *Corr.*, VII, pp. 159-162

129   *Corr*, VII, pp. 182-84

130   Bossuet, *Oeuvres*, XXVIII, p. 657; Guerrier, p. 282; *Vie*, III, p. 212

132   Guerrier, p. 277; Langlois, IV, p. 411

133   Bossuet, *Relation*

134   *Vie*, III, p. 225 ; *Corr.*, VII, p. 192; *Vie*, III, p. 226

135   *Vie*, III, p. 227

135   Bremond, *Apologie pour Fénelon*, p. 140

137   *Corr.*, VII, pp. 208, 209; Guerrier, p. 287; Bausset, II, p. 331

137   Bausset, II, p. 430

142   *Corr.*, VII, pp. 208, 209

142   Bossuet, *Relation*; *Vie*, III, p. 230; Guerrier, p. 293; Langlois, V, p. 6

144   *Vie*, III, p. 234

146   Langlois, IV, p. 463; Guerrier, p. 304

146   *Corr.*, VII, pp. 224, 225; Guerrier, p. 304

148   *Corr.*, VII, pp. 229-38

149   Langlois, V, p. 32

153   *Corr.*, VII, p. 218

154   *Corr.*, VII, pp. 245, 246

155   *Corr.*, VII, pp. 247-250

156   Guerrier, 311

158   *Corr.*, VII, pp. 286-97; Langlois, V, p. 117

159   *Corr.*, VII, p. 228

160   *Corr.*, VII, p. 222

161   Guerrier, p. 317; Langlois, V, p. 87

162   Langlois, V, p. 201

163   *Corr.*, VII, p. 262; Guerrier, p. 318

163   Langlois, V, p. 87

164   Guerrier, pp. 320, 321

165   Bausset, II, p. 199

165   Seillière, p. 223

165   Seillière, p. 221

167   *Relation*, V, p. 2; Seillière, p. 211

168   Seillière, p, 212; Langlois, V, p. 174

169   *Corr.*, VII, pp. 377, 378, 365

170-171   Bausset, II, pp. 182-87

174   Bausset, II, p. 93

175   *Corr.*, VII, p. 407

176   Langlois, V, p. 183

Page 177   *Corr.*, VII, p. 425

178   Bausset, II, p. 109

178   Langlois, V, p. 227

180   *Corr.*, VII, p. 512

181   *Corr.*, VII, p. 523

181   Langlois, V, p. 234

188   Guerrier, p. 404

188   *Vie*, Letter V

189   Guerrier, pp. 406, 407; Bossuet, XXIX, p. 340

190   Guerrier, 408; *Corr.*, IX, pp. 84-9

190   *Corr.*, IX, pp. 79-83

191   *Vie*, III, p. 236

192   Langlois, V, p. 376; *Corr.*, IX, p. 252

193   Langlois, V, pp. 345, 347

194   Guerrier, p. 414

196   *Corr.*, IX, p. 261

201   Guerrier, p. 430

202   *Corr.*, IX, p. 165

203   *Corr.*, IX, pp. 264, 252

204   *Corr.*, IX, p. 303

207   *Corr.*, IX, p. 393

208   *Corr.*, IX, p. 418

210   Guerrier, p. 455

207   *Corr.*, X, p. 165

214   *Corr.*, X, pp. 121-23

215   Langlois, V, p. 400

215   *Corr.*, X, p. 210

217   *Corr.*, X, p. 239

220   Bausset, II, p. 322

221   *Corr.*, X, p. 419

222   Seillière, 258

226   *Corr.*, X, pp. 441, 442

228   Seillière, p. 260

228   *Corr.*, X, pp. 466, 467

229   *Corr.*, X, p. 479

230   Langlois, V, p. 417; Seillière, p. 261

230   *Corr.*, X, p. 574

231   *Corr.*, X, p. 497

233   *Vie.*, III, p. 237; Bausset, II, p. 398

233   Langlois, V, p. 587

234   *Vie*, III, p. 270

238   Fénelon: *Manuel de Piété*: VI, p. 8

241-3   Information about Ramsay and later years of Mme. Guyon in Blois is taken from Cherel's painstaking study: *Fénelon au 18ème Siècle en France*

244   Knox, *Enthusiasm*, pp. 236-38

REFERENCES

Page 246   *Vie*, III, p. 238
    247   *Vie*, III, Chap. 21
    248   *Corr.*, I, p. 217
    250   *Corr.*, I, p. 474

Page 251   Guerrier, p. 493; *Corr.*, I, 202
       (1852 Edit.)
    252   *Vie*, III, p. 224; *Oeuvres*, I, p. 79
       (1852 Edit.)